Borderline

A Memoir

By

Marie Stella McClure

Contents

Part 4 - Redemption

Prologue

March 2016

Borderline Personality Disorder is a serious mental condition characterised by its extreme emotional instability and insecurity which, left untreated, can have devastating effects on the sufferer and all those involved with them. I have suffered this since the onset of adolescence and my life was almost ruined by it. However, despite being in Social Services care, later treated by the local drug services for my prolific drug use, then again by the doctors for depression, I went undiagnosed for twenty-seven years. Now, aged thirty-eight, I finally have an answer to all my rapidly changing turbulent emotions and thoughts, an answer to why I have always felt different, completely self-destructed, threw away all my potential and to why I have always felt that something inside is lost and broken.

My life now is pretty great really if you look at it from the outside. I am a British expat 'living the dream' in Spain with my two daughters. I have some semblance of fame in the Valencian fighting community due to the fact I am a competing amateur fighter who has fought at large events such as Mix Fight. I am seen as a success story amongst my loved ones for having overcome severe addictions and a very troubled adolescence although most would still describe me as erratic and emotionally unstable. I also manage financially as a single parent with no help from my ex-husband in a country where there are no single parent benefits whatsoever to fall back on. Marie Stella, the living success story…oh to be me!

The actual truth of my life is very different. Some days I feel amazing, successful, strong and full of promise, like it all happened for a reason. Other days I want to hide under my blanket, detach from the world and feel safe. My head goes fuzzy like there is a fog in my brain. I can go from happy and excitable to dangerously angry within seconds. I explode and say unforgivably hurtful things to those I love most. I can't handle being in a relationship as I form very unhealthy attachments that make me feel physically sick and the thought of rejection is too painful to handle. When the sadness hits, I cry for hours until my head and eyes hurt. I have been single for over nine years although I have been sexually involved with several men.

Sometimes I feel like I am a freak. Something inside is missing, broken. At other times I feel fantastic, I can do anything…really it all depends on the day. Very recently, I was diagnosed with Borderline Personality Disorder. Devastated though I am as it reinforces my feelings of feeling different, strange and inadequate, it is also a huge relief to have answers to the questions that have bothered me for so long. Why did I go from a good girl to such a bad one? From a convent school education to Social Services care homes? From a talented kid full of promise to a juvenile delinquent, drug injecting addict.

Yes, my childhood had its problems; my mum told me she suffered from severe postnatal depression after my birth and I was kept in the hospital for four weeks while she got better. Then she kept getting ill and could only care for my basic needs and sometimes I would spend days in my cot, no one to play with me and only being picked up for a feed and nappy change every four hours.

My parents were also very Catholic and corporal punishment was the norm in our house. I never felt secure in their love but all that being said, they weren't bad people, just old-fashioned and misguided by their faith. I was never sexually abused (before I went into care), never starved or neglected. What's more is my siblings didn't react the way I did despite having the same upbringing whereas my behaviour caused uproar wherever I went. My memories of my parents' treatment of me are probably amplified due to the way my brain thinks. This book is not written so people think badly of them as I adore my parents now and would never want to hurt them. In turn, they are very proud of me and came back into my life and supported me when I needed it the most. However, I still have burning questions: Nature or nurture? Was I born with a borderline brain or did my upbringing cause it all? Or was it a combination of both factors?

At twelve, I was placed into Social Services care by my despairing parents who had no clue how to handle me or my frequent rages. At thirteen, I started drinking, abusing solvents, using drugs and wilfully self-destructing. I was infamous in all the local police-stations and courts by the time I was fourteen. Despite my catholic upbringing, I slept with anyone who gave me attention from my early teens onward, always unprotected. My mum said I had a self-destructive element which killed anything good in me and for years I was estranged from my family. No one ever knew why I changed so dramatically, least of all me.

Even with my intense level of fight training now, six days a week, two hours a day, I still suffer frequent angry outbursts that leave me shaken and depressed afterwards. I relapse on and off with cannabis; sometimes it takes over my life and I smoke it constantly, usually out of my bedroom window hiding it from my daughters. It ruins my training and I have lost my last four fights due to this addiction albeit it is a lot milder than it was in my younger injecting days. I hate myself for failing so much, seemingly without reason.

My sex life is about as unhealthy as you can get and recently I have slept with men I find physically repulsive, suffering self-loathing and guilt afterwards only to repeat the same impulsive behaviour days later. Lack of self-worth some would say, fear of getting hurt; others would call me a disgusting dirty bitch but no one can criticise me as much as I do myself.

I have been searching most of my life for the answer and now, even though I open my story with this diagnosis, for me it is like coming to the last pages of a book and finally getting clarity on everything that has been hinted at in the story. My true recovery begins now but first I would like to share my story.

Borderline

Part 1

Expelled
From Grace

Chapter 1
Taken into Care

Thursday July 4th 1990

I awoke slowly, wondering at the feeling of dread
enveloping me before I had even opened my eyes.
Then I remembered the previous night's events.
"Don't open your eyes," instructed my inner voice,
"don't open them. Pray. Pray that you are back home
under the starry duvet in the peach room with the
flowery curtain."
I kept my eyes tightly shut as I tried desperately to
visualize my bedroom. *Please, God, I'll never be bad
or lose my temper again, please.*
After repeating this thought over and over, I warily
opened my eyes. And quickly shut them again. The
room was all wrong; small, narrow, light green in
colour. I put the pillow over my head, drowning out
the unfamiliar noises I could hear outside.
I held back my tears. I couldn't cry now. God only
knew what types of kids would be out there. I
couldn't let them see me crying.
There was a knock at the door. A dark haired friendly
looking woman looked in. "Hi Marie, I'm Julie. Have
you got any clothes with you?"
I nodded, not correcting her that my name was
actually Maria, my parents always called me Maria.
"Right, well get dressed, then come down to the room
at the end. All the girls are in there."
Climbing out of bed, I picked up my bag of clothes
which the social workers had collected from my
house before getting me from the police-station the
previous night. So much for God listening to my

prayers. He didn't make it so that I could be back home and all this just a nightmare.

As I noticed that my bag contained my school uniform I felt a tiny shift of hope within me as I realised I could still go to school. Not that I particularly liked school but I would be able to see my Sinead, my best friend. Maybe she'd let me go home with her after school. Maybe her mum would let me stay there instead of here. It was my class's confirmations that night, well, all except mine. Ironic really; I had made my first communion at the age of four, two years earlier than most of my peers as I was considered very holy for one so young but now I wasn't deemed fit enough to make my confirmation. That First Holy Communion had taken place on the third of July 1982; who would have thought that just eight years to the day later, I would be cast out from my family home and put into voluntary care?

Emotion was racing round my stomach, fear building as I left the safety of that small bedroom. I walked down a narrow corridor that had doorways every couple of meters on both sides. As I approached the end I could hear lots of girls' voices coming from the end room. Nervously I opened the door.

"Oh my God, Maria McClure!" a familiar voice exclaimed as I crept into the room.

I looked up and saw a girl I had been at Upton Hall Convent School with. Jessie had signed herself into this home, Wimbrick, a few months back after she had heard about the home's existence through one of its residents, Ella, who we knew from the public bus that we caught to school. Jessie was adopted but didn't get on with her adoptive mother. She'd got off the bus one day with Ella and turned herself into the children's home, just like that. I had lost touch with her since I had left Upton a few months prior and we'd never been particularly close.

"How d'yer know her?" one of the other girls asked, her eyes dancing mockingly over me.

They were all staring at me, about ten of them; I tried to smile but couldn't help blushing. I wished I could be bold like these girls. Some of them looked hard and had rough gravelly voices while others like Jessie had strong local accents but higher pitched cuter voices. All of them seemed to blend together, none of them intimidated by the other yet I feared them all.

"She was at my school but she got kicked out."

This wasn't strictly true but I remained silent.

"Jessie, enough! You always talk too much," Julie admonished her lightly. "Right girls, down to breakfast and then off to school. Marie, can you stay here for a minute please? You won't be going to school today."

I waited until all the girls were gone before saying to Julie, "I want to go to school though."

Julie glanced at me. "Really? We assumed you wouldn't want to go. I'll have to check first with your social worker. He's coming to see you at nine."

I felt a little better at that.

"Do you want to go down and have some breakfast? At least a cup of tea or something," she continued as I started to shake my head.

Julie spoke in a no nonsense way that I didn't dare argue with and I allowed myself to be gently propelled down the wooden slatted staircase. Sunlight streamed in through the open front door making the place look almost attractive. I changed my mind quickly as I followed Julie through the common room area into the kitchen. It looked like a youth club, missing anything homely, completely bare of clutter with a TV and video recorder in a cheap pine unit, a couple of ugly green sofas and uncomfortable looking chairs on the side by the TV and on the other side a bare floor with a battered table tennis game and pool table.

I followed Julie into the kitchen where I was surprised to see two first year boys from my school, one of whom smiled at me sympathetically. There were teapots on each of the four tables and varieties of cereal boxes to choose from. There was also toast waiting to be buttered. I felt surprised at the layout. I had never had such luxury at home and never had much of an appetite anyway. This morning I was even less hungry than usual but caught Julie's eagle eye upon me and hurriedly buttered a piece of toast. I just about managed to swallow it with the sweet hot cup of tea she poured for me.

"First day, you get special treatment," smiled Julie, "tomorrow you do your own okay."

The social worker arrived half an hour late and his stupid, smiling face irritated me. I disliked him instantly.

"Where's my other social worker?" I responded to his cheerful greeting.

"Who?"

"Sister Rose, who my mum has been getting to come and see me, she's a nun from Catholic Social Services."

He was busy scribbling notes in a diary but paused for a moment.

"Well, I'm your social worker now. My name's Terry

and I'm from the local social services who dealt with last night's situation. I'm here to arrange a planning meeting where we can start looking at where you'll live and how often you'll see your family."

"No! I wanna go home," my voice broke. "I don't wanna meeting; I just wanna go home."

I stifled a sob, wiped my nose on my sleeve and rubbed my eyes angrily.

"I'm afraid that's not possible at the moment. Your dad's still very upset."

"Well, so am I," I countered defiantly.

"All the better that you stay here then until everyone has calmed down. Wimbrick is an assessment centre that will assess your needs and what is best for you. That very well may be for you to return home in a few weeks or that we look at another longer term placement for you."

"No, I can't stay here. I hate it, I want my mum."

"Come on now, you've hardly been here any time at all. How can you hate it already? We're not that bad, hun." Julie tried to soothe me.

"When will the meeting be?" I asked.

More busy scribbling.

"Next Thursday at ten o'clock."

"A week! But that's ages."

Familiar feelings of panic and fear jumped around my belly as my mind relived humiliating moments of previous bullying at the hands of local girls. It would surely be worse here. I couldn't deal with any more. I had to get out of here.

"Can I go to school still?"

"Yes, of course. See, you're thinking positively already. Will someone be able to drop her off this morning?" he asked turning to Julie.

"I don't see why not," smiled Julie, who I was beginning to feel a little safe with.

"It's my friend's confirmation tonight at the church," I asked hesitantly, "we'd already arranged to go. Can I still go? My mum and dad will probably be happy that I've been to church too."

"We'll need details of your friend's parents first," Julie replied. "Normally you only have free time on certain days and home leave on others. I'll let your year head at school know this morning."

The social worker put his diary away in his brown briefcase and got up to leave assuring me that he would be in touch before next Thursday. We went downstairs. A friendly looking man with a huge moustache ruffled my hair as Julie told me he would be taking me to school.

"Hello Scruffy Head." he greeted me, "I'm Truck."

I laughed in spite of myself. Julie took me into the office where a few staff members were sitting at a desk. One of them, a little bald man opened a tin and handed me some coins.

"There is your dinner money and your bus fare home."

I had been in receipt of free school meals ever since being at St Mary's due to my family's low income so this meant I could get cigarettes as well as dinner in school and I wouldn't need my bus fare home because I wasn't coming back. If Sinead's mum said it was okay, I could still go to the confirmations and then hopefully stay at Sinead's forever.

I arrived in the school playground at the beginning of morning break. Vicki Morgan, my ex best friend from primary school who hated me now and normally took huge delight in insulting me, ran up to me and hugged me.

"Maria, thank God you're okay."

I wondered how she knew what had happened. At that moment Sinead appeared.

"Maria! I called for you this morning and your mum told me you don't live there anymore. Cold bitch she was too. What happened?"

"Cos I was late last night, me mum went mad and it all kicked off so they called the police and put me in care." I had been out with Sinead the night before.

"Really?" Sinead was incredulous, "but you could only have been like ten minutes late."

I nodded, choking back my tears. Vicki's face was appalled but I knew her sympathy would be short lived and that she was relishing being one of the first to know of this latest drama concerning me.

"They're gonna ring your mum to see if I can still come the confirmations with you. They said they'll let Miss Palmer know."

Sinead and Vicki linked one arm each and we went to the year head's office to find out that I was actually allowed to go to Sinead's and to the confirmations on the condition that Sinead's mum would return me to Wimbrick that night. Sinead promised me that she would lend me some clothes to wear and that she would speak to her sister about getting their mum to foster me. I pinned my desperate hopes on that thought for the rest of the day.

The news of my ordeal was going round school and one of the nicer boys in my year, Stephen, a boy who I had also been in primary school with tried to comfort me. School, once so hostile and unfriendly was now my haven.

No one was nasty to me that day, not even Vicki. Small mercies. Last night's events had taken all of the fight right out of me, not that I had much fight in me where the girls in this school and who lived locally to me where concerned. All my rage was always directed at my family. With other girls I was extremely quiet and shy.

My head was fuzzy, my heart sick, my belly empty; I didn't understand how all of this had happened to me. I had been considered such a good child, praised by every adult who came into contact with me. I had always been different from other kids; I had learnt that immediately upon starting primary school. I was quieter, shyer and my religious beliefs far more advanced and heartfelt than any other kid in the class. Then this last year, these awful rages just started taking over me. Sometimes I would not even know why or how they had begun, I would just find myself in the middle of this huge tidal wave of anger then later I would be left weak and devastated. Deep down, I knew I had blown my last chance of going back home although I banished this thought as soon as it arrived, glossing over the awful reality with the fake hope that only touches the minds of the truly desperate.

During the confirmations in the packed out church of my childhood, I prayed hard. "Please let me go back home, please Jesus, don't make me have to stay in care."

That night however, after buying a portion of chips which we ate in Sinead's mum's car by the Lighthouse pub in Wallasey Village, I was driven back to Wimbrick. Sinead whispered to me that it would be okay but I felt like I was being carted off for

a life sentence as the care-workers locked the front
door behind me.

Saturday 6th July
I was sitting in the TV room when the front doorbell
rang. I heard Sinead's voice asking for me and I
jumped up and ran towards the front door but by the
time I got there I saw only Truck standing there with
another care-worker.
"That was for me, wasn't it?"
"Sorry, no visitors unless by prior arrangement,"
Truck smiled.
I ran back through the pool room in time to see
Sinead and Vicki walking discontentedly past the
windows. I watched them go, powerless to stop them.
Now I wasn't even allowed to see my friends, like I
was in prison or something. The empty feelings I so
often suffered had never been as empty as they were
now. I felt like a robot going through the mechanical
motions of eating, dressing, sleeping and waking.
Bedtime tears dried into a morning desert.
I had spent three nights at Wimbrick by then and had
managed to avoid being alone with any of the older
girls so far. These girls were from the roughest estates
in Birkenhead and I was terrified of them, of what
they would do to me. Jessie, my only possible ally,
had home leave for the weekend and I hardly opened
my mouth while in the company of anyone else; my
awkward shyness like a sentry, positioned in place at
all times hardly letting me breathe.
Later that day, my luck ran out. After an uneventful
drive out in the minibus, I was sitting in the music
room, a small blue room on the corner of the boy's
wing, with a couple of the boys and another girl,

Stephanie. At only just twelve, almost a year younger than me, she was pretty with long dark blonde curly hair and big blue eyes framed by a curling fringe. She was friendly and didn't seem like the rest of the girls. Her voice was more like the girls from my old school, Upton She chatted to me about how she found Wimbrick after two weeks of being there.

"This is cosy," remarked a strongly accented voice. Voices and accents could make me feel safe with a person or intensely afraid of them. I looked up and saw Nina Leyman smirking in the doorway. Apparently she had only been admitted to the home in the afternoon preceding my own midnight entrance and I couldn't believe she was so self-assured and confident already. She walked in and sat down next to Mark, pulling a cushion over his crotch area and putting her hand under it, snuggling up close to him, seemingly established in some kind of relationship with him.

"What yer looking at?" she demanded aggressively.

"Nothing," I quickly averted my eyes.

Nina laughed, "Ah, how innocent. You need a boyfriend I reckon."

I shook my head and made to leave the room.

"Nah, don't go, I'm only messin' wit' yer."

Although Nina's voice appeared light-hearted, I detected the underlying threat and sat down, glancing nervously at Stephanie, who smiled nervously at me.

"What's yer name?"

"Marie." That's what everyone had called me since I had got here and the name change somehow seemed to fit the life change.

Nina removed her hand from underneath the cushion much to Mark's disappointment as she leaned over to the other boy, Keith, a short stout boy of fourteen with beady brown eyes, dark greasy hair and oily, spotty skin, whispering something to which he nodded his head in response, smiling stupidly, his eyes growing hungry as his glance roamed over me. I could feel my cheeks getting hot as Nina narrowed her eyes thoughtfully in my direction.

"Right, well Marie, our Keith, this fit young man here quite likes yer. What d'yer think of him?"

"He's okay," I mumbled nervously, scared of the impact my answer would have on Nina who seemed more threatening by the second.

"Will yer get off with him?" That was the term for kissing with tongues.

Keith shifted uncomfortably in his chair as I glanced at him before taking a breath and responding finally, "I don't wanna boyfriend."

"Really?" She was in her element, enjoying the power trip. "That's not very friendly yer know. He looks hurt. I don't like people who hurt me mate's feelings."

"Leave her alone, Nee. She's just a kid." Mark pulled her closer to him; presumably to finish off what she'd started.

"Right, yer can go now, we want some privacy but Marie, yer best think about getting off with my mate Keith or Auntie Nina's not gonna be happy, like."

That night, it took me a while to fall asleep; my thoughts raced with worries of what Nina would do when I wouldn't kiss Keith. Ew, I couldn't kiss him. This wasn't the first time a girl had made me kiss boys I didn't want to kiss. *Please God, save me from this.* I begged forgiveness of all my sins, especially the violent ones I had committed recently against my mother. This was my punishment. Maybe I deserved it all. My sleep when it came was full of troubled dreams that made me toss and turn all night.

Sunday 7th July

Eventually dawn broke, the sun's first light promising a bright summer morning. I could hear the church bells ringing and remembered that it had been agreed that I go to church at my family's parish church in Wallasey, although since a disagreement with the local priest my mum usually went over to a church in Liverpool. Lots of the kids had gone on home leave the night before and wouldn't be back until later that day. At least not many of them would witness me going to church; cause for more unwanted attention. I knew my dad would be there and hoped if he saw me in church, saw me making an effort to go, that he might soften towards me again and let me move back home. *I want my mum.* I missed her so much, needed the cuddles I sometimes received after hours of crying and begging forgiveness for the latest crazy, blind rage I had subjected her to. How I wished I could turn back the clock. The knowledge of that impossibility left a sick dull ache inside, a misery more intense than ever before, overwhelming me, making me cry through moments of solitude and retreat inside myself while in the company of others. The emotions I was experiencing were so strong I couldn't switch off from them. My body sympathised by losing any appetite for real food, as if it just wanted to be left to its own devices and fade away to nothing.

Entering the church I felt a little comfort. The scent of candles and incense reminded me of a nicer time in my life, a time when I didn't know heartache, betrayal and total, utter abandonment. I saw my dad standing at the back with the other collectors. He nodded at me briefly, more rejection in that simple curt nod.

I stayed until halfway through the sermon, which spoke about God's love for us all and barely able to stomach the hypocrisy, I left. I walked to the shop and managed to get someone to go in to get me some loosies. I had enough for five cigarettes with the fifty pence collection money I had been given and chain smoked them, one after the other.

I was surprised to find a real Sunday roast waiting back at Wimbrick and despite my recent lack of appetite, I managed to eat everything. We were all assigned tables to sit at, five kids at each table with one care-worker and the rota for dishes was sorted by table; each table took their turn for one day with one kid washing, one rinsing, one drying and two clearing. The care-workers would supervise and help where needed. I sort of liked the routine as it made me feel safe.

That evening, I was playing pool with one of the boys, when my mum came to visit. I was polite throughout the visit as was she. It was an awkward conversation and a heart-breaking time for both of us but at the time I couldn't see my mum's pain which she always managed to hide well. When it was time for her to go, I started begging her to let me return home.

"Mum, please. I'll be good. I´m sorry. I'll try harder. I'll play the clarinet again and go to the church orchestra. Mum, I'll do anything. Don't leave me here. I hate it here; you don't know what it's like."

"Well that boy seemed very nice, I bet it's not as bad as all that."

"Mum, it's horrible..."

I faltered, I couldn't tell my mum about Nina as she probably wouldn't believe me due to the fact she thought I was a violent little thug. She would never believe that I suffered immense quantities of fear when faced with confrontations with other girls.

"No, not now. We have a meeting Thursday, let's see what happens then. You´ve said all this before and you never change. Why would this time be any different?"

My desperate tears meant nothing to her, however, she had given me a glimmer of hope by saying we'd see what happened at the meeting. *The meeting, the meeting*, if I could just get through until then, maybe I would be okay. Nina wouldn't be back until later that evening and I had school to escape to all week. I would just stay near the care-workers at all times while in the home and Nina wouldn't be able to get me. My thoughts just kept racing around Nina.

I might have settled down for the days preceding the meeting if I hadn't been called into another girl's room that night. Tracy was fifteen. Long, light, brown hair fell down her back, but the front and sides were short, framing her thin, narrow face. She looked hard and spoke roughly.

"I heard yer after Keith." Her face was inches from mine.

"I'm not."

"Listen girl, Keith is mine okay and I don't want no little sluts sniffing round him. If I find out yer bin near him, yer gonna get this." She waved a solid looking fist in front of my face.

I tried to convince her that I wasn't after him but she got more irritated as I stuttered away. "Don't tell me yer life story, yer silly bitch, just stay away from Keith."

I nodded miserably. If I told Tracy about Nina and her threats it would probably make it worse; best to keep quiet and stay out of their way.

"Well, night then." Tracy dismissed me easily as if she hadn't just been threatening me.

Again, sleep evaded me. Thoughts racing, panic intensifying, *Nina, Tracy, who scares me more? Keith ew, I don't wanna kiss any more horrible boys.*

They're gonna go after me. Nina, Tracy, Nina, Tracy. Rewind, repeat.

Chapter 2
Escaping Harsh Reality

Monday 8th July

The news of my ordeal had got around school and I was the centre of attention. Louise Fila, the hardest girl in our year, was impressed and asked me all about which girls were in the home with me. She warmed towards me, as if my care status was something to be proud of. The school day flew by now I had something to dread at the end of it and that afternoon, unable to face returning to Wimbrick, I went home with Sinead.

"Where yer gonna go?" she asked as she handed me a sandwich. "My mum's not allowed to let you stay here. Your mum said no. It's like she'd prefer that you rot in care."

"I dunno. If I go me mum's now, they'll probably call the police and have me removed."

"God, it makes me so mad. D'yer think they'll let you go home after the meeting this week?"

"I hope so, I can't handle that place."

The meeting, the meeting, it'll be okay at the meeting.
I left shortly afterwards as Sinead had to go somewhere with her mum. As I walked into Liscard, I saw Will the Wanker and one of his mates by Macdonald's, on their bikes.

"A finger of fudge is just enough to give Maria a treat." Will chorused the hated chant that so many sang at me ever since an embarrassing incident in which I had been caught in the school shed with him; a total set up by a group of bitchy girls but still, my reputation was destroyed.

"Shut yer mouth, Will. As if I ever let yer."

"You would have if we hadn't got caught."

"As if!"

"Where you goin' anyway? I thought you were in care now. Thought you weren't allowed out."

I didn't reply.

"Are you on the run?" he asked, looking momentarily impressed as I nodded slightly. "D'yer wanna get off with me?"

"No, I don't! Fuck off."

"If you don't get off with me, I'll tell the police where you are."

I was relieved to see my bus pulling into the busy road and quickly climbed aboard. I had decided to go to my Uncle Dom, my dad's twin brother in Rock Ferry. Surely he wouldn't turn me away. How wrong was I? Nice cup of tea, slice of cake and, unbeknown to me, a sly phone call to report me; the social workers soon arrived to take me back.

Back at Wimbrick, I couldn't face sitting in the girls' common room upstairs knowing Nina and Tracy would probably be there so I sat downstairs with the younger kids where Stephanie was also sitting. We chatted to me for a while about her own mum and little brother at home. Apparently she was out of control too, like me, and that's why she was here, although she appeared angelic, not at all like the others. She wet the bed at night too, something which she was extremely ashamed of yet no one bullied her for it. I heard some of the girls clattering down the stairs and froze as Nina entered the room, her malevolent eyes gleaming at me. Thankfully, at that moment, Julie came in.

"Right young ones, bed time. Marie, Stephanie, go get your baths. Your bed time is in half an hour."

Normally I hated baths but right then I was grateful as I could lock the door and have complete privacy. Nina couldn't come into the bathroom as there would be a care-worker sat on the landing and if I stayed there until bed time, she would have no chance of getting me. In the morning, the landing was too overrun by half-dressed girls screaming for hairspray and hairdryers for Nina to even think of coming over to bother me and I was not going to come back to this hell hole after school, no way.

Tuesday 9th July

After school the next day, I left with Anna, another close friend, who was certain that her parents would let me stay for a couple of nights.

"I just need somewhere to stay until the planning meeting," I told them, trying not to sound too desperate.

Anna's mum was sympathetic. She made some phone calls and came back smiling.

"They agreed but just until Thursday. You have to be either with Anna, at school or here. No going out on your own."

Thank you, God!

There was a school disco that night and as I only had the clothes I stood up in, Anna found me some dungaree shorts and a tight T shirt to wear. After several lashings of hair lacquer to get our fringes backcombed up as the current fashion demanded and multiple coats of mascara and lipstick, we were ready. It was a sunny evening and we walked to the disco, meeting Sinead and Vicki on the way. We shared a couple of ciggies between us and I felt happier and more relaxed than I had since being put into care.

Staying at Anna's made me feel like a regular kid. My friends were popular girls and recently, so was I in my new found notoriety.

At the disco, I noticed Jay Spears looking at me with even more interest than usual. We weren't going out officially but I'd had a crush on him for years. He was an altar boy, the perfect match for me, the daughter of the staunchest catholic family in the church who always sat in the front bench much to mine and my younger sister's embarrassment. However, it had given me good eyeballing time with Jay who returned my looks with his own fiery blue gaze. Since starting St Mary's, we'd kissed quite a few times and my stomach flipped as he came over to me. A boy I actually wanted to kiss!

All our favourite songs played, Maxi Priest, MC Hammer, Madonna, Snap, the sounds of the early nineties blared through the speakers. Cheap lemonade and crisps were being sold outside. Despite it all, I managed to enjoy myself and switch off a little from my current situation.

I slept soundly both those nights I stayed at Anna's and felt like a regular kid going to school with the girls in the morning. A temporary relief from the emotional turmoil. It wasn't to last despite my many begging prayers and silently repeated decades of the rosary said under the covers at night.

Thursday 11th July
The meeting started at ten o'clock in the girls' common room. My parents were there, my new social worker, Terry with his female team leader and three of the Wimbrick care-workers, among them Julie and Mr Rodriguez, the boss.

Everyone introduced themselves and chose biscuits and tea from a tray, laughing and apologising as they bumped hands accidentally. I felt enraged that they were treating this, a meeting which held my future in its hands, like a church coffee morning. I could hardly contain my impatience to get down to the matter at hand, my imminent return home. I was convinced, absolutely convinced I would be going back home now. A whole week had passed. The last time they had put me in care a couple of months back, they had allowed me back after four days.

The meeting began. Julie joked about the fact that they hadn't had a chance to get to know me too well due to the fact I had spent the week running away, to which Mr Rodriguez answered that I would have to settle down if I wanted to be granted free time and home leave. I waited for one of my parents to speak up and say I wouldn't need home leave as they would be taking me home but nothing was forthcoming.

"Erm, is there no chance of reconciliation with the family?" Terry inquired of no one in particular, throwing the words out into the group where the awkward silence picked them up and chewed the very idea out of them.

Eventually my mum sighed. "No. We have talked long and hard about it. I have taken advice from the church and we don't think it would be good for anyone if she came home now."

I swung between rage against the church and my mother's cold decision to an awful feeling of devastation, so deep it was like a physical blow to my stomach. How could she sit there so resolute and hard as she handed me over to the authorities? I looked around desperately.

"But, but I thought I would be going home today. You promised."

"I didn't promise, Maria," my mum sounded tired, hard done to, "I said we'd see and all you've done all week is run away until you got your own way about staying at your friend's, even though it was against our wishes. That's the manipulative behaviour I don't want in my house, never mind your temper."

What could I say? She would just call me an attention seeker if I tried to tell her I was scared of the girls, a slut if I mentioned the boy I was going to be made to kiss for she would think immediately that I was up to my old, alleged tricks of playing fingers in dark places, a liar if I tried to say anything against my family.

"Mum, I'll change. I promise. I haven't kicked off all week, have I, Julie?"

"Pet, you've not been here all week, but yes, she was good at the weekend wasn't she Pete?"

Pete, one of the other care-workers present nodded encouragingly. "It's not that bad here, love, and it's not forever anyway. Wimbrick is just an assessment centre that will assess your needs, what's best for you and your family."

"Well, can I get fostered if my mum doesn't want me?" I looked defiantly at my mum who raised her eyes to the good Lord.

"There is no way we would inflict you upon another family, to destroy as you almost have this one."

"Mum, please, just give me another chance. I'll do anything."

"No, we can't take you back now. That's final, you need to accept it."

"Dad..."

"No, don't look at me after the trouble you've caused." His tone was clipped and abrupt.

"Let's plan some free time and home leave," Julie cut in brightly.

"No, we would prefer to leave it for now."

I couldn't believe my mum. Now she didn't even want to see me, not even for an hour a week.

"Well," Julie contested gently, "how about if we sort out times and days now, for the sake of the meeting but schedule it to start in a week's time, dependent on Marie's behaviour?"

It was agreed that to start with I would visit home on Tuesdays and Thursdays after school and return to Wimbrick at eight pm. Overnights would follow once some trust had been rebuilt and my behaviour was more settled. My free time would be on Saturday afternoons for now.

"Does that sound fine to you?" Julie appeared to genuinely care and I had to force myself not to cry.

I couldn't stay here. Rage exploded. I jumped up and ran out of the room shouting, "I'm going to school and am not fucking coming back."

"Well, Miss, think about that, you don't want your free time stopped before it's started." Julie raised her voice slightly.

I heard my mum muttering, "You see what we had to put up with? Always the same."

I need you, Mummy. I hate you, Mum.

My dad looked very unimpressed to see me when I arrived there later that afternoon, having gone there after school to beg yet again for one more chance. "Why are you here, Maria?" my mum asked me coldly, looking up from her cooking.

I didn't realise then that my mum's coldness was a facade, an act to hide her pain. She saw me as bad, evil personified and this was the only way she could prevent herself from breaking down in front of me, something she was sure would show great weakness. My dad, in contrast, showed his anger. His brother's and sister's kids were all model pupils at school, my own brother and sister didn't cause any problems; I was the only one in the younger generation of our family who was out of control. He didn't look at the vulnerable pre-teen that I was, couldn't see the turmoil, the confusion or the heartache. He just saw a mutinous, sulky, attention seeking, bad tempered, foul mouthed little brat and often told me this.

"I bet you're here without permission," he presumed correctly

I swallowed before saying, "Please give me one more chance. I've learnt my lesson."

"Absolutely not!" he thundered. "How can you turn up here after everything you've done? You are not welcome in this house a second longer."

I turned wildly to my mum, hoping she would be a little more loving.

"Mum, please," my voice broke.

I needed her, craved having her arms around me to protect me from everything, to turn back the clock, to repair the damage. Her eyes showed no emotion as she looked at me.

"Don't turn on the crocodile tears my girl," barked my dad. "It's always the same with you. Little girl lost or light the blue touch paper and stand well back. Your tears don't wash with us anymore. NOW GO!"

I shot out of the kitchen, past my younger siblings who looked at me warily as I rushed upstairs into the bathroom. My dad chased me up the stairs but reached the bathroom just seconds too late as I locked the door.

"THAT'S IT! I'M CALLING THE POLICE!"

Inside the bathroom, I was hunched up on the floor, curled up in a ball trying unsuccessfully to stem my sobs and catch my breath. It was like a physical pain in my chest and I felt sick. I could hear my dad on the phone downstairs, demanding that the police come for me immediately as I had locked myself in "HIS" bathroom like I was some kind of intruder.

I wanted to die. I couldn't carry on. Life hurt too much. Rummaging through the mirrored cabinet, I found some of my mum's headache pills, a new packet containing twenty co-codomal. I filled a glass and began shoving the pills into my mouth only to remove them and start again when I balked, unable to swallow tablets at the best of times but I forced them down, all of them. If they didn't want me home, I really didn't want to live any more. Death would be a blessed release.

I looked in the mirror, hating what I saw. My blue eyes were red rimmed and puffy, shrunken from crying. My hated zits looked far more inflamed and seemed to have multiplied since the previous week, especially on my chin which was red and sore everywhere. My dark hair was drooping and flaky bits of hairspray hung off tendrils of my fringe now fallen from its backcombed heights. *How long would the overdose take to kill me? Would I fall asleep? Faint? What?*

Suddenly my dad hammered on the door making me jump.

"The police are on their way."

I shouted through the door, "it doesn't matter now Dad, 'cos I´m gonna die anyway. Then you'll all be happy."

"What do you mean? What nonsense are you talking now?"

"I've taken an overdose," I screamed hysterically. "All of mum's tablets. Hope you both feel good and enjoy my funeral."

"Catherine!" bellowed my dad, running downstairs, "Catherine! She's overdosed."

I could faintly hear my mum's shocked response and was glad that something had finally cracked the ice queen. I heard my dad on the phone again, this time telling the operator to send an ambulance instead of the police. I prayed that I would die before anyone got there.

After a few minutes, I felt a little calmer, slightly fuzzy. I heard the front door opening and wondered idly why the doorbell hadn't rung first. My dad ran back up the stairs and banged again on the door, this time accompanied by a different voice asking me to unlock the door. Then my dad amazed me as he yanked the door open, breaking the lock and sending splinters of wood flying. He had never been able to do that before and God knows he'd tried enough times as the bathroom was my favourite place to run when escaping his temper.

Two green clad ambulance men came in to the tiny room, my dad behind them shouting, "What have you done?"

"Calm down please, Sir. Let us handle this. Maria?" I looked at him.

"Maria, we need to know what you've taken. Can you tell me, or show me please?"

I pointed at the empty packet of co-codamol on the window sill above the sink.

"How many?"

"About twenty."

"How long ago?" He was taking my pulse as he questioned me, checking my pupils, all my vital signs.

I shrugged as my dad said he thought I must have taken them about fifteen minutes ago.

"Right, we need to get you to hospital. Don't worry hun, you're just gonna go for a short ride in the ambulance."

I sat in a brightly lit casualty cubicle looking at the plastic cup full of thick brown liquid that the nurse held proffered out towards me. It looked disgusting.

"Come on love, you have to drink it."

"Will it make me sick?"

Why hadn't I died yet? My eyes hurt from the bright lights and my head was pounding, probably from all the crying.

"No, luvvie, it won't make you sick. It will just clear the medicine you have taken."

"Promise?"

My dad tutted that I needed to hurry up and take the stuff before it was too late. *Shut up, Dad.*

The nurse nodded, smiling encouragingly as I began to take the liquid.

"Go on, just three big gulps and it's done. I've got some juice here as well, to take the taste away. If you haven't taken it in the next two minutes we'll have no choice but to put a tube down your throat and pump your stomach which is very painful."

The nurse had blatantly lied to me. A few minutes

later I was throwing up like I never had before, many long, horrible minutes of constant vomiting and guttural retching, each time more forceful and painful than the last as my stomach struggled to clear itself of every last bit of liquid, solid or tablet that I had consumed in the last week if not the last month. The nurse stayed with me throughout, replacing the bowl, offering tissues to wipe my mouth, soothing me, telling me I was doing well, that I was brave. *I want my mum.*

"You won't do this again in a hurry eh." The nurse smiled kindly as my stomach was finally empty and I cried weakly.

"I wish it had worked. I wish I was dead."

After my stomach had settled, I was taken up to the children's ward. I was going to be kept in until I saw a psychiatrist and although I didn't relish the idea of seeing a shrink, at least it meant I wouldn't have to go back to Wimbrick just yet. Within minutes of my dad leaving, sleep mercifully took me, allowing me to dream vividly of forgotten memories from long ago.

Chapter 3
Childhood heroes
(Jesus, Mary and Uncle Paul)

3rd July 1982

I twirled in front of the mirror in my pretty white dress. Today I was going to make my First Holy Communion, two years earlier than all the other kids in my class. I had already made my First Confession and was very good at listing all my sins, baby crimes which I deeply regretted as I prayed out my penances, filled with guilt. I was desperate to please my sweet Jesus, for Holy God's love. I didn't want to go to hell when I died where the bad souls went unless they repented before death. Children were safe; apparently God didn't send little ones to hell but the ones who weren't catholic didn't go to heaven either, they went to Limbo, a harmless place in between but one where they never knew God.

I also knew that the devil could begin his evil work on little ones and this scared me. I believed that making my Communion this day would save me from the devil and the dreaded loss of God and Heaven, ensure my family's love and prevent any bad things from happening again.

I was also sure that the fact I was making my first communion today had made Mummy love me more. I was the centre of my Uncle Paul's attention too and this made me proud as he was a holy catholic priest; one of God's men on earth. We had lots of special talks together and I always came out with answers that showed superior spiritual wisdom for one so young. Mummy would smile proudly and Uncle Paul would affirm how special I was.

Uncle Paul was in the front room waiting for me along with every member from both sides of my family. Mummy fixed the white veil onto my hair and we all walked together in a procession to St Peter and Paul's church in New Brighton. Mummy was proud of me and we smiled every time our eyes met. *She is happy because of me. Today she really loves me.* Mummy had wanted to be a nun but had not made it for some reason I was not quite sure of. I knew that she would have preferred to be a nun than a mummy and although this saddened me, I understood that being close to Jesus was more important than anything, even your own family. I'd already decided to be a nun when I grew up and Mummy was pleased by this.

The service was conducted by Uncle Paul who held Jesus in his hands as he gently said, "The Body of Christ"

"Amen," I replied as he put the host onto my tongue. I knelt on the stone cold marble by the altar and the devil whispered in my ear that things would change now, that I would go back to being nobody's girl, the bad things would happen again, *nasty cheeses sandwiches, choking, eat them now, bad girl, naughty girl, do as you're told, crying, vomiting* and that Uncle Paul wouldn't visit as much but I pushed the thought away, certain I had pleased Jesus so much that nothing bad would happen again.

The next evening, I was the one to lead our daily rosary prayers, revelling in the importance of being the one to say the first half of the Our Fathers and Hail Marys and admiring the rainbow sparkles glinting from my new sapphire beads, a communion present from Uncle Paul, while the rest of the family droned off the second half. After prayers, there was always a bible story, for which we were allowed to sit down and rest after kneeling for so long. I always had something to contribute to the bible story discussion and prided myself on being God's best student of my age group on earth. When I was allowed to choose the hymn, I usually picked Ave Maria, liking it mostly because it contained my second name. My full name, Stella Maria, meant Star of the Sea, (one of Our Lady's titles) although I was always known as Maria.

Summer 1982

Uncle Paul always came to stay for a week during the school summer holidays. Every morning during his stay, we would get up and watch various cartoons. Then, after everyone was dressed, Daddy would go to work and Mummy, Uncle Paul, Teresa, Liam and I would go to church where Uncle Paul would say a private daily mass attended only by my family.
I was allowed to read the Psalms and use the big microphone and as I was never picked to do any speaking parts in school because I was timid in front of most people, this was a real novelty.
When Uncle Paul wasn't being a serious priest, he was a lot of fun. My parents were always in good moods while he was there and I was in my element. He had so much time for me and always endeavoured to answer my never ending questions such as, "What's a skeleton? What is in a heart? Where do ghosts live?" He would get the encyclopaedia and teach me whatever I wanted to know. He told me lots of stories, funny ones and scary ones. Due to my extremely active imagination, one of the ghost stories scared me

so much I was afraid to go upstairs alone for weeks so Mummy had to put a stop to them.

Due to my overactive mind I suffered lots of nightmares as a child and some nights I woke up screaming the place down. My ghost dreams were so intense they felt real and on one of these occasions I couldn't be consoled until Uncle Paul and Mummy had taken me all round the house to prove to me that there was nothing there. Uncle Paul opened every cupboard and door and would not leave me alone in my room until I was reassured and finally sleeping again. His never ending patience and his complete and utter understanding of my needs made me secure in his love.

I was an avid student, both in school and with the extra-curricular lessons my uncle gave me. He taught me to play chess and after only a few weeks, at just five years old, I was always able to beat my mother, nearly always managed to checkmate my father and sometimes even my uncle in just a few short moves. He was my best friend. Grownups weren't supposed to have favourites but they did, they just didn't admit it. I knew that Liam was my mother's favourite, Teresa, my father's and I was my Uncle Paul's. For my part, I regarded him as my personal property.

We would go to Spital Woods and he would hide, leaving trails for me and the rest of the family to find him. Sometimes, we would buy Saveaways, tickets that allowed us to go anywhere by train in Merseyside. One of us would point at a random station on the Mersey Rail route and we would just go there and explore the place. During the train journeys, I loved looking out at the fields, the peaceful landscapes, fantasising about living neither here nor there; just the place in between. We went to Chinese restaurants in Liverpool and Southport, the Little Chef in Eastham, countryside pubs in Bromborough and I developed a love of eating out.

Uncle Paul had told me that once he had a very bad temper but learnt to control it out of love for God. I couldn't believe he had ever had a temper; he was always so calm and even when I was naughty in front of him, like if I lost at a game or got irritated with my brother and sister, he would just look at me reproachfully and say my name. That would be enough; desperate to please him I would immediately stop and he would say "good, Maria," and we would carry on playing.

My uncle was the best person in my life and I adored him. I felt the Holy Spirit around him and the whole house seemed lit up from the inside when he was there; I rarely fought with my sister when he was visiting and my parents never smacked me. It was when he wasn't there that the darkness fell. I was always devastated when it was time for him to go back to his parish in Liverpool and often cried or got sulky after begging him to stay longer. I hated that I could only see him once a week on a Wednesday. Even though I knew it wasn't his fault I still felt abandoned and my feelings of insecurity, always bubbling under the service, tormented me. I just wished he could stay forever and never have to go home. Why couldn't he be a priest at our church instead of the one in Liverpool? Life would be perfect then.

In the September after my communion I started my second year in the infant school. I loved learning in class and was on the top table for reading. There was some very competitive reading at our table. The books had spines of various covers, each colour signifying which level the book was. I had beaten Sarah Howden to yellow level much to her annoyance, made worse by the fact that I couldn't help but gloat at this victory.

In school I was considered very clever and well behaved. I unfailingly got good reports in everything except PE, which I hated. I was too scared to climb up to the top of the metal apparatus in the dinner hall that passed as a gym, terrified I would fall. On sports day I had taken so long to complete my egg and spoon race that everyone cheered when I finally came in a good five minutes after the others had finished. Mummy had been proud and told me it didn't matter if I had come last; the fact that I hadn't given in was really good and that I was the only one who hadn't cheated and held my egg. *Oh, so good was I.*

In the November of that year we went to Lourdes to visit the grotto where Our Lady had appeared. Uncle Paul accompanied us and I was hoping to be visited by Our Lady while I was there. At the airport, Uncle Paul had beeped going through one of the machines and we both got pulled to one side. Uncle Paul had thought it was hilarious and I ended up laughing with him.

"I must look like a criminal," he whispered conspiratorially as the big policemen patted him down.

I wondered how they could mistake him for a criminal. Didn't they know catholic priests were good and would never do anything naughty? Lourdes was our only foreign holiday as a family to this date but it was my Uncle Paul who made it a special memory for me.

Christmas 1982
After returning from Lourdes, my class began preparing for the Nativity play. Last year I had been an angel, or, more to the point, one of what I felt was one of the leftover parts. That year I really wanted to be Mary. I deserved it; after all, I was the closest to Jesus and Mary on account of me regularly receiving the sacraments. It was only right I be Mary.
I was very put out when the coveted part was given to Sarah Howden. She knew how badly I wanted to be Mary and smirked in my direction as her name was read out.
"Mary didn't even have blonde hair like Sarah," Mummy comforted me later; "she was dark like you." At that I felt slightly mollified.
After my initial disappointment over the casting, I got caught up in the excitement of Christmas. I liked being dressed as an angel and loved my gold tinsel halo. All of the infants were participating in the Nativity play; the juniors, if they chose, could be in the choir.
The play was held on a Sunday afternoon so that all the parents could be there as no one worked on Sundays. My mother's father, Granddad, had come to stay for Christmas and even though he was an Anglican he accompanied us to the church for the choir service and Nativity play. It was dark and the air was foggy when we left a couple of hours later. I always felt slightly surreal when I was out after dark, as if I was not quite awake and reality had changed. The church was only a five minute walk from our

43

house. Daddy bundled us through the door and had cups of tea ready for us all.

Liam was asleep so for once he wasn't taking Mummy's attention and I sat with my sister on either side of our mother, cuddled into her drinking Daddy's lovely sweet tea. After we had gone to bed, the smell of fish and chips wafted up the stairs, along with the ever present stench of Granddad's tobacco pipe.

We crept downstairs very quietly, pausing at the bottom, waiting for one of our parents to hear us so that we could judge whether it was best to retreat upstairs or venture further.

"Who's that out on the stairs?" Mummy sounded as if she was laughing.

Giggling, we decided it was definitely safe to venture further.

"Can we have some chips please?" we chorused together, turning our big hopeful eyes on our parents. Daddy waited to see what Mummy would say.

"Go back up to bed. We'll shout you down when we've had ours, but don't wake Liam."

We raced back up to bed but a few minutes later we were called down. Although there were only a few chips left, we both declared that they were the best chips we had ever tasted and noisily sucked all the salt and vinegar of the paper wrappers.

I awoke on Christmas morning to a fat red stocking on my bed.

"He came, he came!" I yelled in excitement, tipping everything out of my stocking.

Teresa was doing the same. We had pretty little soaps, chocolates and tubed Smarties. There were tangerines and apples in there too which we ignored. After devouring half the sweets, we ran into our parents' room.

"It's Christmas," we both shouted in unison.

Our parents sat up smiling. Mummy got up to make bacon and eggs, our favourite breakfast.

After breakfast, we were allowed to open one present before church. Teresa and I had a pair of ear muffs each, something we had wanted all winter as they were the height of fashion then. We wore them proudly to church, telling our mother we were too cold to take them off in church.

After church, it was a free for all in present opening. I had a Barbie house, new Barbie clothes and all sorts of little packages of socks, gloves and even a new umbrella. One of my aunties had given me some lavender puffs to put in my draw to make my clothes smell nice. Uncle Paul had bought me a lovely red watch and had already taught me to tell the time. We had picked it out together a few weeks before and I honestly didn't think there was any other little girl in the world as lucky as me when I put it on.

We had a lovely Christmas dinner and spent the afternoon pigging out on crisps, biscuits, sweets and chocolate until we couldn't eat any more. Teresa and I agreed at bedtime that Christmas had been absolutely the best day ever and we both wished it could be Christmas every day.

Chapter 4
Discords in Childhood

In our house, it was Daddy who always washed up and made cups of tea. He also used to hoover up very vigorously, pretending to hoover up our feet which made us scream with laughter. Although Mummy cooked, washed the clothes and ironed for hours while sitting in her armchair watching television, she only bothered about the state of the house when our paternal grandmother who we knew as Grandma came to visit with one or the other of our father's siblings. Teresa and I hated these visits because for some reason we had to do all the cleaning.

We would sit side by side for hours as we attempted to scrub ingrained dirt from the dining room skirting boards, walls and doors. Our hands hurt and went red from the dirty chemical suds. The task was monotonous and the walls never seemed to get any cleaner. Liam never had to do anything on account of him being just a toddler. Then, when the dreaded relations visited, they never came into the newly cleaned dining room at all so it felt like all our efforts had been in vain.

We also had to change our own bedding and make our own sandwiches for school which we just filled with margarine as we didn't like the sandwich spread that was often the only choice in the fridge. As for snacks, I begged crisps and penguin bars from my friends' lunch boxes; rarely was there such luxury for the McClure girls.

Apart from my reluctance for these tasks, I did try hard to be good in every way as I had an extremely over active conscience. Teresa and I had stolen a sweet once from my mother's bag but after a few minutes I had suffered severe pangs of guilt and fears of hellfire and ended up running to my mother and tearfully confessing the theft, convinced I had committed a mortal sin. I also confessed for Teresa much to her annoyance. My mother was pleased with my honesty and rewarded me with another sweet but told Teresa she wouldn't be allowed any for the rest of the day as she hadn't felt any remorse and had even tried to shush me when her name was mentioned. For some reason, she refused to even speak to me for the rest of the day.

I was a sensitive child as well as shy. I was more confident with adults than with children as I always felt a little different from them. They didn't understand me and I felt overwhelmed in school at times. I was too shy to ask the teacher for permission to go the toilet, as sometimes the boys got shouted at when they asked, and this caused more than one embarrassing accident in class, especially if I laughed. To my mortification, pee would just gush out and I would have no control over it. There were many times when I arrived home from school wet, having to stand by the fire to dry myself. If my mother ever noticed the sour smell, she never mentioned it. Although I was bright, I was not physically tough. I was often taunted by certain class mates and called a Goody Two-shoes. Sarah Howden was the worst, she always had something to sneer at me for and no matter how hard I tried to be nice and agreeable with her, Sarah would find fault with me.

As the months passed, I felt that Mummy never had time for me and was always telling me off. She treated Teresa and me differently from Liam and I never felt loved by her. I tried to regain her attention by asking her for regular little talks about Jesus or Mary or other biblical matters. This was the only time when I got Mummy's full attention, other than when I was ill - Mummy was very loving when I was ill -but she seemed to be tiring of the little talks that I constantly needed.

"For heaven's sake! I haven't got time for another 'little chat.' There are two other children in this family you know," snapped my mother one evening after I had requested some time with her alone.

"But it's really important Mummy."

"No! I get the feeling you just use these little chats so you can have me all to yourself. Life doesn't work like that. You aren't the only child here."

"Mummy, please...."

"No, subject closed. I am busy."

I ran upstairs to my room crying. Mummy never even wanted to cuddle me anymore and only last week I had been told that I was too big – I was six by then - to sit on Uncle Paul's knee because it wasn't right to 'maul' him. I loved cuddling him and sitting on his knee but my mother had made out like I was doing something really wrong. I had felt confused, hurt and a little embarrassed. She never had time for me. I felt let down by her and by God who I tried so hard to please and by Uncle Paul who sometimes didn't even come on a Wednesday due to him being busy in his own church. I had sulked so badly the last time that had happened and the following week when he did turn up I had refused to speak to him until just before he went home, breaking my own heart in the process. I had to reject him because I had felt so abandoned the week before but then I had hurt more for doing so.

Mummy called me for dinner and I went downstairs. I could hear my four year old sister complaining, "Don't like macaroni cheese."

My heart sank. Not macaroni cheese again. I hated it and it made me sick, literally. Just the thought of those slimy cheesy things in my mouth made me retch.

"I'm not hungry, Mummy."

"Maria, don't start. Get in here and sit down. You will not leave this table until you have eaten it, ANY OF YOU!"

She glared at my sister and me but smiled adoringly at Liam, who unfailingly ate everything on his plate and everyone else's if he was allowed to, as she noticed him shovelling his dinner into his mouth. I sat down and looked at my sister who had already set her face into a determined sulk.

"Eat it," barked my mother.

"Mummy, it makes me sick. I can't eat it."

"Maria, you always have to argue. At least Teresa keeps her mouth shut. You. Look at Liam eating his without complaining like a good boy. Why can't you be like that?"

I wanted to say I would never want to be like that if it meant being like Liam but thought the better of it. Mummy looked angry and I remembered what had happened last time. I began pushing the food round my plate with my fork. I kept picking it up and putting it to my lips but as the scent hit me I wanted to vomit. It was disgusting. It looked like someone had been sick into my bowl. Teresa just sat there fuming quietly. I was gratified when she gave me a slight smile and smiled back at her.

"And what are you smiling at?" demanded my

mother. "I fail to see what's funny about two girls who will not eat their dinner. It is a sin to waste food."

I dropped my eyes to the table, trying hard not to look at my sister's ferocious scowl for fear of laughing. Liam was licking his bowl clean and Mummy beamed proudly in his direction. Jealousy and resentment pierced my heart. *Mummy used to look at me like that.* My mother finished her dinner and went into the kitchen.

"Not eating it" Teresa stated flatly, "it's howible."

"Let's push it to the side like this, then it looks like there's less."

We both pushed it to the side, declaring loudly, "mmm, this is yummy."

Mummy came back into the dining room and immediately saw that we hadn't eaten anything. She picked up a forkful and tried to force it into Teresa's mouth.

"Nooo," screamed my sister, attempting to fight Mummy's hands. Mummy had done that to me last time we'd had macaroni cheese, making me choke and heave violently before becoming hysterical with sobs. Eventually she gave it up and went back into the kitchen. Teresa recovered herself and looked even more mutinous. I picked up a piece of pasta with my fork and pretended to flick it at her. Teresa immediately did the same back and her soggy pasta flew off hitting me straight in the eye. We both giggled despite ourselves. Mummy came rushing back in, furious.

"Either you can sit here all night until you eat it or you can have a good hiding and go to bed."

"Not eating it," Teresa was in one of her famous sulks

now and nothing could get to her when she was like that.

"Well, Maria? Do I have to force it into your mouth or would you prefer a good hiding?"

She picked up a forkful and pushed it towards me.

"No, Mummy, please just give me a good smack and send me to bed. I can't eat it."

It was the lesser pain. A smacked bottom didn't seem like such a bad idea compared to the other alternative.

"Very well. This will hurt me more than it hurts you."

Mummy, why do you want to hurt me?

"Come here."

I walked slowly over to her and allowed myself to be put over her knee. She slapped my bare bottom several times. I refused to scream but tears of humiliation were flowing freely down my cheeks as I was allowed to climb off her knee and pull my pants up again. I went to leave the room but Mummy shouted. "Sit down!"

"But I thought I could go to bed if I had a hiding."

"Sit down and eat."

I sat, wincing as my red hot bottom made contact with my chair. I couldn't believe I still had to sit there despite the horrible agreement we had just made. I wanted to scream at her about how unfair this was but didn't dare. She was always saying that she never lied but she had just gone back on her word and that was the same as lying wasn't it?

The next day after school, Teresa and I were presented with heated up macaroni but Liam got a nice dinner of fried egg and chips. Mummy was capable of this for a couple of days now until the food became completely uneatable. Teresa and I were unable to eat it, we weren't being naughty on purpose. No smacks followed that time but we got nothing else to eat all night.

The next day was a Wednesday which lifted my spirits somewhat. Uncle Paul's weekly visit surely meant I would no longer be in disgrace because Mummy was always different when he was around. Teresa and I waited on the front door step for him after returning from school. When we saw his familiar, beloved figure, tall and dressed in black from head to toe apart from the white collar he wore, we ran joyfully towards him screaming "Uncly Bunkly" our pet name of the moment for him.

He pretended to be very angry, "Who are you? Get off me you little pests."

We jumped on him and entered the house giggling.

"Hello, Father." Mummy greeted him.

God! Why did she always greet him as Father? Yes, he was a priest but he was her brother too.

"Maria, stop jumping on your uncle. You're too big to behave like that."

I was slightly pacified as Uncle Paul told Mummy I was alright. We watched TV with him and Daddy in our bedroom until dinner was ready. We were dismayed to see the plates of three day old macaroni being brought in for us. Not having had a main meal since Sunday, only being allowed my breakfast and my usual margarine sandwich for school lunch, I was starving. Mummy returned with two steaming plates of delicious smelling potatoes, meat and gravy for the men. When the door was closed, Uncle Paul glanced at me and then spoke to Daddy.

"What's going on here, Paddy? Why have they got different dinners?"

Daddy explained - albeit omitting the part of my chastisement - we had refused to eat our dinner. When he got to the fact that it was the third day we'd been presented with it, Uncle Paul gave me his plate, taking the vomit pile on a plate for himself. He motioned for Daddy to do the same for Teresa.

"This will be our secret, okay girls?"

We eagerly began eating the meat and potatoes. Never had any dinner tasted so delicious!

"Thanks Uncly Bunkly, thanks Daddy," we sang.

Thank God for Uncle Paul otherwise we might have had that dinner forever.

The bell rang at three thirty pm signalling the end of school. All of us from the first year junior class got our bags and traipsed to the door. Mummy informed us we were going to the hairdresser and that we were going to have all our hair cut off.

Teresa and I looked at each other in puzzlement.

"What do you mean, Mum?" I asked.

"Exactly what I say. You have become far too vain recently, Maria, and Teresa is beginning to follow suit even though her hair isn't as nice as yours."

Unsurprisingly, Teresa glared at me.

Mummy grabbed one of each of our arms firmly, putting our hands beneath hers on the handles of Liam's pram and marching us along. I had always been told by everyone how lovely my hair was. Last year, when the boy's playground had work going on, the older boys from the top juniors had shared the girls' and infants' playground and kiss chase had quickly become a favourite game. I was always targeted, probably because I was so small and couldn't run fast and one of the big boys, Lee, had always told me he liked my hair. He had even brought me a box of chocolates for a Christmas present that he presented me with in front of my whole class during morning registration and come carol singing to my house. Our innocent romance had died once the big boys had gone back to their own playground and then he had left to go to senior school.

My mother hated my vanity and often told me, 'Vanity, thy name is Maria' even though she seemed to enjoy her friends complimenting my eyes and hair. She refused to let us wear nail polish and once had removed us from a neighbour's party because our friend's older sister had put mascara on us. On arriving home she had washed it off with soap and water, stinging our eyes painfully. I deduced that this latest punishment was probably because of an incident the other week, when Teresa and I had rubbed our cheeks raw with a face cloth, thinking we looked like we had blusher on and failing to realise until it was too late that we had actually rubbed the top layers of skin off our faces. Our cheeks had stung painfully for a few days and Mummy had said it served us right for being so vain. I thought that we'd already learned our lesson; I, for one, would not be rubbing my cheeks like that again.

Millie, the blonde hairdresser, looked horrified as my mother explained that she wanted our hair cropped. "No. surely not? Look at their beautiful hair. You don't really want it all cut off, do you?"

Mummy assumed a pained expression and explained that there was a nit problem in the school and that our long hair was too hard to deal with. *I had suffered nits once in my entire life.* I fixed my eyes on to Millie, hoping she would refuse to do it but she just sighed

and put the gown around Teresa's shoulders. My sister
was too proud to cry and sat there glaring at the
mirror. I stared at myself in the mirror feeling like a
tragic heroine. My hair looked so beautiful, even
unbrushed as it was now. I fought back tears. I didn't
want my hair cut like a boy's. Everyone at school
would laugh at me. Thank God Lee and the kiss-chase
boys wouldn't see what had become of me.
After what only seemed like a few minutes, Millie
had arranged Teresa's hair into a bowl head type bob.
It was awful but definitely preferable to a boy crop.
Teresa was fuming silently. Sometimes she fought
like mad and my mother had confided to me once that
she worried that Teresa might go right off the rails
when she was older. I had also felt my sister's wrath
before now and hated that I sometimes came off
worse than her when we got physical. She had bitten
me on occasions and broken the skin on my shin one
time after she had kicked me in school in front of all
her friends when I'd been trying to boss her about.
According to Mummy, the day she'd turned three,
Teresa's behaviour had become atrocious and had
stayed that way for months. She then became very ill,
spent many nights in hospital and almost died but
when my mum had prayed all night to Our Lady, she
had healed miraculously, her behaviour too, but she
still sometimes went berserk when she threw a
tantrum. Today, however, my younger sister was not
saying a word. Probably wouldn't say anything for a
couple of days. When she sulked, nothing could get
her out of it and she wouldn't speak to anyone, no
matter who had upset her.
"Is that okay?" Millie turned Teresa to face Mummy.
"It suits her like that, no need to go any shorter, I

don't think."

"I suppose it will do," muttered Mummy ungraciously, "although it's not what I asked for. Do Maria's in a crop."

"But Mum, why can't I have mine like hers?"
I thought my sister's hair was awful but at least she had some left covering her ears.

"No, you are having a crop. Don't start your arguing in here please, we are in public."

"Right, come on love, your turn." Millie smiled brightly, masking whatever she really felt about the situation.

"No, please Mum, everyone will laugh at me. No one else has boy hair."

"I don't care about anyone else. Nuns have their hair cut off before entering the convent and you always say you want to be a nun. You will sit there and have you hair cut now."

At that moment I decided I was NEVER going to be a nun! I wanted to be pretty and popular and now I would be neither of those things. I closed my eyes, already tears were pricking them and I had to stifle a sob as I felt the cold scissors cutting the hair by my neck and ears.

After about twenty minutes, Millie informed me she had finished. I was devastated. Words couldn't describe what I felt now as I gazed at my reflection. My ears stuck right out and they looked huge. My face resembled a pixie's. I was really and truly ugly. My cropped hair clung to my head like a little shiny cap. Determined not to cry, I allowed the hair dresser to take off the cloak and help me into my coat.

"I'm sorry sweetheart." This was whispered in a voice too low for my mother to hear.

How was I going to face the kids in school the next day? I was never going to live this down.

"Stella Maria, Star of the Sea, more like flipping Skinhead of the Sea!" laughed Hayley from Junior 2. I fixed my eyes down towards the dinner table, my cheeks flaming for all to see. I hated Hayley for mocking the title I was so proud of. Apart from Madeleine Bell and Gillian Bremner, everyone had laughed at me all morning. The boys had been terrible. The teacher had had to tell them all to stop pointing and jeering when I had arrived in the classroom that morning.

"Why though? Why did you want your hair like that? It's horrible." Hayley seemed genuinely confused.

"Not so pretty now are you?" The spiteful voice belonged to Lucy Roberts, a cousin of Sarah Howden also in the next class up. Just then two older boys ran past, one of them slapping the back of my unhappy head.

"Slaphead!"

The girls sniggered again, except for Madeleine and Gillian who smiled sympathetically at me. Their pity was too obvious and I fixed my gaze again on the table trying to ignore the snide comments.

Eventually I looked up and stated bravely. "Sticks and stones may break my bones but words will never hurt me."

This was a saying my mum had taught me but it made everything worse. There was an explosion of giggles.

"Oh my God Maria, you're priceless."

Lucy and Hayley started mimicking my words in squeaky voices. *Thanks Mum for that great piece of advice.* I wanted the floor to swallow me up. I was the laughing stock of the school. I just prayed my hair would grow back soon.

Two weeks later, Teresa committed some small misdemeanour and was marched back to the hairdresser's. She returned home with a crop identical to my own. Although I was relieved that I wasn't the only one with boy hair, I felt very sad for her as I comforted her noisy sobs in our bedroom when we were alone after dark.

Chapter 5
The Watch

When I was almost eight, my mum sat us down to tell us some exciting news. We were going to have a baby brother or sister in about six months' time. I was ecstatic. I had forgotten my jealousy of my brother's birth and although I was told I had also been very jealous when my sister had been born, I had been too young to retain any memory of this. My mother seemed happy and talked to me about the process of pregnancy and childbirth. I felt very grown up to be taken into her confidence.

Two weeks before school broke up for summer, I caught whooping cough and was told I would be sick for at least six weeks, meaning I would miss the end of summer term, the most exciting part of the school year. Liam was also ill so he was moved into my bedroom with me and Teresa into his so that she could sleep through our frequent, prolonged coughing fits.

All this I could have coped with if my mother had been able to be there with me, stroking my hair back off my face, soothing me to sleep and dosing me with medicine but due to the baby in her belly, she was advised not to have too much contact with either myself or Liam. A couple of weeks into my illness, my mum had to go to hospital. I remember right before she went, her coming into my bedroom to say goodbye. I had a very bad feeling that the baby was dead and that it was my whooping cough that had killed it. *I want my mummy.* I sobbed noisily as she was leaving, causing myself to cough so much that she rushed back into the room.

"Whoop, Maria," she urged me, rubbing my back.
"You're convulsing again."
I was scared of whooping as it hurt so much but
eventually, after my face had practically turned blue, I
whooped, drawing the breath back into my body. The
ambulance pulled up outside and took my mother
away.
A few days later, she returned home red eyed and
unhappy.
"I lost the baby. He or she is in heaven now."
How could God be so cruel as to take a baby away
from us before it was even born and while I was so
ill? I was seriously beginning to doubt God's love for
us all but immediately after having these thoughts I
felt guilty. I didn't get better until two weeks after
school had started meaning that I had been ill for ten
whole weeks and also for my eighth birthday. I
returned to school a second year junior, quite subdued
by the summer's events.

After the miscarriage, my mother became evermore
wrapped up in her faith. She went to church more
frequently, both for daily mass and to talk with the
priests. She also began doing the church cleaning, for
free. The church was on the same grounds as the
school, which meant all my classmates could see my
mum entering the priests' house every dinnertime.
Mortifying! Eventually, much to my relief, she had an
argument with one of the priests and started going to
a church in another part of Wallasey.
This church was smaller and had a warm feel to it. I
loved the smell of incense that they burned more
frequently here. The priests were friendly and I liked
them. One day, she announced that she was going to

start doing something called "The Watch" and that during all school holidays we would be going to church at ten thirty every morning and staying until after midday mass ended at twelve thirty.

"Two hours every day? That's ages!"

She looked at me reproachfully as she replied.

"Maria I'm ashamed of you. You used to love going to church and now you can't manage a couple of hours for God, He who has given you so much. Ever since you turned six you have changed."

This was something she had told me a lot over the last couple of years. Even Uncle Paul had begun to criticise my behaviour recently. Although he never shouted at me, his quiet reproachful looks when my mum told him bad things about me stung and angered me as he only ever heard her side.

"How can you argue about doing God's work?" she went on. "The church has to stay shut every day due to vandals and thieves. That's where we come in. I've told Father James that we will happily sit in the church every day so it can be open. No one will try to damage the church while I'm there."

God forbid they would! *Mum, why are you like this?* No one else's mums went to church so often even though they were Catholic too. My mum wouldn't even let me go to Brownies like my friends, simply because it was held in an Anglican Church hall. The fact her own dad was an Anglican didn't come into it. Every morning throughout the holidays we either walked or got the bus to the new church. While there, we weren't allowed to speak, laugh, or even move without our mother's permission and she only permitted us to bring prayer books and rosary beads with us. Even Liam got told off by her for being too noisy during The Watch.

The worst part of The Watch was that Mum seemed to feel it gave her rights over the front bench and refused to move out of it even when there was a funeral on. We would stay there for the entire service, forcing the bereaved family to either sit behind us or in the other aisle. I felt ashamed as everyone looked at us, silently questioning why this strange family was at the funeral. *I am sorry, bereaved family. I don't wanna be here either.*

We were soon the most regular of all the church regulars. There was another family a bit like ours with two girls of a similar age to Teresa and me. To pass the time we would have dirty look competitions and pull impressive, terrible faces or simply stare each other out like we had seen older girls do. We did however meet a nice old man called Tommy who slipped us pound coins and sweets after mass sometimes. He went to church every day too but I think it was because he was old and lived alone. Church must have been the highlight of his day. Then there was Sheila, who lived in the local mental home and came to church daily. I remember being really embarrassed that my mother almost came to daily blows with Sheila over who could get into the sacristy first after mass had ended. In the end my mum got so determined to get there first that she began collecting all our prayer books up while the priest was still saying the final prayers and bustling us out of the pew immediately after the priest and his altar boys left the altar, practically joining the priest's sacred procession. If Sheila got there first, my mum would be annoyed all day about it. It was on one of these days that an incident happened that I would never forget.

Mum had gone on about Sheila all the way home to her sister Rose, who had come to meet us for mass with our three cousins who were similar ages to Teresa, Liam and me. I had asked for some sweets when we got off the bus but she'd said no. I honestly didn't think I had pulled a face about it, I certainly hadn't meant to but my mum got very angry.

"How dare you be so insolent? Say sorry now!"

"I didn't do anything."

"Now you're lying. Admit that you just pulled a nasty face at me."

This had happened before with other trivial little things that I honestly had no memory of doing and I would end up being smacked for lying as well as the misdemeanour I had supposedly committed. It confused me to say the least. I said nothing, hoping that if I didn't argue maybe she'd forget about it, on account of Auntie Rose being there.

When we got home, the interrogation began. I insisted I hadn't pulled a face but she told me that if I didn't admit it I would be in for a hiding, this time with the riding crop. I gulped; the slipper and the hairbrush hurt enough but a riding crop… I knew that even if I admitted it now, I would in effect be admitting that I had lied all those times and would get the crop anyway. Teresa and Liam and our cousins were watching me with fascinated horror.

"Say sorry."

"No, I haven't done anything wrong. Why don't you ever believe me?"

"Because you're a liar. Remember the crosses on the stairs?"

I remembered only too well. A while back, for some

reason I don't remember, I had drawn little crosses all the way up the stairs with a pen and when Mum had questioned us, I had vehemently denied it, terrified of what would follow. I had tried to blame Liam, knowing he would get away with it. She had conducted an investigation the FBI would have been proud to call their own, getting all the clues together to prove once and for all that the crime had been committed by me, her wicked liar of a daughter. The most damning evidence was the fact the crosses had been drawn on the left hand side and I was left handed.

On the closing of the case, sentence also had to be passed, something which took days as my mother decided to ask Sister Agnes, a nun from one of the many convents we visited, for her advice. The old nun had looked at me and said in her gravelly Irish tones, "Make no mistake; there is a devil in that child. Take her home and give her a good hiding. It will hurt you more Catherine but you have to be strong."

How would it hurt my mum more? Up until then I had thought nuns were nice old ladies. I was sure Jesus wouldn't have told my mother to do that to me. I had watched her set her face into a martyr like yet determined expression. The waiting was worse than anything. Knowing all the way home I was going to be punished and degraded either with a slipper or a hairbrush or several sharp smacks on my bare backside was unbearable.

"Answer me or you will get the riding crop."

"I didn't do anything."

"Liam, get the riding crop."

"Don't want to," he replied warily.

Mum was incensed that he would talk back to her.

"Go and get it now, unless you want the same."

"Which one?" he asked, tears welling up as usual although I was slightly appeased as he threw me an apologetic look.

"The red one. The one of the liar herself. I think that's fitting."

I was very proud of the red riding crop encased in black leather that had been bought for me as a present to congratulate me on my fast improving horse riding skills. We went every Sunday after church to the riding stables in Moreton and my mum had been really impressed with my fast progress. I rarely used the crop on the horses although I had been reassured it didn't hurt them. She took the scarlet stick from Liam. I wished Uncle Paul was there, she'd never do this if he was.

"Last chance."

God where are you? Can't you see what's happening?

"Bend over."

I refused. She pushed me face down onto the stairs, smacking me as hard as she could with the riding crop. I screamed. Lashing, burning, stinging whips, burning legs, bum and back. *Please be over soon.*

"Mum, stop, please!"

The physical pain and humiliation of this happening to me in front of my cousins was tremendous. Only when I was crying uncontrollably was her anger was spent.

"Get upstairs to your room and stay there."

I went; my breath kept catching in painful hiccups. I tried hard to calm myself, not wanting to be sick like I had been when a similar incident had taken place in front of those same cousins and a school friend. I had cried myself to hysterics that time before vomiting all over the floor.

Usually at the time of punishment I truly believed I didn't deserve it and but later when Mum spoke to me again, I always felt sorry and realised that I must be a very wicked little girl who was ungrateful for all her gifts. I would crave my mother's love, her arms around me to make me feel safe and loved again and would say sorry just to get back in her affections. My mum never said sorry to me, or anyone, as far as I could make out although she spent hours in confession.

At least Dad bought sweets afterwards and although he didn't say sorry, he did say over and over that he didn't like having to do it and if I could just be a good girl he wouldn't have to. After he had punished us, he was always nice and friendly for a while but slowly he would begin losing his temper over nothing, lashing out at us, with that scary look where he would bite his tongue between his teeth as he pounced, his palm open for a good slap. More and more recently, the slipper had become his best friend, accompanying him through the tide of his temper and smacking our backsides so hard it couldn't have hurt any more if someone had set fire to it.

Mum was more controlled. She took her time thinking over the punishment. Sometimes it would seem like hours after the alleged crime before she finally passed sentence. Teresa and I would have to wait in our bedroom while she decided what to do with us. Then she'd tell us that we were to have the slipper and that Dad would be doing it when he came in from work. That meant we could have a further hour to wait before the dreaded slipper beat us into more angry, humiliated reflections of ourselves.

Once, when I'd told her that I felt like phoning the NSPCC about them, she'd been surprised, saying that I wasn't a battered child, I never had bruises or black eyes and that I came from a good respectable Catholic family and I should think myself lucky.

After a couple of hours, Auntie Rose came into the bedroom.

"Look what she did to me." I urged her, showing her purple welts rimmed with angry pinkie red splattered all over my back and thighs.

She put her hand on my shoulder and said they would get better soon and that I should try harder not to upset my mum. I knew then she would never help me or stand up for me. My opinion of adults was becoming bitterer and the storm within me was getting stronger. One day I would show them all that they couldn't hurt me anymore.

As Mum increased the amount of time she spent in church, she used our prayer times to further beat us into submission. She would demand of me that I name one good thing about myself. When I invariably couldn't because I knew she wouldn't agree - there was anything good to be said anymore - she would then direct me to list all my faults. Now that I was good at! I knew only too well what my faults were and she grudgingly told me that at least my conscience was still working correctly.

"See? All your arguments are pointless, because even you know you're wrong. Your list says it all."

There was nothing I could say in my defence. I was not a good girl anymore. I was an argumentative liar; jealous, bad-tempered, lazy, vain... the list was endless.

She began monitoring our behaviour with various little schemes, the most memorable being The Ladder. We children coloured the cardboard cut-out ladder in ourselves according to our mother's wishes; the top, symbolising heaven, had bright pretty colours such as pink, purple and blue, the middle rungs, earth, were coloured green, orange and yellow, whereas the bottom rungs, comprised of greys, browns and black, signified hell.

She cut little slots into each rung then cut out three angels from an advent calendar to represent the three of us and placed them onto the middle rung. She explained that every time we did something good we would go up a rung and on reaching the top, we would receive a reward such as extra pocket money or more sweets after dinner. If we were bad we would go down the ladder and woe betide anyone landing in hell!

At first, I thought that this was a great idea. I'd be so good that I'd earn lots of pocket money on top of the weekly pound from my dad but I never managed to get more than a few rungs above the green one no matter how hard I tried and if I did manage to get my angel onto a pretty coloured rung, I would always be demoted quite quickly. When in hell, I feared for my immortal soul because surely if I died at the time my cut out angel was in hell my soul would also go there. I would also receive a hiding, lose my pocket money and/or be grounded.

I desperately hoped God was more forgiving than my mum, but I believed deep down that God was very angry with me and Jesus very hurt. I didn't dare speak to my Uncle Paul about anything. To me, my parents represented God, my uncle, Jesus, and as Jesus would obviously stand with God, so would my uncle stand firm with my mum. Nothing I did ever seemed to be right anymore and I couldn't help arguing back and making it worse for myself.

One incident with the ladder left both my sister and me feeling extremely bitter towards our younger brother, more so than usual that is. Liam knew all he had to do to make us be nice to him and give into him was to threaten to cry. If we wouldn't let him play with us, he would take in a deep breath, building himself up to a crescendo which would release itself into a high pitched wail. We would have those few seconds of his intake of breath to stop him from crying. If our bribes interested him, the wail would die in his lungs, but other times he would let rip and scream the house down and Mum would rush in to see what we were doing to her precious baby, never listen to our side and pick him up and give him a treat while warning us our punishment would arrive duly. On this occasion, Mum had given us all ice cream for pudding and said whoever ate all theirs first would go to the top of the ladder. Teresa and I immediately began shovelling it into our mouths as fast as we could. We finished within about thirty seconds, both of us suffering a little from brain freeze.

"Yay, we won!"

Liam was eating very slowly and deliberately, unusual for him as he usually gobbled everything in sight as fast as he could. Mum watched him fondly. She got up and moved Liam from his place two rungs beneath the green one, right up to two rungs beneath the top and removed ours from where they'd been near the top for once, putting them down to where Liam's had been..

"Mum, that's not fair...." we began simultaneously.
"Yes, it is, I am not going to reward you for your bad manners."
"Mum that is so unfair! You said whoever finished first, not whoever ate nicest."
"MARIA!" she shouted, "You always argue, well for that you are going further down the ladder."
"That's so unfair," I exploded, "isn't it Teresa?"
My sister's eyes met mine but she didn't answer. She knew better. My angry mother marched back to the ladder and threw my figure to the floor.
 "Hell is too good for you."
I was horrified. *Too bad for hell!* I ran upstairs and locked myself in the bathroom. I burned with injustice. I simply couldn't win. However hard I tried to please my mother, she just loved Liam, that was so obvious and as for God and the devil, well, the devil was probably fairer. I cried and fumed for what felt like hours but eventually had to come out of the bathroom and go downstairs for prayers. My dad was home by then and desperate not to be smacked, I apologised to my mum.
"It's okay but you have a lot of work to do to pull yourself back up from the bottom of the ladder."
In a show of forgiveness, she took me into the kitchen and placed my angel figure a mere two rungs from the bottom.
"That's for being humble enough to apologise," she explained magnanimously.
I was so grateful not to be punished physically and to have escaped hell that I managed to squash my previous anger and spent the rest of the evening snuggled up with my mother on the couch, revelling in the maternal love I felt emanating from her and

promising myself that in future I would try harder to behave.

Chapter 6
A child with potential

I had begun recorder lessons in school during dinner time and often brought my recorder home to play. Unable to read music very well at first I would work out how to play familiar songs without any sheet music. My mother was very impressed. When I told her I just sort of worked out how to play the songs she looked thoughtful. The next time Uncle Paul visited, she told him that she suspected I was musical. Apparently playing by ear was a sign of talent. At Uncle Paul´s request, I happily entertained them with the various hymns and Christmas carols I had taught myself.

"That is very impressive, Maria."

I glowed with pride.

"I love playing music, Uncle, but the recorder doesn't have many notes so I can't play everything that I want to."

He looked at me thoughtfully.

"What instruments do you like the look of? One of my favourites is the clarinet, a beautiful instrument."

Immediately I replied the clarinet although I would have loved to play the piano. The next week, we went to the music shop and when we left it was with a second hand clarinet that my uncle had a paid a whole ninety pounds for. I was so excited. A clarinet of my very own and best of all it came in a small case, similar to the one that Uncle Paul always carried with him. I felt very proud to carry it home and hoped that everyone who saw me would know that I was carrying a clarinet.

My mother arranged for private music lessons as my

school only offered clarinet lessons to the top two junior years. Every week, a man called Mr Smith came to the house. He affirmed that I was extremely talented and I learnt quickly to read music, play scales and little pieces of classical music. Uncle Paul was very encouraging and bought me some classical music tapes by composers such as Mozart, Beethoven and Tchaikovsky. Mozart was my favourite; his melodies spoke to my soul.

Teresa couldn't play a note and was tone deaf. Our headmaster had taken her to one side once during choir practice and asked her to sing quietly, later commenting to me that she sang like a frog, something I couldn't wait to tell her later. My sister was always trying to outdo me with everything so this little piece of revenge tasted good.

Music became a very important part of my life and I practised dedicatedly every day. As a reward I was taken to a concert at the Liverpool Royal Philharmonic and I decided my ambition was to be a professional musician.

That year, my uncle finally managed to teach me to ride a bike. For all my intelligence, I still lacked confidence in physical activities. I was always the last to be picked for teams at school during PE and still couldn't swim despite weekly lessons at Leasowe Leisure Centre. I was terrified of drowning and in PE I was so frightened that the ball would hurt me that I always dodged it when it came my way. With regards to bike riding, I was terrified of falling. My mum said I hadn't walked until I was sixteen months old as I had been too frightened to let go of her skirt. It was surprising how good I was at horse riding given my fears of all things physical.

Uncle Paul had been teaching Teresa and me how to ride the bikes my dad had bought us and one day he just simply let go of my saddle without me noticing. I continued riding just fine and when I came to the end of the pavement, he came running up; full of pride as he cheered that I had done it alone. I was ecstatic. Teresa learnt a couple of weeks later and we spent many a happy weekend with the local kids riding around the block by our house. Liam was among the younger ones who had trikes and scooters, innocent, carefree times.

We also had some rabbits, a budgie and a canary which we had to help our parents care for. I have happy memories of helping my dad clean out those rabbit hutches on Saturday afternoons. In some ways my parents tried hard to make us happy.

However, despite the good parts of my life, music, horse riding, pets and bike riding with my friends, I was not happy deep down. The punishments still continued and ever since the haircut I felt ugly and hated how I looked in the mirror. My mother told me repeatedly that vanity was a sin and I knew my uncle agreed with her on that. I just wanted to be like my friends, to look like them, be pretty again, but with the scarecrow imitation my shorn hair had now grown into, it was impossible. I kept all my feelings bottled up; expressing them only through the sad melodies I played on my clarinet.

I was very excited. I was nine years old and going away from home for the first time for a musical weekend in Anglesey in North Wales with my Saturday morning orchestra. We were going to be sleeping in dormitories, just like the ones I had read about in my Malory Towers and St. Clare's books. I wondered whether we'd have a midnight feast and hoped someone would suggest it. I was the youngest kid going and although I was nervous because there were so many big kids, I was really looking forward to it. Teresa, however, was extremely jealous and kept annoying me with snide little comments. I had been trying to ignore her but she had become infuriating.

"You think you're so good but you're sooo stupid," sang Teresa, "I'm glad you're going away, we won't have to listen to your stupid clarinet all weekend."

"Shut up, you're just jealous."

"Of what? You? As if. "Teresa stuck her tongue inside her lower lip and pulled a face at me.

Before long we were fighting, pulling hair, grabbing flesh and smacking each other as hard as we could. The door burst open.

"What on earth is going on in here?" Mum shrieked, "You're like a pair of little savages. Where is my fight book?"

Recently she had begun keeping record of all our fights, in a little blue notebook. After every fight we had to list with her who had done what. She would then decide on a suitable punishment for the one she found guilty of starting it and the other would get off with minimal consequences. The problem was, by the time we were interrogated, we usually couldn't remember who had done what and would have already made friends again. "Too late now," she'd inevitably answer, "should have thought of that before you acted like a couple of wild animals."

We had to answer to every insult, punch, scratch, bite and kick, learning nothing except how to put the blame on the other one in order to save ourselves.

"Mum, this time it wasn't me. You know how jealous she's been about me going to Anglesey, she started it."

"Teresa, is this true?"

"No, I don't care about stupid Anglesey," she stated belligerently.

"Well, that tone says to me that you are jealous. I am inclined to take Maria's word for it this time."

By the time the fight book was found, Teresa was in a terrible sulk that rendered her silent, enabling me to give solely my version of events. I left out any parts that painted me guilty.

"Okay Maria, go and get in the bath. You, Madam, stay there. Your father will be up to deal with you in a minute."

Teresa visibly paled and I felt a pang of guilt for what my sister was to face but quickly consoled myself that I had been blamed enough times for Teresa and this time she really had started it. I went to the bathroom and shut the door as I heard my father enter our bedroom. Teresa's wails started up almost immediately. I shuddered, thanking God that this time it wasn't me.

I got into the bath and lay back, letting the water cover my ears and completely soak my hair. I was interrupted by a loud rapping on the bathroom door. Startled, I sat up in the bath to hear my dad bellowing through the door.

"Teresa has told us the truth now you filthy little liar. We know it was you who started the fight and she has been chastised by my own bare hands because of it. What have you got to say for yourself?"

"Dad..."

"No, save your breath. What has just been done to

your little sister is waiting for you, only twice as bad. I will be up when you are dressed."

God help me! This time would be worse than usual because, in my father's eyes, my lies had caused my sister to suffer. I really wished Teresa hadn't had what came to her but I had known the only way to save myself was to put all the blame on to her.

I began washing my hair again, then every part of my body with painstaking care, repeating my actions obsessively to put off the inevitable. I knew every minute was bringing me closer to what felt like a death sentence. Eventually, I towelled myself dry, rubbing the cheeks of my bottom really hard in the hope it might ward off the pain coming. My dad's chastisements felt like fire raining down on me so I figured that if I made my skin hot now, it may not hurt as much. Since I had got older my dad no longer smacked my bare bottom but even through clothes, it still burnt. Briefly I thought of staying in the bathroom all night but knew that was impossible.

Teresa looked up as I entered our bedroom, her tearstained face caught between indignation and apprehension of what I might say.

"It's okay, I'm not mad at you, I'm just scared 'cos he's gonna kill me now."

"I wish I hadn't told them my side now," whispered Teresa, "but I was so mad at you."

"What am I gonna do? He's gonna hit me twice as hard this time."

"There's a Yellow Pages in here. You could put that in your knickers under your nightie and hope he won't notice."

The phone directory stuck out so much that despite the severity of the situation and our previous fight, we couldn't help laughing. Our laughter was hysterical, out of control and born from fear.

"I'm sorry, Teresa."

"I'm sorry too, I was jealous. Let's not fight anymore."

"I wish we never fought."

I really did wish that but sometimes when my younger sister annoyed me, a red haze would take over. No one else could anger me like Teresa and I wouldn't have dared to hit anyone else. I ended up putting three pairs of knickers on to try and keep the Yellow Pages in place under my nightie. I tried to walk round the room and the large book stayed in place. I heard my dad coming for me and felt tremors inside my belly.

"Let's be having you."

His voice was short and curt and I walked nervously into my parents' bedroom.

"Lie face down."

I climbed onto the bed and lay down. Immediately, I felt my dad's hand hit the book. He obviously felt it too as he grabbed the offending article, enraged.

"How dare you think you can make a fool of me? Didn't you think I would notice? Do you think I'm stupid or something?"

He threw the book across the room then thrashed my backside as hard as he could. The familiar scorching pain was not softened by the three pairs of knickers I was wearing and I tried hard not to cry out. This seemed to make him double his efforts in breaking me. The molten blows rained down without ceasing. Eventually I broke and screamed, "No, Dad, no more."

"Be quiet!" He smacked me a few more times for

good measure.

I could hear his heavy breathing and I hated him, absolutely hated him and my mother too. Always on about religion and God yet treating us like this. A repressed anger poisoned my heart.

He came back into our room about half an hour later with two packets of fruit pastels to make up for our punishments. I allowed him to kiss me on the head but didn't say a word. My mum came in before going to bed but I turned away from her, giving her the mouthful of hair she claimed to always get when she kissed me goodnight.

She always said that she 'refused to let the sun go down on her anger' but this time it was me who was angry. I had always found everything easy to forgive but hatred was beginning to take hold. I was sick of trying to be good, trying to make my parents love me when all they did was hold kangaroo courts, dreaming up justifications for painful, degrading punishments. My weekend away was ruined. All I wanted to do was to hide away. I was even quieter than usual, too shy to speak and too unhappy to care.

When I returned from Anglesey, I told them I'd twisted my ankle and was taken for an X-ray at Mill Lane Minor Injuries Unit in Liscard. This was a trick I had learnt a while back after I had twisted my ankle for real playing chase in the school playground. It had earned me a lot of sympathy at the time and I never got hit while I was wearing a bandage. Neither was I expected to play PE and therefore suffer the humiliation of always being picked last or, if I was lucky, second to last.

I began to complain regularly of twisted ankles and wrists, even making myself fall on purpose, fooling my parents every time. After a few visits, the hospital said I must simply have a weakness in my joints, usually sending me home with a tuba grip, a tight white bandage designed to support the affected joint without bothering to X-ray. In my eyes though, this was a good form of visual evidence that supported my claims of being injured. Sometimes, I wished really could break something and be put in plaster, that way, I would never be punished or ridiculed in anyway. Six weeks in plaster was a long time but so far I had never managed it.

Around that time, the physical punishments seemed to stop. I don't know why but I was glad of the reprieve. Prayers, The Watch and our devout religious lifestyle continued but my parents did lighten up somewhat. By the time I was a top year junior I felt almost like a regular kid for a while. I was allowed to choose my own clothes with my tenth birthday money and I was allowed out a lot more on my own. My dad had given me my own house key and always made sure I had money for emergency phone calls home. Life became easier and less repressed for a while.

Chapter 7
The Stirrings of Rebellion

December 1987 –August 1988
I became friends with Vicki Morgan from my class
during the Christmas holidays of the last year in
primary school when she dared me to go with her to
smash one of the school windows. Despite my
misgivings, I went along with it and in doing so
proved to Vicki that I was a worthy friend to have.
From then on, we got up to all sorts, making silly
prank phone calls on people and calling out fire
engines to local addresses although I didn't really
enjoy doing this; I just enjoyed being friends with
someone who was tough.
I thought Vicki was really pretty. Her brown hair was
permed and she had big dark eyes that sparkled with
mischief although at times they appeared hard. She
was bigger than me but was very well proportioned
and already beginning to develop the curves that my
tiny frame still lacked. She was confident and
although often in trouble at school for her behaviour,
she was bright and witty. Being Vicki's friend helped
to destroy my Goody Two-Shoes image and I paid
Sarah back for the previous years of suffering she had
caused me, taking great delight in calling her names
and putting fake insects and plastic dog poo into her
desk, laughing at her screams when she found them.
Every week, I went to first aid classes with my dad
who was a very advanced first aider and had been part
of the St. Paul's Ambulance for years. He had
certificates all over the walls at home and I was
following in his footsteps, having won a competition
recently that had led to me having my picture in the

local paper.

"I can't wait to go to St Mary's, Dad." I announced one evening as we walked home from first aid class.

"Um, well about that," he seemed awkward, "your mother and I are putting you in for the Upton exam."

"Upton Convent? Why?"

"Because it is a far better school and will help immensely in your religious education as well."

"But, Dad, I wanna go to St. Mary's. All my friends are going there."

"It's not about your friends; it's about securing you the best possible education. If you pass the exam you'll get an assisted place meaning we only have to pay a small amount of the fees. You're more than capable of passing."

"Dad, it's a snob's school full of posh girls. I don't wanna go."

"Maria, Upton is the best girls' school on the Wirral, you should be grateful. Your mother and I have discussed this. You're doing the exam and that is that."

I told the girls on my table the next day and was surprised when Madeleine and Gillian said that they too were going for the exam. They actually seemed pleased about it. On the day of the exam, my two friends were so nervous about the exam that Gillian was actually sick when we got out of the car. Personally, I didn't see what the fuss was about, I would have been happy to fail. *I could fail it on purpose...*

I looked at the papers after the supervising nun ordered silence. The sums were easy but I deliberately put the wrong answers in all of the boxes. It might have been better to have done some right but

I wasn't taking any chances. With the English comprehension I wrote the wrong answers and while writing the essay, I used terrible grammar, misspelt words and omitted any punctuation.

However, despite totally failing the exam on purpose, my parents and headmaster believed me when my appalling results arrived a couple of weeks later and I gave them the excuse of having had a headache. By some miracle they managed to arrange for me to take the exam again. Two weeks later, I took the bus to Upton with my mum and was ushered in by a smiling nun, who I hated on sight, to a warm, cosy room on the ground floor. There was another girl of my age, pretty with big dark eyes and long straight black hair. She didn't look snobbish at all and spoke with a strong Birkenhead accent. Jessie smiled at me once our parents had left the room, telling me that she didn't want to come to this school but her adoptive mother was making her come.

"One day I'll run away and find me real parents," she announced confidently, "and get me hair permed too." I laughed nervously, unsure of what to say. I hadn't been expecting this type of girl to be at Upton and felt a little intimidated by her. The exam was easy and I really didn't dare to fail it again so I did my best. Might as well prove how quick my brain was if I was going to be coming here anyway.

A week later, I was told in front of all of my class that I had passed with flying colours and would be going with Madeleine and Gillian to Upton Convent in September. My cousin Shona had also passed the exam and my dad, always somewhat put down by his sisters, was very pleased indeed that I had also managed to get in to Upton.

Despite the fact that Upton Convent was hanging over me like some kind of bad dream, I enjoyed that last year at primary school more than any other. I joined the school chess club, the only girl able to beat all the boys at chess. Our class went away for a weekend to Colomendi in North Wales which was exciting. I was now confident enough to take leading roles in plays and I continued playing the joker and acting the part of the rebel. When the weather got warmer, Vicki and I often went to New Brighton Baths although I still couldn't swim much; a certain freedom represented in the pop music blaring out over the smell of chips and candy floss made me long for something more than my uptight family home and religion.

At home, prayer time still remained firmly in place, every evening at six-thirty. *Please God, don't let anyone ring the doorbell.* If they did, one of my parents would go out and tell the caller that we were saying prayers. On more than a few occasions it was Vicki with some of our class mates, who thought it hilarious that I was still a little church girl at home when I tried so hard to be tough in school.

The bible frustrated me. I found so many contradictions in the stories, especially between the New Testament and the Old Testament. My mother's answers never satisfied me and I always felt like I was going round in circles with her. She told me I should be a lawyer as I seemed to thrive on arguing, which was partly true but I really did feel frustrated at the hypocrisy I noticed in my religion. I wanted to understand the bible and have the innocent unquestioning faith I had had as a child but my mind questioned every detail.

To my mind, God was an angry God who judged us all harshly; sending people to hell left, right and centre, a complete contrast to the sweet Jesus who had been described to me as a child. Gone were the days when I waited faithfully for my Uncle Paul who now criticised my appearance and my sulky demeanour. I was more interested in playing out and pop music. I would spend every Sunday evening listening to the Top Forty on the radio, recording the popular songs that I liked on my cassette player. I rarely danced though after my mother had caught me one day and told me that for all my musical ability, I had no sense of rhythm whatsoever.

She banned me from listening to Madonna, my favourite singer, and took all my tapes away, claiming all her music was about sex. I had been confused at the sex reference and my ignorance caused her to sit down and lecture me once again on every sordid detail of the 'sexual act' something which disgusted and horrified me. I still didn't see what Madonna's songs had to do with sex though; such was my naivety at that time.

The sex talk reminded me of another horrible little lecture that I had been given as a very young girl on the evils of masturbating. All I knew was that it felt nice down there and when I was ill it made me feel better to rub myself on whatever ridge I could find in my mattress. I never touched there with my fingers, just stimulated it as secretly as I could under the privacy of my covers. My mother had informed me, after catching me in the act one night, that masturbating was a grave sin; dirty and very selfish. Every time I had indulged in it since, I had felt ashamed and dirty but I couldn't help doing it, especially if I was ill but I felt dirty and guilty every time I did so and I could never, ever confess it in confession meaning I never truly felt forgiven and cleansed as I knew God saw everything.

The last day of primary school was emotional. There was a leaver's disco and everyone signed each other's shirts wishing one another other luck although most of them would be going to St. Mary's together in September. It began to hit me that I really would be going to the dreaded private school and it obviously hit Vicki too. She began distancing herself from me over the summer holidays and picking on me whenever we were together.

Every day she would laugh at my clothes and my recent hairdo – a terrible misunderstanding on the hairdresser's behalf which once again had me looking ugly and ridiculous with horrible short layers.

Even Will, a local boy who had told everyone he fancied me, had presented me with a bar of chocolate one evening as I'd played in my friend's front garden and had pestered me for months to kiss him, said he didn't fancy me anymore right in front of everyone.

Vicki got nastier and one evening she and a few other girls told me they were going to hide in some old man's garden but instead shoved me in, locking the gate behind me. It was more like a jungle than a garden and they wouldn't let me out for ages. Insects attacked my face and lodged themselves in my hair. My so-called mates laughed outside the gate calling me a little wimp.

"Let me out," I pleaded several times, only to be mimicked cruelly by the girls.

Eventually, Vicki let me out and said I had best get home because I would be on baby bed time as always.

I only cried when I reached the safety of my bedroom where Teresa patiently picked all of the greenflies out of my hair and promised not to tell anyone. It was a rare moment of closeness between us that we hadn't experienced for a long time.

Sept 1988

That first day of Upton, I awoke and dressed in the ugly second hand uniform my mother had obtained. Nothing fitted me properly. Why did my parents insist on sending me to this stupid school for rich girls when they couldn't even afford a new uniform that fitted nicely? My hair, which still didn't seem to have grown an inch, was atrocious despite the wet look gel I had applied after wetting it to make it appear longer, something I had resorted to doing all summer.

I had to leave the house at seven-thirty as Upton was two bus journeys away. I picked up the envelope containing my first week's dinner money and new bus pass that my dad had purchased for me a couple of days earlier. He had told me several times that he was proud of me, that I was growing up and that Upton would be the making of me but I was still outraged by my parents' decision to send me to a school I had protested against repeatedly.

My dad kept saying he wanted me to have the chance he never had. Apparently he had been refused entrance to St. Anselm's, the private catholic boy's secondary school due to failing the eleven plus exam by half a mark and although the Wirral Grammar School had been prepared to offer him and his twin a place due to the fact Uncle Dom had passed the exam by a couple of marks, their parents had put their Irish Catholic feet firmly to the floor and said if it wasn't Catholic it wasn't good enough. They had ended up at the local comprehensive.

My dad had never had it easy. Born three months prematurely, he and his twin were given so much oxygen to save them that their eyesight was irreversibly damaged. My dad's eyes had been affected more and he had always been the weaker twin, bullied mercilessly and called Specky Four Eyes by students and teachers alike. He didn't do well at school and had worked in a factory for a few years before being made redundant; eventually becoming a postman in the local sorting office. He'd recently had a promotion and always referred to himself as Postman-of-Higher-Grade. He genuinely wanted me to have a better chance than he had but I couldn't see that at the time.

There weren't any classes that first day; we were introduced to our form mates, given a tour of all the classrooms and a weekly timetable which we had to copy out carefully into our homework diary. Books were given out, a multitude of rules and regulations explained and several teachers introduced. Our year was split into three forms. I was in 1U, the same class as Madeleine and Gillian and we all had to sit in the alphabetical order of our surnames.

At the end of the day, we left our classrooms, five minutes earlier than the rest of the school as was custom for first years. I went with Madeleine to the cloakroom. Katrina, an African girl I had met that morning at the bus stop who happened to live round the corner from me in Stoney Hey Road introduced us to another girl, Natalia, a blonde girl who appeared much older than her eleven years who would also be taking the same bus route as us. Neither of them seemed snobby in the slightest.

We decided we would be doing our homework on the bus once it started being given out the following day despite being told precisely we were not allowed to do that. "Homework is to be done at home!" Natalia mimicked the dulcet tones of the teacher who had given us all a long lecture that morning about expectations.

"I'm not scared of any of those stupid bitch teachers," I announced defiantly.

I didn't feel so brave however when I bumped into Vicki a couple of streets from my house immediately after saying goodbye to Katrina.

"Look at the state of you! Oh my God!" drawled Vicki. "That uniform looks worse on you than most. And I see you're hanging round with niggers."

"Don't be like that. She's nice."

"A nice nigger? Whatever! How was the convent then? Bet it suits yer well yer little goody two-shoes."

"I hated it and I'm not a goody two-shoes."

"Well, you should have made more of a fuss then and told yer parents you didn't wanna go. Anyway, gotta go, I'm starting Mary's tomorrow like all us normal kids and don't speak to me again. I don't wanna be seen talking to you."

I was crushed. Blaming my parents for Vicki's behaviour - I knew this had been caused by them sending me to Upton - I let myself into the house.

"Well, come on then, how was it?" beamed my mother from the sitting room.

"Fine."

"Well? Tell us how it was."

"I don't wanna talk about it." I slammed up the stairs, ignoring my mother's surprised, hurt voice floating upstairs behind me.

Nov 1988

A couple of months later, we moved house. Our house on Shiel Road was barely acceptable by Upton standards but at least it was a semidetached and had double glazing, albeit only the downstairs. The new house, in Rice Hey Road, Egremont, was terraced, with single pane windows and felt oppressive, as did the neighbourhood which was full of rough looking kids who swore and shouted at the tops of their voices. I pleaded with my parents not to move there but was told that it was because they couldn't afford the current mortgage. I suspected it was because my mother wanted to be an official member of her beloved church parish, regardless of the fact Teresa and Liam would have to change schools.

At school, the girls crowded round me and asked me what the new house was like.

"How many rooms?" asked Zena.

"Nine," I added a couple of rooms although this made no difference to Zena, who in my opinion was the ugliest, snobbiest girl of them all.

"Nine? Is that all? Our house has eight bedrooms and eight other rooms and that's not including the attics and cellar." Zena had made comments before in her stupid, posh affected voice about the fact that my dad was only a postman and hers was a bank manager but none of this surprised me. Wasn't it exactly as I had expected it to be? When I complained to my mother about the snobbery she told me I was an inverted snob, meaning that I looked down on people just because they came from nice backgrounds and rich families. *Mum, you don't understand anything.*

Not all the Upton girls were like Zena and although Gillian and I grew apart, I remained very close to Madeleine as well as making good friends with Katrina, Natalia and Becca, a girl in my class who had a huge mane of curly hair and mischievous, intelligent eyes. Becca, Natalia and Katrina, had sturdier figures than me, I was tiny in comparison to them and they often teased me good-naturedly about my slight frame, laughing that my legs were like two pieces of string hanging down from my skirt, a popular insult in those days. I started wearing two pairs of over knee socks to make my legs appear bigger and wished desperately for a stouter figure like those of my friends. These girls didn't possess a hint of snobbery though and accepted me for exactly who I was.

My first sleepover was at Becca's house in Hoylake, a lovely place filled with huge Victorian looking houses, far nicer than the squashed terraced rows in Egremont. That night we went to a school disco at Upton, especially thrilling because the first year St Anselm's boys were also invited. Jessie, the girl I had met when I retook the entrance exam, even snogged one of them, causing great excitement as she was the only one out of all of us who had ever snogged a boy. We watched videos all night when we got back to Becca's, all deciding passionately that Lost Boys was the best film ever made and that Corey Feldman and Corey Heim were the fittest boys ever. Boys were becoming more and more interesting to us all.

When Becca's parents drove us home the next day, I made them drop me at the top of the street as I didn't want them to see the scruffy little house in which I lived. The glaring contrast between my home life and school life affected me. I dreaded non- uniform days on which I wore the one single nice outfit I had, something which certain girls always felt the need to point out. Mum didn't understand that the girls dressed in really fashionable, classy outfits and that I looked terrible in comparison. I never had anything to talk about after the school holidays either; the other girls' foreign, exotic holidays made my street playing seem pathetic. The differences between us, in my mind, were huge and I became evermore defensive. Despite the fact it was a private school for highly achieving girls, I wasn't allowed to take the clarinet in school as I was so advanced, already working towards my Grade 5, a G.C.S.E. equivalent, at home. It was decided that I learn the violin in school. Life had so many pressures nowadays. I left the house at seven every morning, strictly speaking I didn´t really have to leave until half past - Katrina and I liked hanging round the school early before anyone else got there – and often didn´t get home until five most evenings. After dinner and daily prayer ritual, I would be sent upstairs to practice the clarinet for an hour, the violin for half an hour as well as having an hour and a half's worth of homework. Saturday mornings were for my clarinet lesson, followed by orchestra and music theory, then weekly confession and midday mass. Sunday mornings were for obligatory mass, where I also had to play the clarinet, and afternoons for homework.

I began to lose interest in the clarinet, becoming frustrated with it when I couldn't get my scales perfect, sometimes throwing it across the room, daring it to break. I also started to really slack off with every subject in school except English, which I loved. The old English teacher, Mrs Rough, was a lady who demanded respect and excellent standards of essay writing. Hers was the one class I really tried hard in it, always got good marks, which she didn't give easily and it was through her I first discovered I had a love of writing.

Somehow I managed to pass my Grade 5 clarinet exam but to my mum's disappointment, I was only awarded a scrape through pass and not the distinction she had hoped for. When my school report came at the end of the first year, she was disillusioned again. Although I had received mostly B's, with a couple of A's and C's, most of the teachers reported that I had put in very little effort and if I wanted the A stars I was capable of, I really had to work harder.

At the time I didn't see the privileges that I had were what lots of children would have loved the chance of having. I felt determined to do worse rather than better. I was sick of it all. The things I wanted to do well in, PE and Art, I was terrible at apart from an unexpected talent for cross-country I had discovered when I came in fifth out of the entire school year. My mum wasn't concerned about those subjects though.

Chapter 8
Painful Adolescence

Aug 1989

As I entered puberty, shadows entered my mind and ripped it apart with their violent storms of obsessive thoughts, heightened emotions and complete lack of control over my reactions to them. My twelfth birthday brought with it my first period and with it, something dark entered my life, something that went beyond hormonal changes.

My mum instinctively knew what my tummy pains were and explained to me all the possible, physical symptoms that can accompany a period and although she did explain that some women could be a little weepy while bleeding, I was never made aware of the angry form of PMT some women could suffer, something that may have helped us both in the coming months. However, for years I have blamed my hormones for it all when no one had a clue what was really happening to me. Borderline Personality Disorder symptoms are highly triggered by a woman's menstrual cycle and in my case, if I could pin point a time in my life when I it started, it was then. My poor mother had no way of knowing any of this.

At the time when my periods started, I also began having fantasies of myself naked with a boy. These brought me physical sensations in my privates, which I couldn´t help but give into when alone under the privacy of my duvet. I felt dirty and ashamed of myself. I was certain there was something wrong with me. *Surely twelve year olds don't get those types of urges?* Life and my perceptions of the world were changing rapidly. That winter, a dark entity seemed to take over my mind and I was never the same again.

September 1989

I was on my way to the local shops one evening when I noticed a couple of girls my own age heading towards me. I recognised one of them as Leanne Oak, a girl who was a year younger then me with whom I had exchanged plenty of dirty looks whenever we saw each other in the street. Leanne said something to the girl she was with, making them both laugh. I felt slightly uneasy and tried to walk past without looking at them.

"Oh! Not so tough now are yer?" Leanne drawled.
"Where yer goin'?"

"The shop."

"Oh are yer? Well I wanna talk to yer first, and me mate Sam does too," she said menacingly.
"Gorra sister?"

"Yeah," I mimicked her accent to sound tougher than I was feeling, "Teresa, from your school."

"I'm not at that school now, startin' St. Mary's next week. Have yer gorra older sister?"

"No," I faltered, for some reason fervently wishing that I had.

"Well, I wanna know why yer been givin' me all those cocky looks?"

I said nothing. The other girl, Sam, looked hard and she was of a far heavier build than me. Leanne was taller than me but skinny, not scary on her own but with Sam…My face jerked up in stung surprise as Leanne slapped me. I didn't dare hit her back because Sam moved even closer to me.

"That's what yer get for being a cocky little bitch.

Aren't yer gonna hit me back yer little wimp?"
She slapped both of my cheeks, harder this time and
Sam laughed. "God, how pathetic! Her face is red
from your slaps and she won't do nothin' back. Slap
her again."
Leanne obliged willingly and although the slaps
didn't even hurt that much I was burning inside from
humiliation. I was pathetic like Sam said. Some little
kids of about five years old wondered up to us.
"What yer doin'?" One of them, a blonde haired,
tough looking boy asked, taking in the situation as he
looked me up and down.
"Teachin' this slag a lesson," sneered Leanne. "D'yer
wanna punch her too?"
The kid immediately punched me right in the face
with his balled up, grubby fist. I wanted to cry, I felt
so degraded. There were loads of them surrounding
me now.
"Lay a finger on him and I'll kill yer meself,"
threatened Sam.
Leanne spat in my face. I automatically moved my
hand to wipe it but Sam slapped it down. "Nah leave
it there, makes yer face look better, you ugly fuckin'
slag."
I had no choice but to stand there, feeling the spit
gradually turn cold and make its slimy trail down my
face.
"Come on kids, whoever wants a go, punch her now."
I hated Leanne at that moment but something stopped
me from doing anything to help myself. The little
blonde boy and his mates took turns punching me. It
didn't hurt but it was so humiliating.
"What time yer gorra be home?"
"Eight."

I could hardly speak. Getting whacked at home was different. It was because I was bad and deserved it and it didn't involve humiliation techniques such as this. It was controlled and at least I knew it would be over at some point. They hadn't hit me for years now either. I hadn't got a clue how long Leanne was going to keep me there or what else she might do. I felt so stupid and pathetic. *God, are you asleep? Help me.*

"Well, looks like yer gonna be late tonight," Leanne crowed in her nasty sing-song voice. "What will yer bible basher mum and dad have to say then, eh? She's a right little nun this one you know Sam, goes the church all the time and goes the snotty posh school run by nuns. Think yer better than us don't you?"

It was dark by now, a fast approaching autumn made the night air sharp and frosty but everything was surreal and detached, like I wasn't really there.

"Eh, what's going on?" A local man called over.

"Quick, let's go," Leanne looked at me, "You can go now yer slag but am not finished with you yet and if you ever look at me again I'll knock yerrout."

As I entered the front garden my dad flung the door open.

"Where on earth do you think you've been? We've been worried sick. Well, you're grounded now," he ranted, dragging me into the house.

Repressed anger and humiliation exploded.

"Get off me!" I yelled, "You stupid man, you know nothing, it isn't my fault."

My dad completely lost his temper and ragged me into the back room screaming "Don't you dare shout your mouth off at me. It's never your fault is it? I'm gonna teach you a lesson you little madam."

"GET OFF!" I shoved at him with every ounce of my

strength. "I just got battered in the street, then I come home late 'cos of it and you fuckin' start!"

I hadn't meant to swear but I was so upset it just came out. My dad swiped at me, catching me hard around the head, knocking me dizzy. I turned and saw my mum.

"Mum, please, it really isn't my fault; some girls had me and wouldn't let me go. It was scary..." my voice broke.

"Oh stop the crocodile tears, you have a filthy mouth on you, my girl, whatever happened was probably your own fault."

"No, Paddy, wait," my mum cut in. "She does seem upset, give her a chance."

He let me be as he demanded, "Who was it? Where is she? I'll go down and see her parents right now."

The thought of him going down there shouting the odds was horrifying.

"No, Dad don't, you'll make it worse."

He ignored me and started putting his coat on.

"Dad, don't. You're gonna make it worse. Mum, tell him." I grabbed hold of his arm now but he threw me off. "DAD! FUCKIN' LEAVE IT!"

Desperation not to have him go down there and secure my future reputation as a grass plus the pent up humiliation and repressed anger at the fact that I couldn't defend myself earlier made me scream, curse and yell. The swearing, so strictly forbidden in our house, made him see the proverbial red but as he went to hit me, my mum stopped him.

"Don't lose your temper, Paddy, she isn't worth it."

I was crying loudly by then but they didn't care. My mum looked at me coldly as she told me, "Take yourself and your noise to bed Maria."

I cried myself to sleep.

A week later, after doing my best to avoid her, I saw
Leanne walking down my road after returning from
an outing to Hoylake with my dad to buy an item I
needed for my PE kit. I had actually had a nice time
with him and the change of scenery had done me
good. Leanne smiled tentatively as she approached
us.
"Sorry 'bout last week, Sam makes me like that."
Relieved that Leanne wasn't going to be starting on
me anymore, after all, she had apologised in front of
my dad and everything, I smiled back.
"What was that about?"
"Nothing, Dad."
Later that evening, I was in my friend's garden at the
bottom of my road when Leanne and Sam walked
past.
"Alright, Maria?" they seemed friendly, both of them.
"Alright."
"Come round to Sam's with us," invited Leanne.
My instincts were telling me not to go with them but I
couldn't refuse. As we sat outside on Sam's front, I
was quiet and felt uncomfortable; the malice from the
previous week was infecting the air around us.
"Talk, will yer," complained Sam. "God, is she
always like this?"
"Dunno, hardly know her meself."
Timothy, a little boy of around four years old, who
lived on my street walked past, squinting at us
through his unfocused eyes. He lived in a squat and
was permanently filthy, always out alone until all
hours with barely any clothes on. Sometimes the kids
would go in the house to try and rob pennies out of

his mum's purse but more often than not, there was nothing in it. His dad was always drunk and his mum was obviously not right in the head.

Leanne looked at Sam, her eyes gleaming and leant forward to whisper something to her. Sam laughed and called Timothy into the garden.

"Sit there, next to Maria," ordered Leanne. "Maria, have yer ever got off with anyone?"

Ashamed to admit that I hadn't, I lied.

"Nah, no way, I don't believe yer."

"I have, a boy at one of our discos," I protested weakly.

"Well, whether yer 'ave or not, yer gonna do it now." Leanne smiled nastily.

"Who with?" I asked nervously.

"With our cute little Timothy, right here, right now." Sam laughed at this but her expression froze in hostility when her eyes met mine.

"But, he's only four." I was horrified.

"Oh, so you like him then? Just worried 'cos he's only four? Told you she was a dirty bitch Sam."

"No, I don't, that's not what I meant."

"Haven't you learnt yer lesson yet? You don't give me cheek, right? You do what I say."

"But I thought you were sorry," I faltered.

"I thought you were sorry," mimicked Sam. "Did you say sorry to her, Lee? What for?"

Leanne replied easily that she had only apologised in front of my dad in case I grassed on her for last week. "And so's we could get her round here now," she added, looking at me scornfully. "As if I'd say sorry to a little slut like her.

I smarted inwardly at the insults; I wasn't a slut, I had never even kissed anyone. My throat constricted as fear raced through my heart.

"Open your mouth Tim, and stick yer tongue out," Leanne advised the scruffy little boy, who squinted vacantly back at her. "D'yer wanna kiss her?"

Tim nodded slightly although it was obvious he hadn't got a clue what was going on.

"Ah, Maria, don't be an arlarse, he wants to kiss you." Leanne was enjoying every moment of the power she was wielding over us as she demanded threateningly, "Kiss him, on the lips and use your tongue."

I refused. The thought of having to snog a little boy, barely more than a baby revolted me.

"Do I have to slap you again?" Leanne spoke as if I was a wayward child disobeying its mother.

"Please, Leanne, no, I don't want to."

She slapped my face twice. *God where are you? Asleep again or just handing out more punishments through these girls?*

"Now do it, put yer tongue on his, or next time it'll be Sam who slaps you."

Sam suddenly thrust her face in mine.

"Yer best fuckin' do what she says."

Revulsion choked fear. Unwillingly, I leaned forward.

"That's it. Get off with him. Put yer tongue on his, now."

Sam grabbed my hair and shoved my head towards Timothy's.

"Stick yer tongue out."

Sam twisted my hair even harder in her grip. I put my tongue out and met Timothy's waiting one. It tasted horrible. I felt sick and tried to pull away.

"No, not yet. Snog him, Twist your tongue round his, you dirty bitch. Look, she's lovin' it." Leanne crowed in excitement while Sam held me there, preventing me from escaping.

"Tim, lick her tongue, mate, we'll give yer some choccies later."

He licked my tongue a few times while I closed my eyes and tried to block out what was happening to me. I felt sick, dirty and completely powerless. After what seemed like forever, Sam's mum shouted her name from inside the house.

"Right, go on; fuck off, the pair o' yer." Sam pushed both of us towards the front gate.

That night I had a huge row with my family, swearing and shouting terrible insults at my mum which resulted in my dad losing his temper and whacking me before sending me to bed in the little cold room at the front of the house, the room in which I was to spend many miserable nights in the near future. The repressed anger had made me crazy and I had needed to vocalise it, regain some element of strength but after it had ebbed, I sobbed hysterically for hours, feeling battered from all ends.

After going downstairs several times, each time crying and apologising more than the last, my mum finally forgave me. Her eyes were red but she seemed composed.

"I just wish you wouldn't lose your temper with us. It sets your dad off and upsets us all."

I cuddled up to her, wishing things were different, that I was a little four year old again, the apple of my uncle's eye, living in a world where all that existed was my immediate family and the Holy Family of heaven.

Winter 1989

After the incidents with Leanne and Sam, I constantly felt frightened and threatened when out in my local area. Everything seemed dark there, oppressed like some bad horror movie. The local girls, the ones who were around my age, now appeared very intimidating indeed and always laughed at me for being from a religious family and a private school. In contrast, at school, I wasn't intimidated by anyone, posh girls weren't the not the fighting type and I was the aggressive one, always starting arguments and sometimes physical fights.

I lost interest in washing myself, and went through the routine once a week on a Sunday night although my changing body meant I really should be showering more. I even took to sleeping in my uniform, wearing it under my pyjamas to save time on the chilly mornings. I was the opposite with my teeth though, constantly cleaning them, so much my mother complained that I would scrape all the enamel off them.

My behaviour at home grew steadily worse. I pushed harder against my upbringing and began shouting abuse at my mum every time she took me to task on anything. This resulted in my dad losing his temper, me being hit or grounded and then crying hysterically, lots of heartfelt apologies from me, followed by some comfort from my mum. An unhealthy pattern had been born and none of us had any control over it. On the one hand, I craved my mother's love, on the other; I rejected her in every way.

Now I was a second year at Upton, Sarah Howden had transferred over and I went out of my way to pick on her. Eventually, Sarah learnt to ignore me at the times when she couldn't avoid me and I grew bored of my games. I was also annoyed at the fact that Sarah became friends with my cousin Shona, like Shona was good enough for her and her for Shona but I had never been good enough for either of them.

School was a different world from home and I fitted into neither. I didn't realise at the time that if I had simply used my brain and studied, I could have got into Upton life. I didn't have to go out in the streets and be bullied; I could have stayed home, studied, practised, prepared for my future and got away from there. Hindsight is a great thing but at the time my brain just seemed to stop functioning properly. It was like there was a dark blanket there, my whole reality was distorted.

My first real kiss was with Rob, a fourteen year old who lived round the corner from me. Lila, a loud, bossy, blonde eleven year old from the next street had been quizzing me over who I fancied and on discovering I had a little thing for Rob, she told me he said he would either go out with me or get off with me. I didn't really understand the difference and I was eager to try proper kissing and also to erase the sickening memory left over from the Leanne incident. We went down an alleyway and he tilted my face to his. I was nervous but he laughed and said he had got off with four girls before and that he would show me how. We only kissed for a few seconds when he stopped and asked if he could finger me. I was unsure what that meant but didn't want to appear stupid so I said yes. He put his hand inside my knickers and then inserted a finger into the same place where my period came from. I felt embarrassed, no one had ever touched me there. He pushed his finger up and down and I let him, glad it was dark and I didn't have to look at him. When he pulled it out, he simply said "see yer" and left me there. I didn't know what to think but I was glad I had finally got off with someone properly.

I obsessed over Rob from then on but he showed no further interest. Every morning on the way to school I would look out for the milk van in which he worked the early morning round, my heart beating wildly when I saw it approach. I lived for those few seconds every morning. I was confused. Although he always smiled and waved from the van, he didn't want to 'go out' with me now. He told Lila and some other local girls with that he would never put his finger up there again, not until I had put a bar of soap up there. They all laughed and I told him. "Shut up. Look at the state of you and where you live. Fucking tramp!"

I regretted my words immediately as his older sister bounced over to me, grabbed my hair, punched me in the head several times and banged my face up and down on her knees.

"Don't call me brother a fuckin' tramp again you little slut."

God, why is life so harsh now? What did I do?

Apart from my unrequited feelings for Rob, my other crush was on Jay Spears, the altar boy at our local church who was in the same school year as me, but at St. Mary's. Of a slight build, freckled with strawberry blonde hair he appealed to something within me. I would check the altar boy lists and memorise them for weeks an advance, waking up with butterflies in my belly when Jay was serving the ten o'clock mass, which I attended to play the clarinet with the youth orchestra. He always served the Saturday midday mass too which made my own forced attendance somewhat more enjoyable.

We never spoke, simply spent the whole mass staring but only rarely smiling at one another. That was the main attraction church had for me now, although admittedly, I did still find a certain amount of peace and comfort from the pungent incense burned within the cosy church with the pretty stained glass windows. Despite my restless boredom, the incense and candles were homely and familiar to me in a world that confused me more and more every day.

I had been off school with a virus for a few days and on my return, discovered that my best friends, all apart from Madeleine, had begun smoking in my absence. They informed me, slightly smugly I thought, that they all smoked now and were going to go for a ciggie at dinner time. I told them I had smoked for ages, it was no big deal.

"Can you get ciggies from the shops?" Becca challenged me.

"Yeah, course. Can bring some in tomorrow if yer like."

I had perfected a very scouse accent now and spoke like the kids local to me. The fact it infuriated my teachers was an added bonus as far as I was concerned. The deputy head, Mrs Smith spoke to me in her rich, well-educated, posh voice every morning, forcing me to copy her and pronounce my words properly but it was more important to fit in at home with the locals than to please my teachers.

"How do you get served?" Natalia wasn't convinced.

"I get me mate, Jodie from over the road to get 'em

for me. She's fifteen but looks older." Jodie was rough and loud but she was always nice to me.

"What type of ciggies do you smoke?" Katrina persisted.

I was scared I'd be found out at any minute so became aggressive.

"Berkeley, for fuck's sake, any more questions?"

I knew the brand as they were what my mum smoked when she wasn't in one of her non-smoking stages.

"Keep your hair on, we're only asking."

The next morning, I got on the bus at Liscard and greeted Katrina.

"Got 'em. Let's go upstairs."

At that time it was still legal to smoke upstairs on the bus. Getting the cigarettes had been easy. I had gone over to Jodie's with the money, sixty four pence that we had pooled together on the bus coming home, and Jodie had been happy to oblige.

"Just gis a smoke outta them hun," she had said when she'd passed the burgundy coloured packet of ten cigarettes to me.

I was relieved I wouldn't have to lose face in front of my friends. I had enough problems without losing my tough image at Upton. I didn't even want to smoke but couldn't back down now.

When we got upstairs, I removed two cigarettes from the packet, handing both to Katrina.

"Light it for me, I hate the first pull."

I hadn't got a clue how to light a cigarette and didn't want to give myself away. Katrina struck a match and lit them both up, passing one to me. I put it to my lips, pulling on it the way I had just seen Katrina do. I didn't inhale, just kept the smoke in my mouth for a couple of seconds before blowing it straight back out, noting with relief that Katrina did exactly the same. From then on, we both pooled some of our dinner money for me to get cigarettes and matches, spending the rest in the little shop in Wallasey Village, where we waited to catch the second bus into Upton, on sweets, chocolate and crisps. As a result, I hardly ever had any dinner in school and this, combined with my vegetarianism, my latest bid to fit in with my Upton friends, resulted in my weight dropping noticeably. I had been skinny enough already so this was not helpful to my appearance. I was soon smoking regularly and taught myself to inhale after a month or so, the first of my friends to inhale. *Such an achievement!*

Chapter 9
Possessed by the Devil

Spring 1990
Maybe it was the deep unhappiness I felt inside, or
just a horrific puberty that had stolen my former good
looks, all I knew was I really disliked what I saw in
the mirror. The haircuts hadn't helped my self-esteem
but worse were the comments I seemed to attract
more and more regularly of late about my appearance.
Boys on the bus would say loudly, "I wouldn't get off
with her; she has a moustache. Hairy legs and eew,
look at all her spots. Look how skinny she is, that's
not normal." I always pretended not to hear but my
face would burn with shame. My confidence levels
plummeted.

I started hanging round with Jodie from across the
road and her friends. I liked the fact that I hung round
with the older girls far more than the reality of
actually being with them. These girls never bullied
me, not like the ones of my own age, and hanging
round with them assured some form of protection. I
was always too shy while with the big gang to speak
much and was intimidated by their brash scouse
voices. It was due to that I tried to make my own
accent as strong as possible. If I sounded tough, then
people were more likely to leave me alone.

Sometimes, my new friends would get drunk. One
girl, Gina, got so drunk one day she couldn't stand up.
She was thirteen, only a year older than me but
looked a lot older as she was tall and well developed.
So drunk she had vomited several times, rolling round
on the ground on Egremont Prom, talking gibberish.
Two older lads who were about nineteen kept

touching her up and grabbing her boobs, one even put his hand inside her top, ignoring Jodie when she told them to leave her alone. She ended up calling an ambulance as Gina was practically unconscious, and thankfully it came quickly, saving her from any further advances.

Jodie said she was a fool to drink like that if she couldn't handle it and that having her stomach pumped would teach her a lesson. I wasn't sure what that meant so she explained it to me. I was so naive that when Jodie had told me one morning how stoned she had been the night before, I'd immediately asked her concernedly if she was okay, thinking that she had literally been stoned by people the night before.

"Yeah, I'm fine lar, loved it." On noticing my confusion she explained, "I took loadsa tomazzies, proper nice mate."

I understood that tomazzies were some kind of pill as I'd seen her nicking them from the woman's house where she babysat. Sometimes I noticed my friends and the young men we hung round with had extremely small pupils, which made their eyes look strangely bright. I didn't realise then that opiate pills caused this and the change to their eyes frightened me.

They also smoked something called pot, a smelly cigarette which made their eyes go red. The smell was sinister to me but Gina reckoned even her mum smoked it and told us it wasn't harmful, that it actually cleared her lungs. I could never imagine my own mum doing that and I was terrified at the thought of drugs although I kept that strictly to myself. They never tried to force any on me though although sometimes I smoked so many cigarettes with them that I would get sick, my body trying hard to reject the nicotine poison.

When I was out after dark with them, I always felt surreal, like a part of me was missing; fog in my brain. I never told anyone about this. How could I tell my parents that sometimes my mind blanked out? They would think me mad, not just bad and would pin all of my behaviour onto some crazy mental illness. Recently my mum had begun referring to the possibility that I was possessed by the devil and she had also said several times she was convinced the house had an evil spirit.

I had been awarded the privilege of staying at home on a Saturday while my mum took Teresa and Liam to church with her. After a long hard battle with my parents, and several incidents of me throwing my clarinet across the room in temper, it had been agreed that I could give up my music lessons as they realised that they were wasting what little money they had on paying for Saturday morning lessons.

I loved my time alone in the house on Saturdays and pretended I was the woman of the house, tidying it, vacuuming and polishing, often preparing a small lunch of soup and bread for my family when they returned. I was painfully aware that our house was much untidier than any of my friend's houses; even the ones who lived locally had nice front rooms with modern stereos and everyone possessed a video player except us.

Curious about alcohol after seeing my friends drink it and mostly having a laugh, apart from the unfortunate Gina, on one of these mornings I went to the cupboard and poured a small measure of Bacardi into a mug, topping it up with coke. My parents very rarely drank alcohol but my mum sometimes gave us little sips of her Bacardi and coke at Christmas time and I liked the taste. After swigging my illegal drink back, I immediately poured another, this time using far more of the spirit. I still didn't feel any different. After drinking about four of these strong concoctions, it hit me. My eyes lost focus and I felt myself sway. I made my way back to the front room. Everything around me was spinning and I heaved, vomiting all over the freshly vacuumed carpet. Staggering out into the street, I saw my mum, brother and sister at the top of the road.

"Mum," I was incoherent, "I've been sick, very sick but it's 'cos I came on my period this morning."
My mum really wasn't that stupid.
"Come on," she urged as I retched again, "Let's get you to the bathroom."
Too late; I spewed the rest of the contents of my stomach all over the front garden.
"Sorry, Mum. Sorry. I love you yer know."
I stumbled into the house collapsing down onto a sofa.
"What's wrong with her, Mum?" asked Teresa.
"She's drunk. Come on, Maria, you need to be in bed to sleep this off."
My mum half dragged, half carried me upstairs to my room, calling for Teresa to bring up a sick bowl. I kept apologising and repeating how much I loved her. Angry though my mum was with this latest incident, her natural nursing qualities came to the forefront as she undressed me and put me to bed, listening to my drunken ramblings and stroking my hair as if I was a child still. I began to cry, *sorry mum, so sorry* and she

kept reassuring me that it was okay until she finally managed to settle me off to sleep.

When I awoke around five o'clock that evening, my parents calmly told me that I was grounded for a month and had lost my privilege of spending Saturday mornings in the house alone as I had proved once again that I couldn't be trusted. For once, I accepted this punishment without arguing, knowing that they were completely in the right. Privately, I vowed never to drink again and the thought of Bacardi made me feel ill for a long time to come.

The nun had a kindly face but I hated her on sight. Strands of white hair poked out from her dark blue veil and she wore a smart blue jacket and skirt, not the traditional habit usually worn by convent nuns. After my drunken incident, my mum had called the Catholic Social Services, desperate for someone to help me. Sister Rose had arrived the following Saturday morning.

"So, child, why do you behave this way?

"What way?" I asked sulkily.

How dare my mum call the social services on me? Didn't she understand that I really was sorry after my outbursts? It was like a force took over me and turned me into something I had no control over. I tried to contain it but the fire that raged through me at random seemed to have its own life force. My emotions and mood swings controlled me with an angry haze that enveloped me, only clearing when I was dragged out of the room and pushed roughly into my bedroom, sometimes receiving slaps on the way there. The anger would evaporate into gulping hysterics, my broken tears drowning out the fire and leaving me desperate to be held, loved.

"Getting drunk, giving cheek to your poor parents, having them worry themselves sick about your soul?" Her no-nonsense voice had light Irish tones to it but also a hard edge.

"What do you know? You don't even know me. I only got drunk once and I hated it."

"Getting drunk is a sin against yourself and God."

"For God's sake! I only did it once and I suffered for it."

"They don't know how much more they can cope with. They have asked about the possibility of you being looked after in one of our homes but I don't think we need to go there yet. I'm...."

"You what?" I was outraged. "Well, I'll tell you what. I'll go into care. Go on; take me now, you silly old cow."

"Calm yourself down now. Don't dare use language like that with me. You would have a jolly rude awakening in a care home. Let me tell you."

I felt sick with emotion as I contemplated the knowledge that my parents had actually inquired about getting rid of me. I had never thought they were serious when they'd threatened me before with it and I often said myself as a way of rejecting them first, "go on put me in care then, I don't give a damn!" Deep down I didn't want to go away from them and my mind would be screaming out for me to stop even while I pushed them to their limits but I could never stop. How do you stop a fire from burning when there is no water at hand?

"I'd like to come and see you every couple of weeks. Your parents are desperate. They don't really want to send you away. You scare them when you lose your

temper and your brother and sister as well."
"Well what about when they scare me? When they hit
me? And Teresa ain't scared of me. She always hits
me too."
Teresa constantly tried to get me in trouble as I did
her.
"Now, don't start telling lies. Your parents are good
God-fearing people. You're just feeling sorry for
yourself. Really, I have just seen a display of what
they are talking about for myself."
When she left the room, I heard her say reassuringly
to my mum that she was confident that if they all
prayed and that she came often that things would
settle down. My temper pricked at me again as I
heard her mum saying in her special voice she kept
for members of the clergy, 'Thanks so much, Sister. I
know she's difficult now but she was a good girl at
one time."
Sister Rose continued to visit regularly but I hated her
and refused to even speak to her.

A few weeks later I became extremely ill. My
symptoms were flu like but my mouth was covered
with severe black abscesses so severe I could hardly
speak. My mum nursed me through the delirium,
soothed me, brought me cold drinks and stroked my
hair back from my face. My temperature continued to
rage and eventually a doctor was called, who
diagnosed malnutrition. He advised my parents to get
some nourishing foods into me and also to get me to
the dentist for the mouth infection.
My mother lectured me once I was feeling a little
better that my malnutrition made them look like unfit
parents, when the truth was that I had done it to

myself by keeping up the vegetarian act and refusing to eat anything but fried eggs and crackers - she didn't know about the stash of butter I kept in the wardrobe, *anchor butter, mmm, delicious* I used to sneak it home when I did the shopping for my mum and hide it in my wardrobe to binge on when I needed to - one minute I was protesting weakly against any share of the blame, the next, I was screaming like a maniac at my mother with no recollection of how I had got to that state. I just remember being at the top of the stairs, her at the bottom.

"You fuckin old bitch, you ugly SLAG, I HATE you. It's your fault, all of it. I hate my life, especially you and my dad. You're evil bastards and I FUCKIN' HATE YOU!"

I raged on and on, screeching out sheer hatred, until the red mist cleared and I collapsed on to the bathroom floor – again, no recollection of how I got in the bathroom - welcoming the tearful hysterics as they finally overtook me, allowing the sobs to release the anger and the tears to wash away the pain.

I could hear my mother talking on the phone and hoped she wasn't telling my dad to come home or I would really be for it. After a few minutes she came upstairs and knocked on the door. I opened it warily, sniffling back my sobs as I knew they wouldn't wash with my mum.

"Maria, we're going to see the priest. That outburst wasn't normal. You didn't have ability to speak just minutes before. I honestly think you are possessed by the devil. We need to get you sorted out. Father Nick is waiting for us now."

Devil possession! Come on! Even as I angrily rejected the thought, a silent voice asked me, well, where does it come from? I had no control over it. I felt weak and limp now, my body remembering it was still malnourished and unwell and I allowed myself to be taken to the church.

Father Nick showed us in to the warm lounge. The house smelt of delicious home-cooking, comforting. He smiled at me and asked me to sit down while my mother began to make a case for my possession emphasising how violent and out of control I became at times. All the while, the priest nodded sympathetically, kindly, glancing at me from time to time and smiling reassuringly. When my mother was finally done he said soothingly, "I can see you're upset Catherine but we need to look at things rationally. Your daughter isn't possessed; she's just at a difficult age."

I sighed with relief. My mother however was determined to get the priest to agree with her and began raking up more of my wrong doings, becoming angrier and more frustrated as the priest continued smiling and shaking his head at her in a manner that must have felt extremely patronising to her. Finally she gathered herself up and told me we were leaving. After that day, she began going to another church in Liverpool unless she couldn't get over there on a Sunday due to the sketchy bus service that ran on those days. If she did go to our church, she ensured she went to a Mass said by a different priest.

My behaviour got worse, the incidents more frequent and violent. Now my dad would lose it the second I answered back. Sometimes he battered me furiously with his bare hands, whacking me around the head, back, legs, and bottom, pulling me off the bed and hurling me to the floor, only to heave me back up on to the bed, all control completely lost, his despair evident for the world to see. Even while screaming in shock and pain, I would be unable to stop swearing and cursing and hitting him.

One day, I had gone to school after one of these episodes and had put dark make up on one of my eyes, so that it looked like a black eye but my friends just laughingly asked why I had put make up under one eye. *Why? I didn't even know why.*

The first time I skipped school was after one of these episodes. When Katrina suggested we bunk off I was totally up for it although I had actually been trying to behave better in school as it had recently been found out that I had been forging my mother's signature on all of my homework when I had been telling her that I hadn't had any. The school had realised that there was no way that my mum would sign homework of such poor quality and had eventually phoned her about it leaving me with no other choice than to admit that I had been doing my homework hurriedly in the form room in the mornings before class, sometimes copying other's work.

After last night's incident, the last thing I felt like doing today was going to school and getting through the day, having to appear cocky and hard to keep up with my coveted image when all I wanted to do was curl up into a ball and die.

On the second bus we met two older Upton girls who I was now friends with and they decided to bunk off with us. I had recently been going down to The Grand, a club in New Brighton that did discos on a Wednesday night for fourteens and over, with these girls after telling my parents I was at their houses studying and then spend the evenings getting off with older boys. I felt nothing for them but had to keep up with my friends.

We stayed on past Upton until Landican Cemetery from where we could get a bus into town. Katrina then called the school speaking in what I assumed to be her mum's best phone voice, saying she was Katrina's mum and that Katrina was sick and that she had received a message from my mum to say I wouldn't be in school. Stupidly, the other girl did the same for her and her friend all of twenty seconds later.

As we couldn't use our bus passes on the buses that went from Landican to Birkenhead, we had to walk all the way into town. We had soon eaten the sandwiches that Katrina had brought and decided to pool our money to buy twenty Berkeley, a box of matches and some crisps and chocolate.

Despite what seemed like hours of walking, it was only about eleven o'clock when we arrived at the town centre. We had eaten all our supplies and had nothing to do now except wonder round the shops and smoke. Last night seemed far away, surreal, as if it might not have really happened. The monotony of the long walk had numbed my brain and I talked with my friends of boys like a robot programmed to be a regular twelve-year old. I was relieved when it got to half past one and we began the long trek back to Landican.

It was obvious I had been caught out the moment I walked through the door at home. Teresa smiled triumphantly at me as my mum confronted me. I ended up grounded for a month that time but stormed back out of the front door as soon as the words were out of my mum´s mouth.

I made no effort after that day to behave better, not seeing the point. I was always at the extreme of my own negative emotions, angry or unhappy at home, scared and fearful in the street, bored out of my brain in school. The only happy thing at home was the cute little grey kitten my parents had got for us just after moving to Rice Hey Road but even he became another cause for fighting with my sister. Life was oppressive. There was no incentive to be good, just punishments if I wasn't. I was spiralling further out of control. My parents resorted to locking me in my bedroom when I kicked off after struggling between the both of them to get me up the stairs and out of their way when I started. Sometimes they left me in there for hours, overnight without dinner when I had gone too far. Teresa let me out on one occasion but got into so much trouble she didn't dare do it again. My school work was never done, either in class or at home and during the Easter holidays, my parents received a call from Sister Marie Joseph. Exactly what was said in that conversation was never made known to me but I was told that I would be going to St Mary's immediately after the holidays.
I was excited although a little apprehensive at the thought of a new school. Maybe now I wouldn't get as much grief in the street about being a bible bashing convent girl. Loads of local kids went to St. Mary's, it made no difference whether they were Catholic or not. But then again, my parents didn't help matters as they loved to display their strong beliefs, especially at that time of year. There was always a poster in our window, throughout the six week period of Lent that

said, "Jesus died for us." On Easter Sunday, that same poster then unfolded a little more to say, "He is risen." The local kids thought it hilarious but it never occurred to me that it may have been my extreme discomfort at their piss taking that made me such a target rather than the posters themselves.

During those holidays, I began to hang around with the gobby Lila. Although a year younger than me, she was tough and I was glad to that she'd chosen to befriend me rather than fight me. The added bonus was that Leanne Oaks was scared of her and began smiling tentatively at me every time she saw me - Sam had a new mate now. One day Lila and I invited Leanne to the prom to smoke with us and I told her I was going to start St Mary's after Easter. She told me I could get the bus with her. I wasn't overjoyed at this prospect but decided it would be better to have her onside, and thank God she was. St Mary's was not the dream I had thought it was going to be.

Chapter 10
Emotional overload

Summer term 1990, St Mary's

Instead of being welcomed back into the fold of my primary school friends like a long lost hero as I had fantasised, I was all but ignored by most and my former best friend, Vicki, was absolutely horrible. I spent most break times alone. I couldn't tell my parents how unhappy I was as they would have just said "I told you so." Ironically, Leanne was my only friend in the big comprehensive school but as she was a first year and I was a second year, we weren't in the same class.

School felt strange and foreign; in contrast to Upton's rules of orderliness, strict uniform and plain black shoe regulations, St Mary's was full of loud girls in short school skirts, Kicker boots and Reebok trainers and rough boys, voices breaking with adolescence. I retreated inside myself on that first day to an empty desert nightmare and it took weeks to come back out. School, especially break time, sent me to that place.

It wasn't long before Leanne got up to her old tricks of trying to humiliate me in public. Lila was visiting family one Sunday so it was just Leanne and me. When we saw some of the local lads, Rob among them, Leanne turned to me, saying suddenly, "I want yer out."

(Local lingo for wanting a fight). My heart sank.

"Why? I thought we were mates now."

Leanne just smiled slyly and went to slap my face. Something snapped inside me at that moment and instead of cowering away, I grabbed Leanne's hair as hard as I could and pulled her head down, bashing it onto the pavement until Rob and his mates rushed over, pulling me off her. Leanne ran off home crying. "Wow," Rob looked admiring, if a little shocked, "can't believe you girl!"

At school on Monday, Leanne ran to Louise Fila, the hardest girl in my year trying to make out that I had bullied her but God must have been looking out for me that day because Louise actually listened to my side of it and let me off. *Thank you God!* The last thing I needed was her after me, a girl who was infamous for putting a fourth year girl in hospital after battering her with an iron bar. Louise, a pretty girl who always had a wide merry smile on her face didn't appear the type.

Later that week, after being quizzed by one of my classmates on how far I'd gone sexually, I stupidly confided in her about Rob fingering me. She then set it up for me to go in the shed with Will, the boy who had fancied me back in New Brighton, after spreading rumours he was going to finger me. I didn't know how to protest without making myself look stupid in front of my classmates but in that shed I refused to even kiss him and when the dinner ladies burst in a couple of minutes later, I realised the whole thing had been a set up. As the dinner ladies marched me off to the year head, another girl spitefully informed them I had cigarettes in my pocket.

Guilty as charged, the cigarettes were found and confiscated and I didn't speak when asked for an explanation about the shed. My parents were called and unsurprisingly accepted that I was without any sexual morals as well and went through my room to confiscate every bit of makeup I had stashed there.

Things got even worse at school. Girls walked past me calling out slag as they went. Boys whispered to each other and laughed as I went by singing "A FINGER of fudge is just enough to give Maria a treat."

The next set up followed soon afterwards. I found out that Cara Martin 'wanted me out' after school - apparently I had been calling her a slag.

"What? I never called her nothin'."

"Best see Cara now then, before she sees you after school." Stuart Finn, one of the few from my primary who still treated me like a human being, warned me. Familiar fearful butterflies were flying round my stomach as I remembered uncomfortably that when we had been on a school trip to Hilbre Island during the last year of primary school that I had picked on Cara all afternoon, for reasons I failed now to remember. The fact that Cara was now Louise Fila's best friend made me feel even worse. I found her in one of the classrooms.

"Cara, I heard what you said about me callin' yer a slag and I never called yer nothin." My voice masked the fear I felt towards a public fight where I would undoubtedly come off worse.

"Ah, don't worry about it, love," Cara smiled. "Loadsa shit stirrers in this school."

I went back outside to spend another dinner time alone. I wished that I'd stayed at Upton although I couldn't admit that to anyone. After leaving school that afternoon, I saw Leanne outside waiting for me.

"Shall we be mates again? We're even now."

"Yeah, ok but no more startin' Lee, I'm sick of it."

"OK, well don't tell anyone yer battered me though 'cos I'll deny it.

We were walking down Leasowe Road when I heard footsteps running behind me. With dread I turned to see Cara, Louise and some others from my year. Cara wasted no time, "I heard yer bin callin' me a slag."

"Cara, we talked before. You were alright with me?" My voice shook, not so much with fear of the red haired girl, but of the public humiliation I knew I was about to suffer; the fact that Louise Fila was with her made it far worse.

"Yeah, well, yer would've grassed if I'd said anything then." Cara was smiling coldly; already triumphant in what she knew would be a victory for her.

"Anyone joins in an' I'll be joinin' in," warned Louise, smiling at the crowd of twenty or so onlookers who had gathered.

The girls nearest to me moved away as Cara grabbed my hair.

"Fight, fight, fight."

Cara pulled my head down and kneed me in the face repeatedly, only hitting my hands which I had protecting my face. It didn't hurt, she had no power at all. I attempted to kick her in the shin but couldn't muster any strength. When she finally let me up she punched me in the eye. The punch didn't hurt either, not physically, but it was so humiliating. Tears burned the back of my eyes but I managed to hold them back. "Now who's the slag," were her parting words.

After Cara and Louise had gone, a few of the other girls from my year unexpectedly tried to comfort me.

"I'm okay. It didn't hurt."

"Yeah, Cara isn't hard at all, just a bitch who acts it 'cos she's bezzies with Louise. She had no mates til Louise took her on as a sidekick, the toilet Billy we called her. Come on, we'll walk you home. You can hang round with us in school from now on." Sinead Donnelly, a popular, pretty, Irish girl with long fiery red hair and light blue eyes linked my arm.

"And you," she said to Leanne, "Thought you were supposed to be her mate yet you stood there smirking with Louise all the way through."

"No, I just didn't want her to start on me," she protested.

"Do one, first year. Come on Maria, you don't need mates like her."

The next day, lots of the boys who had been in my primary school and who were also in Cara's class now ran over to me saying how out of order Cara was and that they'd told her that if she didn't apologise then no one in the class would be speaking to her. I was surprised to say the least and grateful to Stuart Finn, the self-appointed spokesman of the group.

Sinead was in this class too, along with Jay Spears and some of the others who had befriended me the previous night. They were true to their word, including me in their gang at dinner time and inviting me to hang out with them after school. The girl who had grassed on me for having ciggies came to commiserate about what Cara had done. Cara duly apologised too and Louise smiled at me in class. Although relieved, I was confused, more so than before. Everything seemed to be a game; no one was to be trusted and these girl fights terrified me more than anything.

After this incident, things settled at school. I hung round with Sinead and her friends every day. Our parents knew each other and my mum seemed to approve of her. I became close to her and another girl Anna. Sinead's family were lovely too, her younger brother and sister adored me, her glamorous sixteen year old sister was always nice to me and their mum was lovely, a typical Irish mammy. I felt at home in their house.

Most afternoons after school we would stop behind the pub on the way home to get off with the boys in our group. Although we sometimes swapped snogging partners between us, I usually paired up with Jay, my altar boy. Exploring each other's mouths, tentatively using tongues, we practiced our kissing skills and I liked the closeness. I enjoyed kissing Jay, not like some gross boy Leanne had made me pair up with once, the ugly friend for the ugly friend. I tentatively began to enjoy life at St. Mary's. *Thank you, God for Sinead Donnelly.*

Things deteriorated further at home. I had lost all respect for my parents by now. My anger frequently unleashed itself on my family instead of the bullies who deserved it. My mum and I began physically fighting, hair pulling and wrestling on the floor sometimes. I never bothered with my Uncle Paul at all anymore; resenting his disapproving looks when he came to visit and witnessed me 'acting up'. I refused to even speak to him most times. My family had become the enemy, the people to kick back against. My downward spiral was out of control.

In contrast, the nervousness that I always felt when walking the streets was amplified. I was petrified of suffering more bullying and scared to look at anyone crossing my path. Girls always started on you if you looked at them - it didn't take much to start a fight

where I lived. I was regularly set up by local girls, their reasons always similar to Cara's. "Yer bin callin' me a slag? I heard yer called me mum a slag." Or "Yer after me fella, saw yer lookin' at him." *Nasty fucking bullies with their horrible intimidating accents and voices.*
If I stayed in to avoid whoever it was who was after me, they would send a girl to my house pretending to be my friend, asking me to go the shops with her or to go out to smoke a ciggie in the back alley, then we would "bump into" whoever wanted me out on the way home, crowd gathered, more humiliation. Life was one, long sick journey of emptiness unless filled to its limit with a sickening sense of fear and dread or total rage, anger, then complete despair.

June 1990
My parents called the police out to me one night after I had kicked off and they'd found a knife in my room under my pillow. The knife had actually been used to cut up a pair of trainers, - 'Nasty Nick's,' this particular brand was nicknamed on account of them being so cheap and ugly - in an attempt to get my parents to buy me some decently named ones. My mother had guessed exactly what I had used the knife for - the trainers had obviously been deliberately cut - but I denied this hotly, seeing the chance of the Hi-Techs I wanted going fast out of the window. Stupidly, I shouted that the knife was to protect me from my dad, something which horrified my mother who then called the police. The sergeant who arrived an hour later was awful, accusing me of taking all sorts of drugs and shouting me down every time I tried to defend myself. I was fuming. It was bad

enough being in trouble all the time without being condemned for stuff I hadn't done.

"Anyone can see you're on something," he determined, "look at your spots, pure tell-tale sign and your attitude is abnormal."

He continued to lecture me, on the behaviour reported to him by my parents who believed I was abusing solvents due to the amount of air freshener I sprayed on myself to cover up my smoking. *How the fuck do you abuse a solvent?* He sneered triumphantly when I eventually broke down crying, telling me that he hoped I had learnt a lesson. My parents sat there like mean robots throughout the unfair lecture.

That weekend, there was another huge row at my house. I was caught egging a window along with Lila and some other girls. I hadn't wanted to but Lila had threatened that if I didn't do it she would batter me. She had a loud voice, an intimidating personality and I didn't dare say no. The angry people whose windows got egged called the police and I was taken home in a police car.

My mum was so mad with me that she slapped my face several times, a practice she now employed regularly. I slapped her face in retaliation, as hard as I could. For a moment she paused, shocked, but then she slapped me again. I flung myself at her, like a wild animal, pulling her hair until we were both struggling with each other on the ground. I was crying, fighting with my mum was horrible but I couldn't stop trying to hit her. She was too strong for me to do much damage but breathless in her efforts to protect herself. Teresa and Liam watched, appalled, from the doorway.

"Dad, Dad," screamed Teresa, "help! Maria's gone

crazy."

My dad burst into the room and grabbed me up from the floor yelling, "How dare you hit your mother? HOW DARE YOU? AGAIN!"

He dragged me from the room and flung me towards the stairs.

"Get to your room. You are grounded until further notice."

I snuck back downstairs, taking a pound from my mum's purse on the way out, something I now did often and ran away to a friend's house who agreed I could stay in her shed for the night. Later that evening we went down to King Street to buy cigarettes with my stolen money but as we were leaving the shop, I saw my dad standing outside with the police. I tried to run but the young constable caught my arm and put me in the waiting police car.

"Where are you taking me?"

"To Brynmor."

"Brynmor? What's that?"

"A home for bad girls like you, darling."

Shock penetrated every cell in my body. No, they couldn't mean it. Surely they were just trying to scare me and would take me back home after a short drive and long lecture about my behaviour. My hopes faded as we pulled up outside a large white seafront house in Hoylake. Ironically it was the kind of house I had always wanted to live in and also just around the corner from my old friend, Becca's. I was distraught as I was led up the steep stone steps. A large lady with blonde hair came greet us.

"Hello, chuck, my name's Marge. Don't look so scared, we don't bite."

After the police had left, Marge took me upstairs to

the bathroom and gave me some shampoo, shower gel, toothpaste and toothbrush.

"I'll bring a nightie and leave it outside the shower cubicle for you. Then you need to get into bed. All the girls are asleep now, well they should be anyway."

"I just wanna go home." I stuttered through tears.

Marge smiled, her kind eyes crinkling at the corners, "there will be a meeting next week honey. I've put you in a room with Debbie for now. She'll look after you."

Brynmor was an all girl's home that took girls from fourteen upwards. At twelve, I was the youngest there and to my surprise, all the girls were really nice to me, as if they saw I was at the edge of my pain barrier and really couldn't take any more. I was quiet throughout my stay there, only crying into the safety of my pillow at night. It had been decided not to send me to school until things had been sorted out. I felt strange around the others and hardly spoke unless invited to do so. I was filled with remorse for everything I'd done and did my best to convince the care-workers of this.

On the Sunday evening, one of the care-workers gave me fifty pence for the payphone across the road so I could ring my mum and talk to her in private, away from the ears of the care-workers and girls. I cried, begged and pleaded for almost an hour, repeatedly telling my mum I knew I'd gone too far and that I wouldn't as much as raise my voice again. I was so broken inside.

Four days after being admitted, there was a meeting which my parents and Uncle Dom attended. It was agreed I could go home on the condition I calmed down. There was no counselling or support offered to any of us but I promised sincerely and fully meaning it that I would control my temper. I had promised the impossible.

July 3rd 1990

This fateful day started like any other. I got up at eight, brushed my teeth, dressed and backcombed my fringe up, spraying it with lacquer. Without eating, I left the house, met Sinead on the corner of her road and walked into Liscard to get the bus. Everyone smelt of chewing gum and freshly brushed teeth combined with sneaked cigarettes, hurriedly put out before the bus came. Before separating at school to go to our separate classes, Sinead arranged to meet me after dinner that night.

I promised my mum I'd be back for eight and escaped the house after prayers. We hung around the shops and got someone to go in for us for a couple of loosies.

"Are you coming the confirmations tomorrow?" Sinead asked

"Yeah, probably, if I can get a lift with you?"

"Yeah, course. How come you're not making yours?"

"Cos of my behaviour," I smiled ruefully. "Mum said I have to behave a lot better first before I am deemed worthy."

"Deemed worthy," snorted Sinead, "My God! Who does your mum think she is? Mother flamin' Superior?"

I giggled, Sinead was always so blunt. We hung around Central Park, bored and aimlessly passing the time then went into Will's house because he offered us some more ciggies. Will the Wanker we called him behind his back on account of him being such a tit.

Suddenly I remembered the time. *Oh my God, the time!*

"Sinead, what time is it?" I grabbed her arm urgently.

"Five past...." Sinead started to reply.

"Oh my God. I'm for it. Gotta go."

I set off at a run, much to Sinead's amusement. I was so for it now. My mum would kill me for being late again, not to mention my dad. My mum was standing in the open doorway as I charged through the gate completely breathless.

"Where. Have. You. Been? You're. Late. Again." She slapped my face as she spat the words out, each syllable she uttered equalled a slap. *I was ten minutes late.*

I didn't even have a chance to explain that I'd run as fast as I could and really hadn't meant to be late. By the time she had finished her greetings, my temper exploded.

"How. Dare. You. Hit. Me. For. Nothing?" I retaliated, returning the slaps forcefully.

All thoughts of trying to keep my temper in check went clean out of my head. All memories of Brynmor and threats of being put into care vanished. All I wanted to do now was hurt this woman I loved so much yet hated equally.

"Paddy!" shrieked my mother, "She's started again. Call the police."

"Oh my God! The police again! How dare you treat me like this you fuckin witch, I hate you."

"Police are on their way, NOW CALM DOWN!" My dad yelled at me, grabbing my arms.

"She hit me first."

"SHE is your mother. Do not address her as SHE. You deserved it."

"NO I DIDN'T!" I furiously struggled to escape of his grip. "You bitch, you evil bitch. You're the evil one, Mum, not me. You made me like this."
"ENOUGH!" shouted my dad, "You are going, for good this time."
A police car pulled up and my dad demanded they take me away. I tried to plead with my mum but it was way past too late. Her cold look and unreasonable, impossible-to-grant request that I calm down before I woke my siblings, who I knew would not be asleep at this time anyway, were the last things I remembered as I was driven away and taken into care *For Good This Time*.

Borderline

Part 2

Enter the Furnace

Chapter 11
Care kid

Hospital - 12th July 1990

"Years ago, a man came to the door, trying to sell his wares. He noticed a photo of the two girls hanging on the wall, taken when Maria was around three. He pointed to Maria and asked who she was. When I told him she was my oldest daughter. He paused, as if contemplating whether to tell me what was on his mind. His words were at best disturbing."

My mother´s voice droned on, strangely comforting as I began to drift back into consciousness.

"He said, 'This girl is going to go through a lot of pain. Torment and misery will befall her and she'll suffer greatly. Think of her as gold going through the furnace in order to be made pure. She'll do a lot of good in this world one day.'

As you know Father, psychics are frowned upon greatly by the church and I tried to put it out of my mind but his prophecy lingered like a demon in the dark."

"Yes I can imagine," replied a man's voice.

"Maria was such an angelic little girl. We were so proud when she received the sacraments so young. I privately worried about her for never in my life had I encountered such a good, spiritually advanced soul in one so young. She was so small and timid, a perfect target for Satan. Sure enough, she began to develop little faults, display problematic, attention-seeking behaviour, telling lies and causing fights with her siblings. An unhealthy interest in the material world that put her peers before her family became apparent at around the age of six. And the never ending arguments! She never stops contradicting me, Father. Her good reports from school stopped glowing and her temper holds the whole house captive in its torrent. She had everything, a loving family, a priest for an uncle, musical talents, a good brain, good looks yet the older she's got, the more self-destructive she's become. She is *awful*."

Wow! How much you love me Mum! Obviously you are totally blameless in all this.

"Maria? Are you awake?"

I kept my eyes closed.

"She's awake. I can tell. Look, her eye lashes are fluttering."

I made an effort to relax my eye lids. I didn't want to wake up yet, desired more than anything to go back to the oblivion only sleep could bring.

"Maria! Open your eyes, please."

I slowly moved one leg a couple of inches across the bed and twisted my body towards the direction from which her voice was coming. I opened my eyes and stretched, putting on an excellent display of having just woken up. My mother's green eyes, as usual bare of makeup, surrounded by worry lines and sparse lashes, met mine and for a moment, I saw the beloved mother of my childhood, the concern in her eyes reminding me of times when I had woken from a delirious fever to her cool hands on my forehead. The illusion was broken as I noticed the young priest next to her, also looking at me, his worry for my health obviously mixed with trepidation of what my reaction to him would be. The overdose wouldn't have changed her decision. I already knew it would be put down to the manipulative streak I was so often told I had and that my mum never, ever responded to manipulation techniques.

I searched my brain desperately for inspiration. Maybe I could fake that I had lost my memory, go back to before the worst part of this nightmare had taken place. Surely she wouldn't hold things against me that I didn't even remember having done.

"Where am I?"

"In the hospital. Don't you remember?" my mother exchanged a quick glance with the priest.

"Remember what?"

"The overdose, the reason you're here."

"What? I took an overdose? Why?"

"Maria, don't play games. You must remember. You had us all worried sick."

"Mum, I don't know what you're on about. I don't remember anything. What day is it?"

"July the twelfth. Friday, July the twelfth."

"What? No way! It's May isn't it?"

"Where do you live, Maria?"

"At home with you."

"No, Maria, you don't. You're in care now. You were out of control and we had no choice."

"What? You put me in care? Why?"

"Because you kept hitting me. You were ripping the family apart with your behaviour."

"Mum, I would never hit you." I surprised myself at how easily I fell into the pretence. I began to get into the role I was playing. I felt like a tragic heroine.

She looked at the priest for support. At that time my mum believed she was doing the best for us all, the only thing she could do under the circumstances.

"Well, you did, several times. We gave you chance after chance and you just got worse and worse. We couldn't take anymore."

"Mum, I'm sorry. I really don't remember. I'm so sorry though...for hitting you. I can't believe I went that far."

She looked disbelieving.

"Sinead's mum rang before. Sinead's going to come and see you after school."

She noticed my expression brighten.

"Oh, so you remember Sinead do you?

"Well, yeah, I've been at St Mary's since Easter."

"Yes but you only got friendly with her a few weeks back."

"No, we've always been friendly, I knew her from church too."

My mum raised her eyes to heaven and called the nurses in to inform them of my newly developed amnesia. They told us that it was unusual for an overdose of this kind to cause amnesia of any kind.

"Not that we won't be taking it seriously," the nurse reassured us, "we'll be keeping her in until the psychiatrist has seen her."

A week later

I had outstayed my welcome in hospital, a stay I had enjoyed despite the dire circumstances as I was quite a celebrity among my class friends who came every evening, Jay Spears among them. The doctor who did the morning rounds told me I would be discharged that afternoon, memory returned or not. The psychiatrist had agreed that the best way to get my memory back was to return me to my previous setting in the hope that familiarity would help this process.

"But I don't remember the home," I had maintained.

It had achieved an extra couple of days in hospital but time had run out. Despite the fact that my friend's mum had applied to foster me, my mother had insisted I be returned to Wimbrick. *Doesn't she realise the only way I can survive is to become the worst I can be?*

During the summer holidays, I learnt a lot about surviving in care. Number One - Most Important; never fall asleep next to any of the boys on the minibus. This, I learnt when we went away to Llangollen, North Wales for two weeks' camping along with another home. During the journey to Wales, I was next to the boy my mum had judged to be 'nice' and had dozed off a little. I woke to his hand creeping around inside my knickers but stayed stock still, not wanting to make a scene in front of a load of kids I already felt intimidated by. *God, why can't I speak? Protest this gross invasion? I am stuck inside myself.* He put his dirty fat finger into my vagina, wiggling it about a bit before sneakily withdrawing his hand from my knickers. I felt invaded and dirty. At least I had actually fancied Rob. This boy was repulsive with his round football head and tubby body. I hated myself so much for not saying anything, for letting him do that to me.

I also learned how to shoplift while in Llangollen. *Wow, so easy.* It was a bad idea to let several teenagers in care loose in a tiny Welsh village. We robbed whatever we could get away with; souvenirs, make up, sweets and chocolate despite the fact that we all had a few quid spending money. This, we saved for cigarettes as they were the only items impossible to steal. The shoplifting spree resulted in several complaints from angry shopkeepers and all of us kids from both homes being banned from the village. Our tents were searched; suspicious goods removed and returned to the shops the following day by an angry Mr Rodriguez and his wife who was the manager of the other home. The main culprits (Stephanie, me and two others) were also grounded meaning we had to stay behind with a care-worker when everyone else went on walks up the stream or mountain.

Fed up, Stephanie, the other two girls and I ran away; hitchhiking to Wrexham where we robbed half the contents of Woolworth's confectionery department and some nice lipsticks, before bunking the train to Bidston and walking to Wallasey where we were picked up and taken back to Wimbrick. While being on the run, I learned that neither of the other girls were virgins, both boasted of having slept with four different lads. Stephanie and I had been shocked, for my part despite having had naked fantasies that made me feel good, I was still a Catholic girl where my virginity was concerned.

The others seemed less hostile when they returned from camp and I put this down to the fact I had run away, shoplifted and hitchhiked. Some of the harder kids regularly kicked off on staff and soon I was also kicking off regularly, especially when I woke up with the restless, caged feeling that I experienced more the older I got. Care-workers weren't allowed to hit us, only restrain and did so by shoving our arms up our backs and removing us from the situation.

Although I didn't go to church anymore and my mum couldn't do a thing about it, I started with the pre-planned twice weekly home-leaves, even having an overnight stay on my birthday. One perk to being in care was that they gave me pocket money and birthday money in addition to the birthday presents I received from my family.

Since the arrival of another girl, Vicki Duffy, a fourteen year old girl with dark permed hair, Nina Leyman had become much less threatening. Although the issue of my getting off with Keith had been forgotten in the wake of my overdose, the older girl had continued with her nasty little comments such as like asking me what I'd do if she was to punch me in the face, laughing when I went red and squirmed uncomfortably. One day she had done this when Vicki was there. Fierce looking Vicki, with her stormy blue eyes had got up and almost punched Nina in the face, warning her very aggressively to leave me alone. She had taken a shine to me and from then on made a point of bullying Nina who, like all bullies was a coward, and left me alone from that day onwards. The downside to my friendship with Vicki was that she liked to smoke pot and expected me to smoke it too. She suggested that we walk to the shops one afternoon before Sunday dinner and produced what looked like a small piece of black play-doe.
"D'yer know what this is?"
Stephanie, another new girl, Shirley, and I shook our heads.
"It's pot, girls. Who wants to try some?"
None of us wanted to and Vicki had a lightning flash mood change. With eyes full of aggression, she turned a hard face towards us and told us we had to.
Stephanie shook her head and said "No way, drugs aren't for me man," and skipped off down the road towards home.
Shirley and I looked at each other warily. Vicki seemed like a different person. I wished I had run off

with Stephanie but I hadn't quite dared. She told us to watch how she made the spliff so we'd know how to do it in future. Just the word 'drugs' invoked sinister images for me. They were of a world even I didn't want to enter into. Vicki lit it up, took a few pulls, showing us how to keep the strange smelling smoke in for ages before passing it to me.

I shook my head, "I don't want to, Vick."

Vicki stared at me hostilely.

"Do it, do it," she kept repeating, her voice becoming more and more threatening. "I'm losing' patience now girl. Smoke it!"

Tentatively I put the burning roach to my mouth, inhaling deeply like Vicki had shown me. I took another toke then passed it back to Vicki who promptly passed it to Shirley, a girl who was like me in her inability to fight back against her peers. Vicki brightened again after finishing the joint, her mood change so rapid it was as if we had imagined her previous ominous humour.

I didn't feel any different but when I sat down at my designated table for my roast dinner with the other kids so I was surprised when the care worker on my table started talking about the dangers of smoking pot, all the while casting me pointed glances.

"What yer lookin' at?"

"Just looking at your eyes mate."

"Why?"

"They look like you've been smoking pot."

I caught Vicki's fixed stare from the other table flashing silent warnings.

"What yer on about?" I widened my eyes innocently.

"Hmmm," he looked at me thoughtfully then changed the subject, suggesting we all drive to Wigan for the afternoon activity.

How did he know? What did he mean, my eyes? I felt normal. *Did Vicki set me up?* I quickly dismissed that thought. Why would she do that to herself? I didn't think at the time of Stephanie, who'd probably told him what had happened.

Please God, I don't wanna do drugs. I don't wanna be a bad girl. Please protect me. Unfortunately He was obviously still deaf to my prayers. Vicki always managed to obtain permission to go to the fair on Sunday afternoons when we all had free time. She would make spliff after spliff in the filthy toilets that stunk of pee and give us loads of blowbacks. I came to associate Adventure Land in New Brighton with the acrid smell of the drug as everyone smoked it there.

Although Shirley often went "white" and got sick when Vicki had given her one too many blowbacks, I never felt affected although my eyes would become bloodshot and heavy lidded like everyone else's. I didn't get what the hype was about. *Being stoned? What's that like then?*

Autumn 1990

The upper school at St Mary's was on a totally different site from the lower school, which was only for first and second years. The novelty of me being taken into care had worn off and a couple of girls including Vicki Morgan made bitchy, unnecessary comments to me on a daily basis. On insult could affect me hugely and I would get it stuck in my head, rewind, repeat, rewind, repeat. I hardly saw Sinead in the huge school and I was scared, irrationally so, that it would start turning physical again with the others.

144

Every morning I tried my hardest to get out of school, putting my fingers to the back of my throat to make myself sick, then calling to the care-workers to show them whatever I had managed to vomit into the toilet. They got wise pretty quickly and told me to stop being an attention seeker.

I would leave for school but never turn up there; instead I would head to Egremont Prom and spend many cold, lonely hours looking at the murky, grey waters of the Mersey. The contaminated river reflected my current state perfectly. Even when I was personally delivered to registration by one of the care workers, I would skip classes and hide in the toilets, bored out of my skull but preferring this to being around the others.

Eventually, I was taken out of school altogether and sent to the prefabs in the back yard of the home, that served as Wimbrick's school. The work was ridiculously easy. Most afternoons, we either messed round on the computers or went swimming. It was here that I finally learned to jump in at the deep end and swim a length, an achievement I was extremely proud of although I still feared deep water and would never be a confident swimmer.

My desperation to return to my family had disappeared the day I returned from hospital to Wimbrick. My heart had hardened and I was past caring what they thought of me. It was more important to me that I received approval from my peers and in my mind, running away, stealing, fighting care-workers and skipping school were the only ways I could stay safe from being bullied.

It seemed the social services had given up on me ever returning home either as they began suggesting other possibilities to me about where I was going to live long term.

They took me to see a home on the Woodchurch estate that was actually two council houses joined together. I refused to entertain that idea and told them if they put me there I would run away. I had got used to Wimbrick, my fear had left me and apart from Stephanie, I had been there longer than anyone, as many of the kids who had been there when I had first arrived had left for other homes or even their own home. In addition, the Woodchurch was rougher than Wallasey. *No way was I going to live there.*

I suggested foster parents, again my parents said no. I suggested Brynmor but even though Jessie was there, they told me I was too young. Finally, another home, Othona, situated in a village near Southport was proposed. Apparently there were only a couple of girls there as it had been a boy's only institution up until a couple of months previously. The less strange girls I had to deal with, the better. I would get the chance of going to a nice comprehensive school in the pretty little village with kids who weren't as rough and therefore less likely to bully with their fists. I didn't care about being further away from home, I welcomed the chance.

It was a grey October day the day I was discharged from Wimbrick. After going to school to be officially signed out and saying goodbye to Sinead, Anna and Jay, I felt quite nostalgic. Vicki, Stephanie and some of the other girls had written me little goodbye letters wishing me luck and promising to stay in touch which made me feel even more desperate to stay.

At the last minute I panicked and ran away from the social services office while I waited for my new social worker, Joan Hogarth. Looking out over the murky waters of the Mersey I wondered when I would be back to feel the cold foamy spit and the whip of the Wallasey Mersey wind on my face. After half an hour, I returned to the social services office, resigned to my fate.

I noted with fascination during the drive there how the environment changed as we left the grey dockland areas of Liverpool behind. Seaforth and Litherland were horrible. I felt depressed just driving through the rundown roads lined with disused factory buildings and tiny, cramped, terraced houses. As we entered Crosby, then Formby, the world noticeably brightened and the houses became bigger and more spaced out. Large, beautiful houses were abundant along the winding country roads and residential lanes. I started to feel more positive and hoped this was to be my fresh start.

Oct – December 1990

Othona was a Catholic Social Services establishment in Ainsdale; a beautiful, grey, stone-walled mansion comprised of two units, St Vincent's, where the older kids lived and St Thomas Moore's, where I was to live. The bedrooms all contained sinks and fitted units. There were only three other girls and at least twenty boys ranging from twelve to eighteen.

The two oldest girls, Sherry and Sarah, were hard-eyed, bottle-blondes; their very presence intimidated me. Even though they were never horrible to me, I tried hard to avoid them, absurd in my fear of them. The other girl, Kelly, was thirteen like me and also lived on my unit. She was from Litherland, the grey docking area that I had taken a dislike to on the way to Othona but she was friendly, introducing me to all the boys in the home, telling me which ones she had kissed.

As we were the only girls, apart from Sherry and Sarah who didn't want to know about anyone under sixteen, both of us had our pick of the boys. I didn't fancy any of them apart from one blond boy, Seth who was about a year younger than me. We had a little casual snog sometimes but it was a mutual need for affection and never developed into anything serious.

To my disappointment, I wasn't sent to either of the local schools I would have been eligible for. Kelly still went to her comprehensive in Litherland as it was only about thirty minutes on the train from us and she asked my key-worker if I could start her school. *Thanks Kelly!* I was sick of acting up in order to fit in. At this school, I would be targeted for sure if I showed I had brains. When I tried to plead my case with my key-worker, Tina, she told me it would be easier to start a new school with someone I knew and that I was lucky to get this concession. *Lucky?*

The first day at that high school overwhelmed me. I was crowded by girls who were rougher than anyone I had met before. They swore constantly in their nasal, gravelly voices and strong accents, making Lila and Louise Fila seem soft in comparison. Instead of saying, 'I want yer out,' when they were starting on the unfortunate using the same excuses as the Wallasey girls used like some trivial name calling incident or of flirting with the girl's fella, they would say, "I'm gonna fuck her after school, she's getting' fucked like," with more emphasis on the K than I had ever heard used on the Wirral.

They were more two faced and slippery than the nastiest of girls I had encountered before, all friendly one minute then turning into complete bitches the next. School was full of negative vibes and I felt constantly repressed and intimidated, scared of getting on someone's nerves, of looking at one of them in the wrong way. *Who's harder? Who's harder? Who's the hardest?* Why was this so important to everyone?

I hated the journeys there on the train where I would watch the world go from colourful and safe to grey and dangerous. It was like I could sense oppression in the air of certain places and was affected by the negative energies there. I couldn't discuss my feelings and perceptions with anyone, I didn't know how to put them into words but I was sensitive to the intangible.

After just three weeks in the school, of which I had skipped a few days, I became convinced I was being set up for some kind of initiation girl scrap after school and took eight paracetamol in the toilets before morning registration, going straight to the year head to tell her what I'd done. An hour later, Kevin Sutherland, the head of the home, arrived to collect me. The headmistress informed us coldly that she'd only taken me on a trial basis and that I wasn't welcome to be part of the school anymore. *Well worth the liver damage then.* I was taken straight back to Othona; apparently eight paracetamol didn't warrant a hospital visit.

"I am disgusted with you," Mr Sutherland raged once I was standing in front of his desk in his plush red velvet and dark wood panelled office. "What have you got to say for yourself?"

I looked at the floor, hating the fact I felt extremely intimidated in the face of this large man's anger. He had a formidable presence about him, especially now as his dark swarthy complexion took on a menacing sneer. He made me hold out my hands while he rapped my knuckles sharply several times with my bus pass, scraping and grazing them. He banged the table making me jump, something which caused him to smile briefly before continuing his verbal assault. "It's not surprising your parents couldn't cope with you. Who would want a horrible child like you? Othona is a good home and you have destroyed our reputation with your attention seeking stunt today. Don't think you will be getting out of school either. Your parents have specified a Catholic school so you will have to go to Christ the King in Southport instead, providing that is, that they will take a vile little creature like you. You sicken me to look at you with your dirty hair and spotty face. When did you last have a bath you dirty little girl?"

He ranted on and on. Lots of beliefs I had long held about myself were reinforced by his words, spears that easily hit their vulnerable targets. When I finally broke, he lit up a cigar which he put between his teeth pulling his lips back from them and winking suggestively at me. He was gross.

"Come here."

I hesitated. His mood had changed so rapidly. Again he smiled his cigar smile, this time his voice gentle as he repeated his command. Reluctantly, I walked over to his high backed swivel chair. He pulled me close, hugging my unenthusiastic, tense body, breathing his foul smelling cigar and whiskey mingled fumes all over me. He held me for ages, pressing his entire body up against mine before finally letting me go and ordering me to kiss his leathery cheek. *I don't wanna kiss you.* Grudgingly, I pecked it quickly, stepping back immediately

For some reason, I was never sent to the new school until after Christmas and unfortunately for me, I often ended up back in his office as, maybe due to the fact I had absolutely nothing to do, my already frequent mood swings became worse and often ended with me smashing furniture and screaming at, if not physically attacking care-workers. Mr Sutherland was able repeat this ritual often but I didn't think for one minute about telling anyone as it was too weird and no one would have given a damn anyway.

Chapter 12
Sexually Corrupted

Despite my irrational fears of the older girls, I got on well with most of the kids apart from Tim, a fourteen year old boy who went out of his way to annoy everyone. There were four handicapped adults living there too and I especially liked James, a young adult with Down's syndrome. He was very affectionate and loved hugs from everyone, care-workers and residents alike.

As well as the permanent residents, Othona took respite kids who just came at the weekend to give their families and carers a break. Among them was fifteen year old Amy, who came from Blackbrook House School, a semi secure girl's institution run by nuns in St Helen's. Amy's mum had dumped her and her brother when they were toddlers. She had no other family so came to Othona every weekend for her home leave. She'd been brought up in another Catholic Social Services home in nearby Formby but as her behaviour had worsened with her adolescence, she'd been sent to Blackbrook. We had all heard of and been warned about Blackbrook while at Wimbrick.

Amy took me under her wing and taught me how to fight back when Tim started a fight with me, giving me the home's popular 'yer ma's a slag' insult then kicking me hard in the stomach when I retaliated by calling him an ugly knobhead. He knocked my breath right out of me and I doubled over in pain as he ran off laughing.

"Right, you need to go and find him and fucking knock him out, the dick," Amy stated once I had got my breath back.

I looked at her fearfully.

"Marie, you have to stand up for yourself. If you don't hit him, I'm gonna hit you."

I feared girls a lot more than boys and we went into the hall just in time to bump into Tim as he came back in from the pool room.

"You little knobhead, Tim," Amy said.

"Well at least I gotta ma, unlike you, and she ain't a slag like yours, Marie."

I punched him straight in the mouth. He stepped back, stunned and then put his hand up disbelievingly to his lip to wipe away the blood. *Since when could I punch?*

"You bitch, yer knocked me lip into me braces."

"Serves you right yer ugly bastard. Now fuck off."

Amy stepped towards him threateningly as well and for once he shut his mouth and ran.

"You proper showed him, Marie! Oh my God, you've cracked your knuckle. Remind me not to mess with you. Never would've hit you really, you know that don't you? Just hate seein' you pushed around."

The next day during an outing to Wigan Baths, two boys a little older than me, Paul and Matthew ran up to Tim when he was stood at the deep end, one telling him his 'ma was a slag' and the other kicking him full force in the stomach straight into the water. The lifeguard heaved him out, spluttering and coughing and we all laughed mercilessly. He never hurt me again after that and I began to develop a little confidence. Although I still had no desire to fight with the girls, after this incident I often got into fights with the boys when they upset me.

New kids were admitted to Othona regularly. Amy and I made friends with Kate, a pretty, dark haired girl from Blackpool and spent most weekends causing trouble in the posh surrounding villages. We bunked trains all over the Northern line, jumping off at stations where the ticket inspectors got on. We would hang around Moorfields and Lime Street for hours, messing round on the escalators and in the lifts, playing a teenage version of hide and seek.

Amy taught us how to rob the tampon machines in various supermarkets and we did this every time we went out anywhere, developing quite a knack for getting the money tray out within seconds. Usually there was only about three or four quid in them but it was enough for some cigarettes and munchies. We only got one pound fifty a week pocket money from Othona so this little trick came in very handy.

17th Dec 1990

"Quick, we can make it if we get across now."

Kate was already on the tracks and through the darkness I could see the light of the approaching train. My heart pounding, I scrambled on to the tracks after her, terrified of stepping on the electric rail that Uncle Paul had always warned me about. The train tracks were the best route of escape as the care-workers would never put themselves in danger by chasing anyone this way. We got caught straight away by the minibus if we used the road.

We hid outside the station then raced for the train the second it pulled onto the platform. Once we got past the ticket office and onto the train we were safe as there were rarely ticket inspectors at that time of night. When we arrived in New Brighton, two trains

later, we went to see my old Upton school friend,
Natalia who lived near the station. She had let us stay
there the last time we'd run away but this time she
shook her head.

"My mum went mad last time, I can't."

I knew that Natalia had a tin containing quite a few
ten pound notes in her bedroom and I was determined
to borrow some, especially if she wasn't going to help
us. Smiling at her I asked if I could use the toilet. I
ran straight up to her bedroom, opened the tin and
took four ten pound notes. Well, we needed it more
than Natalia whose mum was rich and would
probably just give her more anyway. After nipping
into the toilet and flushing it, I hugged Natalia
goodbye and left. *No more painful, guilty, little
conscience anymore.*

Kate's face lit up when I produced the money.
Minutes later we were leaving the off license armed
with snacks and cigarettes. We wondered off down to
the arcades where we saw some girls I had known
from St. Mary's with a few older lads. We joined up
with them and walked off down the prom towards
Egremont where Kate and I ended up pairing off with
two of the lads, Paul and Lee, both eighteen years old.
Paul, the one I was with, had hard blue eyes, which
both excited and unnerved me. Kate snogged Lee all
the way back to the bedsit where they had said we
could stay the night. She got in the bed with Lee
leaving me to sleep with Paul on the floor.

Paul kissed me for a couple of minutes, lying me
down on my back and after I had stiffly allowed him
to fondle my tiny boobs, still practically non-existent,
he moved his hands inside my trackie bottoms and
began to finger me. I tensed at first but let him carry

on, part of me excited by this attention. However, he was rougher than Rob and the nasty kid at Wimbrick had been and I started to feel a little scared, more so when he took my hand and put it inside his boxer shorts. I had never touched a penis before and pulled my hand away but he was persistent, catching it, forcing it back there. He moved it up and down for a minute, making me feel all of his hardness, completely ignoring my resistance.

"Suck me cock," he breathed.

I shook my head, appalled.

"Suck it."

"No," I whispered.

I would have been happy to let him continue fingering me but I couldn't suck his cock. He brought his not so fresh smelling crotch up to my face, making me recoil. I noticed the bed where Kate was, moving rhythmically and knew that they were having sex. I didn't want to go that far.

"No," I spoke more strongly, "I can't."

He paused, "Well, let me fuck yer then."

"I'm a virgin."

He smirked and moved himself again, pinning me down with his weight, his body forcing my legs apart. He moved up and down, his cock straining against his boxer shorts, hard and threatening against my pubic bone.

"Let me fuck yer," he was more forceful now.

"No," I was so scared.

"You either suck it or fuck it. Yer gonna suck it?"

"No."

"Right well I'm gonna fuck yer then, okay?"

I don't want to. I'm scared. Why can't I say no? Shout? Scream? Silence? Did I nod my head?

Whisper yes? It's all blurry. I lay fearfully in the dark as he pulled my knickers and trackies down and then his own boxers. His cock looked monstrous as it sprang free in the shadowy moonlight and I closed my eyes to block out its image. I couldn't escape. I felt the end of his cock pushing at me, shifting up and down against me, rubbing backward and forwards until he took hold of it and placed the tip inside me. He thrust hard and I felt a ripping pain which made me cry out.

He grinned, oblivious to my pain, moving faster, filling me up. *It hurts.* No matter how hard I tried to blank out what was happening, I couldn't. I was completely under his control, he was inside me, an alien presence and I had to just lie there and bear it. The gentle, teasing feelings of lust that his finger had induced had been violently chased away by something far bigger. *Stinging, painful, unbearable!* I begged him to stop. He ignored me, panting heavily as he derived his pleasure.

"Please, I need the toilet."

I tried futilely to push him off but he gripped the tops of my thighs, his fingers digging into my delicate flesh, forcing my legs to spread further while he thrust deeper and deeper until he shuddered, letting his whole weight fall on me before rolling off.

"Go the toilet then."

Shakily I got up. Something sticky ran out of me making a warm dirty trail down the inside of my thigh. I made my way to the toilet where I sat for a few minutes, scared to pee because the stinging pain I'd felt was burning now and I knew that peeing would make it worse. When I went back into the room, he appeared to be asleep. I curled up miserably on the floor, after getting fully dressed, as far from him as I could. I felt defiled and disgusted with myself. The realisation that I had lost my virginity at the age of thirteen gnawed at me, appalling my dreams as I slept fitfully. I didn't cry; I was numb. Paul simply said "see yer" in the morning as we left, not even a kiss goodbye like Lee had given Kate. Total rejection. I wanted him to, I don't know? Acknowledge what he had done? Say sorry? I had meant nothing to him, he hadn't cared about my age or whether I'd wanted to do it or not. Now he was discarding me like a piece of used rubbish, not that I wanted him near me again, but maybe some show of acknowledgement would have helped. I felt dirty and used. *Dirty little bitch.*

The police picked us up as we were on our way to the train station. For once I offered no resistance and I was taken to Manor Road police station. The grey, bleak detention room reflected my mood perfectly as I waited for the social workers. I actually felt relieved to be going back to Othona.

23rd Dec

Mrs Field had been on shift since two pm. Most of the care-workers were called by their Christian names but Mrs Field was old school. She had a raspy voice, coloured by a Scottish accent and was strict, firm and fair with the kids in her care. The unit was peaceful; Mrs Field must have been reluctant to wake me, knowing that the second I was up, the tranquil atmosphere would vanish. I was constantly causing trouble by then. Since returning from that horrible night, I had got worse, taking innocent comments made by care-workers and kids alike and turning them into World War Three. "Just with the boys and the staff though, never the girls eh?" Mrs Field had noted wryly much to my annoyance.

At four o'clock, she finally came up to see why I hadn't been downstairs all day and found me running a fever and mumbling to myself. She put her hand onto my forehead covered by my dark messy hair and was shocked at the heat emanating from me.

Addressing the other care-worker with her she exclaimed, "She's burning up. Call the ambulance. Marie, honey, sit up."

I tried but my head rolled back against the pillow.

"Marie, we need to get you to hospital. How long have you been like this for?"

"I don't know. Didn't want to. It hurts."

Mrs Field filled a glass with water, and encouraged me to sip it.

"We need to cool you down," she stated the obvious, placing a wet flannel on my forehead.

"Gonna be sick, blood in my wee." I lurched out of bed, attempting to get to the sink but my yellow bile splattered the carpet.

Half carrying me, she helped me downstairs where we met the ambulance crew who took me straight to Southport Infirmary.

Christmas Eve

I awoke screaming, ripping the IV tube from my hand as I thrashed about wildly. Disturbing images of monsters holding me down filled my mind. I was so hot and full of fever, every single joint in my body ached. A nurse rushed to my bed, pressing cotton wool onto the blood coming from my hand and trying to calm me down. I kept screaming, crying and muttering half formed words. My hospital gown was up around my hips and I was pushing at an invisible force.

"Get off, leave me alone! Get off me."

"It's okay, Marie. No one's going to hurt you. You're in hospital, you're safe here."

"Stop, please, get off me."

"No one's on you honey, I'm just holding your hand," she stroked my hot hand and attempted to pull my gown back down. My delirium held me between two worlds; I didn't know what was real. Hallucinations danced in front of my eyes as she took my notes from the end of my bed, scribbling something on them. She put cold, wet towels on my face and stayed with me until my fever calmed and I was able to sleep.

After spending the most miserable Christmas of my life on the brightly lit children's ward without a single visit from my family, I was discharged the day after Boxing Day with instructions to drink lots of water to help clear my kidneys from the serious infection they had suffered. The pain I had felt when the doctor had touched the kidney area of my back had sent me shooting into the air in agony. It still hurt to wee but at least the blood and foul smell had gone.

Sitting in the doctor's surgery waiting for my follow up, I knew I was going to have to mention the symptoms I was suffering down below. The stinging had been apparent since that horrific night and I was all red and sore down there. There was a nasty discharge too that seemed to be getting worse. I felt so embarrassed at the thought of mentioning this to the doctor as I instinctively knew it had something to do with that night.

I had already denied knowing the cause of my bruised inner thighs that the nurse must have seen while I was crazy with delirium and then reported. A very concerned paediatrician at the hospital had questioned me gently about them after diagnosing the kidney infection the next day. I felt Mrs Field's disapproval as I nervously told the doctor now about the symptoms in my private area. The metal clamp inside me felt cold and threatening as he took a sample, a process which was uncomfortable, embarrassing and a little painful. Mrs Field held my hand throughout the invasive procedure.

"It's okay, relax, I'm finished now," the doctor reassured me as I tensed my vaginal muscles together tightly.

"Chlamydia," he announced a few minutes later and then began asking me all about my sexual history. *A dirty disease for a dirty little bitch. A punishment from God?* Shame washed over me as I admitted I had slept with someone a couple of weeks earlier.

"Just some lad from New Brighton, when I ran away. That was my first time," I whispered shamefacedly. Mrs Field seemed to take some comfort in that. Probably glad there wouldn't be an outbreak of STDs at Othona.

"I'll prescribe you some oral antibiotics and some cream for the discomfort. It is imperative you sleep with nobody at all until the antibiotics have worked. You are far too young to be indulging in sexual relations, let's hope this is a lesson to you."

Jan/Feb 1991
After recovering from my illness, I rebelled further. If I ever went home, I would steal fivers out of my

mum's purse until she stopped leaving it in sight when I was around. I was cocky and full of myself at my new school in Southport that I'd started a couple of weeks after Christmas and the kids seemed a little in awe of me due to the fact I acted tough and came from a care home. The novelty wore off quickly for me. I hated being confined and having to sit still all day. My once quick brain struggled to concentrate on anything; I needed to constantly be moving or I would feel totally agitated. After being escorted to the classroom by the care-workers, I would stay for registration, leave amidst the rush to get from the form rooms to the first lesson and then jump the train back to Ainsdale where I would meet with my mini Othona gang.

There were six of us in all; Matthew, my 'boyfriend' a fat ginger kid who had a crush on me. Terrified of his hugely obese sister turning up and battering me as she'd threatened if I didn't go out with him, I sometimes allowed him to kiss me although this made me feel sick. Kate was getting bullied at her school and had a genuine reason to bunk off. Then there were Ste, Paul, and Jamie. We would jump the trains over to Birkenhead, avoiding the ticket inspectors and spend our days in The Pyramids Centre, stealing from shops and smoking our dinner money.

I was an accomplished shoplifter by then and always filled my ski coat with all sorts of beauty products from The Body Shop and Superdrug. Sometimes, Mr Sutherland caught us on our way back, pockets and sleeves bulging with our ill-gotten gains, and he would confiscate the lot, which he later sold cheap to the older girls! When he called us separately to the office for a lecture, the boys would pale visibly and I would take the piss out of them. I hated his lectures and cigar breath and as for the compulsory kiss on his cheek at the end of his forced embrace, horrible, but I wasn't as scared as what the lads seemed to be. *I thought they were meant to be hard?*

We also ran away from the home overnight on several occasions, once ending up in Blackpool after robbing the bingo in St Helen's only to hand ourselves in after two freezing cold days of walking round the pier and arcades. Being on the run was always exciting at first, the lads would sometimes carry out a successful graft and Kate and I would top up our illegal earnings with our tampon machine money. However, that place in between, the no man's land which numbed me from all emotion would eventually become empty and lonely.

Alcohol was not easily available to us but another type of high was, in the form hairspray and which we inhaled through a towel pressed to our open mouths. The buzz was electrifying and very short lived although the hallucinations and alternate realities experienced while high seemed to last much longer. We robbed giant canisters of Insette and spent hours squatting in parks with broken glass all around us, alleviating the boredom and depression that sets in when you are on the run, cold, hungry, thirsty and fucked up. Inevitably, we always got picked up by the police after a couple of nights but it was never long before we ran again.

During one runner, I slept with Paul; a surreal experience in a confessional box of the big Catholic Church in St. Helen's town centre while the others had gone to suss an earner. I have no idea what possessed me to sleep with him, I wasn't attracted to him in the slightest. Maybe it was a silent rebellion against being Matthew's girlfriend, my up yours to God, *fuck you for the first time, God,* I don't know. In that place in between nothing was real.

That action had consequences, not of the sexual disease type that time, but Matthew, spurned by the rejection of a love that existed in his mind only, absolutely battered me. His punches landed on a numb body, it didn't hurt. Thank God for small mercies, he also 'dumped' me and I was free from that particular oppression although there was one further occasion when I was drunk one night, spewing all over my room when he came in and tried his luck pushing his small willy against me. *Hmm, even I could never be that drunk.*

Matthew got together with another girl, Sue, probably due to more of his fat bitch sister's strong persuasion tactics and I got with Jamie from our gang. A year younger than me, he was handsome, strong and well developed for his age but he wasn't a man and that made me feel safe. He had a mop of black hair that curled when left to grow and deep emerald eyes fringed with dark lashes that all the girls were jealous of. At first I'd seen him as no more than a friend but we often play fought and he would pin me down with his body on the couch or floor, which soon progressed into more. My feelings for him got intense very quickly. I loved his kisses, his soft mouth, his taste; the strength in his arms as he held me down, kissing me forcefully, holding me close, before setting me back and kissing me softly, lovingly. It wasn't long before we were having sex.

I took comfort in an act so different from my first time in its gentleness and the inexperience of my lover. Although always over within minutes, it felt nice and I craved the affection. We would hold each other close and tight. I would pull him into me as deep as I could. *Never let go.* We were far too young for the type of relationship we were having but we both craved love. Damaged kids are incapable of healthy love but sex and obsession is easy. At Othona everyone was sleeping with someone. I adored him.

Chapter 13
Self-Destructive

March 1991

Among the many new kids was thirteen year old Bev from St. Helen's. Six months older than me, she spoke with a Lancashire accent, and despite her nerves which caused her hands to constantly shake, she was a tough girl who had been kicked out of school for stabbing a teacher with a pen. She had a statement banning her from mainstream school and was taken every day with the other statement kids to Clarence House Residential School. Bev took an instant shine to me and looked out for me when Amy wasn't around. Even though she was on the other unit, her bedroom was next door to mine and we made a large hole in the dividing plasterboard wall so that we could sneak into each other's rooms at night, covering the hole with posters from our Smash Hits magazines. By then, I was regularly abusing solvents along with Kate, Amy and the lads. Bev soon joined in and we would steal huge cans of Glade air fresheners from the cleaning trolleys when the cleaner wasn't looking then spend the morning getting out of our faces. The girls and I often went to the local shops where one of us would distract the shop keepers while the others stole canisters of lighter gas to buzz off in the local graveyard.

My key worker, Tina, was aware of my solvent abuse and got angry with my wilful self-destructiveness. She stopped my pocket money and refused me privileges such as going to Blackpool Fair on the minibus with the others. This didn't help matters as I found myself with more time on my hands and the frustrated boredom I often felt increased.

My relationship with Jamie became volatile as my solvent induced mood swings triggered deep rooted insecurities and when we argued I would scream and shout abuse at him, sometimes becoming physical. Similar to how I'd been at home, I would scream the worst things I could, before being overtaken by floods of tears. When we had fallen out, I was unable to think of anything else but him. I craved him with everything I was. I would sneak into his room, press my body against his and make him forgive me.

Despite the fact I was sexually active, I only bathed if I was made to and even then I would convince Kate or Amy to sit in the bathroom with me while I hid myself under the bubbles. I had no personal hygiene standards and I hated everything about myself, my skinny body, my wild dark hair and the face troubled by fiery red spots which glared at me in the mirror every day.

I stole some peroxide from Superdrug and bleached my hair to a brassy yellowy orange. I actually saw this as an improvement. I was subconsciously rejecting everything nice and good about me. I drew loads of black eyeliner drawn on to my lower rims each day thinking it made me look tougher but in truth marred the beauty of my bright blue eyes, making them appear far smaller than they were. I drowned myself in Dewberry perfume which didn't mask my unwashed smell.

In the March of that year, I was expelled from Christ the King. In between my frequent truanting, I had corrupted a few of the girls by getting them to try their first cigarette and caused trouble between my classmates and some older girls which resulted in a big fight. When taken to task by Tina and told that they were running out of options with me, that I was a spoilt little madam who had a good life offered to me at Othona, *yes fabulous,* I blurted out that Mr Sutherland wasn't as holy as he made himself out to be.

"I don't like being made to kiss him, it's gross! He's not my dad, why the hell should I kiss his fuckin' cheek? And why should he make money out of us? He should take the stuff back if he thinks it's wrong to rob, not make on it!"

Tina seemed concerned and promised she would get to the bottom of it. Later that day she summoned me to go to Mr Sutherland's office with her.

"What trouble have you been trying to cause this time?" he thundered. "You have a twisted mind, my girl, making out that I am some kind of pervert, a dishonest one at that."

I looked at Tina for support but her disapproving eyes stared coldly back at me.

"Kicked out of school, yet again! You are a disgrace." The usual put downs were thrown at me in between his justifications that he only kept the stolen toiletries because taking them back would result in the arrest of the me and my robbing gang. He claimed that the products served as a reward to the older girls who were only allowed to buy them cheaply if they had earned the right. How they earned the right, he never actually said. He told me I didn't deserve the fatherly affection he offered me, I didn't deserve love as I threw it back in the unfortunate's face; no wonder I had ended up in care. "Dirty little girl, disgrace to yourself, your poor parents…" until again I was crying and he held me closer and for longer than usual.

"There will be a meeting next week to decide what to do with you," he winked at me, then at Tina, bared his cigar smile back in my direction and sent me on my way.

I started on Tina later that evening, insulting her in front of all the kids.

"Fat cow. Fuckin' midget, slut, look at all yer make-up, is that 'cos yer a slag or 'cos yer so ugly you have to cover up?"

She made the mistake of trying to get hold of me to get me out of the room. I fought back hard, hitting, twisting and kicking. Tina pulled my hair so hard, my orange strands were entwined her fingers.

"All this after I have tried so hard to help you. I'll be telling Sherry and the girls on the other unit what you've done. They'll see to you."

I was shocked that this woman, employed to care for me, would threaten me with my worst fear, thus using whatever information she had managed to glean from me previously in the guise of key worker support sessions. *Fuck you, you fat paedophile lovin' little bitch.* I hated her from then on, only speaking to her if I wanted a cigarette and had run out of options with the other care-workers.

The threatened meeting took place the following week. I hated these meetings where everyone discussed me and even if they did ask me what I wanted or how I felt, they never took any notice of my responses. I was incapable of expressing myself calmly and always ended up kicking off and storming out of every meeting.

As usual, my terrible school attendance was dragged

up but this time with the extra news of my latest expulsion. My shop lifting habits, (I had been arrested and cautioned for the first time recently), my anti-social behaviour, and solvent abuse were mentioned, none of which I could argue with as it was all true. Then Mr Sutherland read out a report written by Tina, detailing worrying behaviours such as my promiscuity with all the male residents including the handicapped young men! Although I had sex with Jamie regularly, I loved him and that wasn't what they were talking about anyway. *In Kevin Sunderland's twisted mind my innocent hugs to a handicapped young man are sexual.* The report's implications filled me with disgust.

"What? That's not true."

I saw my mother's eyes go heavenwards and my father's mouth set in a grim line.

"Don't start Maria," ordered my mother, "you've done enough. Save your lies. No one believes them."

"She is a danger to herself. We have no choice I'm afraid but to send her to Blackbrook House." Kevin Sutherland's deep voice sounded sincerely apologetic. "It is a lot more secure than Othona. Maria, (he used my parent's name for me) won't be able to leave the premises until she earns the privilege. It is run by a nun called Sister Mary. Your daughter will have no choice but to toe the line there. What do you think?"

I was horrified as my mum nodded in agreement. Blackbrook had a terrible reputation where the girls flushed your head down the toilet and jumped you when there were no care-workers around. My one consolation was that Amy lived there during the week and would surely look after me but that didn't serve me much in that moment. I told them all to go and fuck themselves and slammed out of the meeting. I don't know what affected me more, my not too distant future prospects of being locked up with the nuns or the horrific accusation made about me which everyone believed.

N.B. Although he was regularly abusing the children in his care and had actually been trying to groom me, Kevin Sutherland (bastard's name changed) wasn't actually reported for another seven years by his victims, something which resulted in him being convicted of thirty-two sexual offences including buggery against both the boys and girls in his care spanning many years including this time period.

April 1991

Bev was devastated at my imminent departure and the worry of what would happen to me at Blackbrook, contrary to Jamie, who didn't seemed too troubled at all. I had spent the morning doggedly trying to convince him to run away with me but he'd refused, his excuse being that he would be sent to Redbank, a secure unit in Manchester. *But I would do it for you…I love you.* I think he was relieved to be rid of me.

Now I was leaving, I remembered all the good things about Othona; my freedom which I was about to lose, the late nights at weekends, the pool table, the way some of the care-workers always gave us smokes, all the stuff I had taken for granted. Several times, I tearfully begged Tina to get me another chance but she told me I'd had more than enough.

Despite jumping out of Joan Hogarth's car on the day of my transfer and hiding under a bridge for a while in Ormskirk, I gave up and was admitted to Blackbrook one sunny afternoon in April *adios freedom* by a red-haired, bearded man, the dreaded Mr Toms who Amy had warned me about. His disapproval at my late arrival was evident as he warned me that this type of behaviour wouldn't be tolerated at Blackbrook.

He escorted me up to unit on the top floor of the main building; the most difficult to escape apart from the actual secure unit. I was introduced to nine other girls, all of whom were older than me. Amy lived on the unit below mine. If I was ever to run from here I would have to make it out of my unit, down three flights of stairs and a long, seemingly endless corridor, past the senior male care-workers and out of the front door which, to keep in with some ridiculous protocol about it not being an actual secure unit, had to be kept unlocked.

There were three more separate houses on the premises. George House was a large detached house opposite the main building, far easier to escape as it was set alone in the grounds and had its own front door. There was a secure unit which was just like a prison and lastly, an 'independent' house where the oldest and most trusted girls were allowed to live without care-workers as they prepared to return to the big wide world. They came to the main building for school but were allowed to go out alone and were only checked on by care-workers twice a day.

The girls seemed friendly, not scary like rumour dictated and although I felt very shy, I wasn't afraid. The strongest emotion I was feeling at that moment, and for many days to follow, was a devastating loss at being ripped away from Bev and Jamie. Kate had been sent away some weeks before and although I'd missed her when she went, it was nothing compared to what I was feeling now.

I was issued a used school uniform, which was even more badly fitting than my Upton one, comprising a huge grey skirt, light blue shirt and shapeless green cardigan. The inmates also had to wear socks pulled up to their knees and brown Jesus sandals. The nightclothes were long and flowery, reaching our feet, just like my mother's. The many rules were explained to me by the stern faced manager of Orrell House, Mrs Jackson.

"Two supervised cigarettes a day, one after tea and one before bed, as long as all twenty two forks and fourteen knives are in place." On seeing the puzzled look cross my face she explained, "Girls have been known to use them to unscrew the window blocks." (Each window had a sturdy wooden block on each side of the frame to prevent them from being opened more than three inches).

"You will receive four pounds a week pocket money, £1.40 of which will be taken to pay for the cigarettes and £1.60 to save leaving you a pound to spend on what you choose. You will bathe every night at seven unless you are menstruating, in which case you will be woken at six forty-five in order to bathe before breakfast, which is at seven thirty. You will go to assembly at eight thirty where we say prayers and then be in your classroom at nine. You will not have any home leave for the first four weeks of your stay," she paused for breath.

"You will be allowed to go out unaccompanied by staff only when you have been here for at least six months and that is subject to excellent behaviour and you choosing a suitable activity to participate in. Two of our girls go to sea cadets twice a week and are allowed to go into town on Saturday afternoons together. We have a video night every Sunday where the girls from all the units, can watch a film in the main hall. You get an extra cigarette at the interval too," she winked unexpectedly. "Any questions?"

"How often will I get home leave?"

"Once every three weeks to begin with, increasing to fortnightly, then weekly, subject to behaviour." Brusquely she continued, rattling off her instructions with the air of one who is absolutely sure all her rules will be adhered to. "You will have a planning meeting in two weeks and then a review meeting every three months."

"How long will I be here?"

"At least twelve months."

My heart sank further. Amy hadn't told me any of this and she had been here two years. Still, she got weekend leave to Othona most weekends so at least she could look forward to something. I had nothing. Four weeks without any freedom was an eternity. I needed Jamie so badly. The desperation I felt to get out of that place and see him was already overwhelming.

"After two weeks, behaviour depending, you will be granted permission to go to town on Saturday afternoons with some of the other girls and your key-workers. Your parents can visit on a Sunday, once a fortnight. Friday nights are phone nights but you're only allowed to receive calls, not make them. You are permitted to write letters at weekends. The care-workers will send your bedding, nightwear and uniform to the laundry but you are expected to wash your weekend clothes by hand along with your underwear. There is one box of washing powder allocated to the unit every month, when that runs out you use hand soap. Bed time is nine pm and anyone caught out of bed after lights out spends the night in the quiet room. We supply all sanitary items. Tampax is not allowed under any circumstances."

The quiet room was another name for 'Pin Down.' It wasn't locked but there was an alarm on the door that went off if it was opened, alerting the male senior care-workers. They would burst into the unit, restrain the culprit and pin them down to the bed until all the fight had left them before leaving them in the 'unlocked' room until they'd learnt their lesson as I found out to my detriment a few weeks later.

"There is a token system, where you can earn the right to extra home leaves, get your hair done at the hairdressers or request phone calls. Make-up is only permitted for home leave or in-house parties. Right, you can go to your room and put away your things. It will be time for tea very soon."

"I need some sanitary towels please. I came on this morning."

Mrs Jackson gave me a few sanitary towels, which looked more like nappies with loops in them, Doctor White's. They were the sanitary items that all the lads from Othona had laughed at most. I was given clean, floral printed bedding and told to make my bed. Every choice I had taken for granted, including the freedom to choose my own sanitary wear had been taken from me. My head was spinning with all the rules. My mouth was dry from crying earlier and I was craving a cigarette. Blackbrook was a huge intimidating place and I doubted I would ever get to grips with the rules and regulations. How had Amy coped with this for so long?

At first, I cried myself to sleep every night grieving for Bev, Jamie and my freedom. Bev and I wrote regularly; but to my disappointment Jamie only ever scribbled a couple of lines on the end of one of Bev's letters. Despite his lack of contact, I continued obsessing over him for weeks. The highlight of my life was after tea when the cutlery count was complete, the pile of letters brought in and our first cigarette given out, *blissful nicotine, so much more enjoyable in its restricted quantity*. I received letters from my parents too and Amy posted letters to me while on home leave so I had more mail to open, making me laugh with her funny drawings and piss takes on care-workers.

I had no trouble from any of the girls; my close friendship with Amy ensured protection as she was friends with the toughest girls and always referred to me as her little sister. At school, I was one of the brightest despite being the youngest. I also loved the aerobics/dance class we did for P.E. We had to choreograph a dance for an open house night where all the units performed a dance. I enjoyed dancing in sequence with the others and the song we danced to 'I wanna give you devotion' always reminds of those first few weeks at Blackbrook.

For the first time since being in care, I behaved myself. I gained the maximum amount of tokens allocated every week both from school and the house unit, although this was more because of the fact that I was still quite new and intimidated by the regime rather than any real desire to be good. My parents visited me every other Sunday and these visits, although a little strained, didn't end in the usual arguments.

After the designated four weeks, I was allowed home leave, which went well despite the fact that Jamie avoided me when I went to visit him, apparently having taken up with some fifteen year old girl who had moved in just before I left. The rejection almost killed me especially as I was also told in no uncertain terms by Tina that I was no longer welcome at Othona and if I came back again the police would be called. Surprisingly it was Matthew who accompanied me to the train station and hugged me goodbye and my mother who comforted me when I arrived back home.

The head of Blackbrook was Sister Mary, a tough nun who was very respected by all the girls. She was strict but sometimes liked to surprise us at break time by giving out an extra cigarette. A ripple of excitement would go round the room when the foil pie wrappers that served as ashtrays were produced and given out; the atmosphere that pervaded was almost euphoric. Film night was every Saturday in the hall with all the residents and care-workers from the other units including the ghostly pale secure unit girls. Mr Toms, infamous also for his love of Mars Bars, usually handed them out in addition to the much desired cigarette at intervals.

On Sunday mornings, although there was a chapel attached to the main building, we weren't forced to go to church and often went for rambling country walks with care-workers through Sankey Valley. It was during one of these walks that I became agitated with one of the staff for the first time since I had been at

Blackbrook. I can't remember what the argument was about, but before I knew it, I was banned from smoking for a week. By the time we had arrived back at the home, I had wound myself up to epic proportions.

"Marie, I think it's probably best if you go to your room to calm down," remarked one of the care-workers.

I told her to fuck off. Immediately, the alarm was pressed and the other girls were ordered out of the room. Mr Black, the senior worker on duty that day, burst into the unit through the double swinging doors, launching himself at me, grabbing both my arms and shoving them hard up my back. Overwhelming pain and fear made me react like a psychiatric patient, desperately hitting out, trying to kick and bite. I was half lifted, half marched to the quiet room by him and one of the female workers where I was put onto the bed face down and sat on by Mr Black. I quickly realised the only choice was to be quiet and stay still. If I tried to move, my arms felt like they were going to come out of their sockets. I was left in the room for several hours and eventually let out at tea time, subdued but simmering quietly.

The week that followed without cigarettes was a nightmare despite the fact Amy managed to sneak me a couple of halves which I smoked in the bath.

Although I lost my unit credits for that week, that incident was a one off and I soon began earning more and more credits that I chose to spend on going to the hairdressers to have a spiral perm. The perm bleached my ruined orange hair to a dark brassy blonde and I had obvious black roots. I was a long way from the dark haired little girl who had twirled and pranced her way into Jesus' grace nine years earlier.

Chapter 14
Beating the System

June 1991

"Come on Marie. We won't get another home-leave together for ages."

Amy had accompanied me to Wallasey rather than leaving me in Liverpool to go to Othona as she usually did.

"Yeah but Amy, it's Father's day and my unit's going camping next week and you said yerself, camping's proper good."

"Father's day! Pfft! Like your dad cares about you. We'll bunk the train to London, go to Centre Point. They take in care kids as well as homeless tramps and we'll never have to go back to shitty Blackbrook again."

I hesitated.

"Marie, yer meant to be my little sister, remember?"

"Yeah, I know, but..."

"I look after you all the time. Come on, if we go there they'll get us foster parents together like real sisters. They won't make us go back to Blackbrook."

I didn't want her to go off to London alone. "Ok, but I wanna go me mum's first, just to see them."

We had a cup of tea with my parents who were polite to Amy but not keen, I could tell. They told me that Lila had begun bullying Liam as well as putting out rumours that I was pregnant.

"Right, well if I see her, I'll sort her." I was full of bravado now when I was at home.

"Well, don't go getting yourself into any more trouble. You've been doing well recently."

I felt a pang of guilt at the first praise I had received

from my mum in years, knowing I was about to let her down again. *Why did Amy have to have home leave that weekend?*

I made an excuse to my mum about going to visit Sinead who I still saw and marvelled at how she had changed. She looked older than her thirteen years, had gone really skinny, took poppers regularly and went to The Quad in Liverpool every weekend. When I'd tried poppers with her, they'd given me a pounding headache. *Give me a can of gas any day.*

I kissed my mum goodbye and left the house with Amy, on my way to break their hearts again. On the way down the street, I saw Lila and bounced over to the scraggy blonde, "Oy, Lila. What's this about yer pickin' on our Liam?"

"What? Yer think yerrard now cos yer with yer mate? Cos yerrin care?" *Well, yeah.*

I got right up in her face. "D'yer wanna try me, you nasty bitch?"

Backing down immediately Lila replied, "I was only messing with him yer know."

"Well fucking don't, right, or I'll fuck yer next time I'm down. And do I look fuckin' pregnant?" I shoved Lila hard and left my previous tormentor looking more than a little shocked behind us.

Instead of London, we ended up opting for Manchester as Amy said she was sure Manchester had a Centre Point too but that night as we walked the streets around Piccadilly asking everyone where Centre Point was, we got nowhere. One man tried to drag me onto the bus with him telling me he had a spare room I could sleep in but Amy jumped on him, knocking him to the floor.

"Leave my sister alone you dirty perve," she yelled,

pulling me to safety.

Eventually we got talking to two homeless workers who took us to a soup van where we could get hot tea and soup at designated times of the evening. They gave us a number for an organisation called 'Safe in the City' which helped children who had run away from care or home by liaising with social workers for them.

These workers came and picked us up and took us to a cafe but their organisation was a drop-in service not a safe house. They offered to get in touch with the emergency social services to see if they could provide an emergency bed for the night but we refused. Our other choice was to rough it for the weekend then call them on Monday when they'd be able to speak to our social workers and also offer us a place to stay for a night or two. They informed us that if we had anything to report, things that may have happened to us while in care, they were the people to talk to. They also let me phone my parents to tell them I was okay *so magnanimous was I* and I was actually surprised and hurt when my dad slammed the phone down on me.

After getting the Safe in the City workers to drop us back at Piccadilly bus station we mooched around for a while then spent Saturday night in the back of a robbed car that we had seen someone abandoning and all day Sunday traipsing the city scavenging for food, money and smokes. It was a sweltering hot day and the dehydration exhausted us. My body was exhausted from spending so long without food or anything to drink and I felt minging. I had developed good hygiene habits again since being at Blackbrook and hated feeling dirty now.

In the evening, a young Irish couple took pity on me when I begged them for a cigarette and let both of us go back to their house to sleep on the sofa. I opened my heart to the sweet faced woman who woke us with hot sweet tea and toast in the morning; confiding in her about my experience so far of the system, the rejection from my own parents and the prison which Blackbrook was. Her husband phoned Safe in the City and within a couple of hours two workers arrived who took us to their drop-in centre where we were able to shower and get our clothes washed and dried. We had no idea of the storm we were brewing when we told the two counsellors of the rules and regulations of Blackbrook. They were shocked when I told them I'd been restrained and kept in the quiet room just for swearing at care-workers and had witnessed others suffer the same treatment. According to them, 'Pin Down' had been banned by the Children's Act a month before in May. After assuring us there would be an investigation, they called our respective social workers and arranged for Amy to go to Clarence House and for me to go to a children's home in Liverpool.

I ran away the next day, managing to bunk the train straight back to Manchester where the counsellors met me at the station and reluctantly called my social worker to tell her I would prefer to be at Blackbrook after all. *Better the devil you know.*

I was in disgrace when I returned. The other girls were away at camp and I received a long lecture from Mrs Jackson as well as a reproachful phone call from my parents followed by a letter of hellfire and damnation from my mother. The letter, which described in vivid detail a documentary about purgatory, disturbed me deeply. Despite having rejected my religion, I still feared what would become of my immortal soul.

July 1991
My quarterly review meeting was attended by my parents, social workers, my key worker and a senior care-worker from Blackbrook. The promised investigation still hadn't begun and evidently they were still unaware of the allegations I had made. Apart from the runaway, everyone was very pleased with my behaviour which had had no choice but to improve dramatically. When the subject of my alleged promiscuity was brought up, I blurted out that I had been raped in December but had been too scared and confused to say until now. All of them, including my mother, actually believed me.

Truthfully, I wasn't entirely sure myself whether what had happened constituted as rape or not and felt a bit of a fraud. On the other hand, I suffered frequent nightmares featuring Paul, from which I awoke screaming uncontrollably. Plenty of care-workers had been witness to these nightmares as they often woke me after hearing my screams and seeing me toss and turn through the window of my bedroom door.

The following week, two members of the child protection team came to take a statement from me. They called me back a week later to tell me Paul had been arrested and charged and that the hospital had sent my records over, confirming the bruising I had incurred and the tell-tale positioning of them. They'd also requested the reports from the GP of the chlamydia I had suffered and accessed Paul's medical records which proved he had been treated for the same disease.

They assured me we had more than enough evidence to convict him in court. They also recommended that I go for HIV tests. I had to wait a week for the results, a week in which I tortured myself constantly that I was HIV positive, all for nothing as they came back negative. I wouldn't have to go to court for quite a while so I did my best to put it all out of my head and forget about it.

Amy returned to Blackbrook after having realised she couldn't lord it over Clarence House like she could over Blackbrook. Bev was now at Clarence House too and I wished the three of us could have ended up there together, at least they had some freedom, but for some reason this request had been flatly refused. Amy went to live in the independent house as she was fifteen and a half now and often brought me little gifts to school like smuggled Tampax, *true luxury*, sweets, cigarettes and funny little notes to make me laugh.

I had grown very tired of the Blackbrook regimes since the Manchester runner and began running away again, taking someone different with me each time I ran. The first time I went, I blagged some new girl that once we got out we'd go to Bradford, her home town. In reality I had no intention of going to Bradford; I had just needed her help to distract the care-workers. Once we got to St. Helen's town centre, we met a couple of lads who took us to a little flat in Parr where they squatted.

I liked one of them, Reece. He dealt pot and also took a lot of speed - according to his mate he injected it but I had never seen him do so. At seventeen, he was four years older than me. I stayed in the squat for a few days, no water, no bath, filthy but not caring, smoking weed from morning until night - though I still never felt affected by it, maybe a tiny bit tired - and I ended up having sex with him when he turned to me in the middle of the night and kissed me. This time I knew what was expected and I was a willing participant. I confused sex for love and didn't take his many subtle hints about handing myself in before I brought him 'on top'. Eventually he told me the police were on their way, gave me a lump of weed and sent me home.

Within days I was back there again but came up against some of the other girls on the Parr estate who told me to fuck off when I asked for Reece. I was crushed when he came out of the squat with another girl he was now seeing, laughing at the silly kid I was and denying me publicly.

After that I went back to Blackbrook and stayed put for a couple of weeks, living a fantasy that I could be pregnant. *A baby would make Reece want me back.* I was desperate for someone to love me, need me, to put right what had gone so wrong. I looked at my photos of me as a baby, chubby, cute, dark curly hair, bouncing on my mum's knee; a time that seemed so far away it could have been a different life.

Girls at Blackbrook were known to try and get pregnant on purpose while on home-leave as pregnant girls were sent to a mum and baby unit where you got your own money to look after yourself and your baby and the care-workers were meant to be really nice. A girl from the unit downstairs was pregnant and boasted happily of all the luxury she had to look forward to.

My belly got harder and more bloated as the days went by and I prayed I would miss my period. When it was two days late I told the care-workers I needed a pregnancy test and was taken straight away to the local surgery. The test was negative and my period started almost instantly. I couldn't believe it; I had convinced myself of pregnancy so much it felt like I was losing a baby. The period brought with it another kidney infection, which, although wasn't severe enough to have me hospitalised again, was enough to knock me off my feet for four days.

More running away, hitch-hiking, escaping randy truck drivers who tried it on with minors, no awareness or care of the danger I continuously put myself in; I just acted on overwhelming impulses to escape, experiencing a type of tranquil solitude when I was on the run, where nothing was real. The motorways were similar to the railway lines of my childhood summer day trips, neither here nor there, simply the places in between where I felt more at peace than anywhere else.

Autumn – October 1991
Our numbers were diminishing fast. After my fourteenth birthday there were so few girls left that the ones from downstairs were all moved into my unit. I have some happy memories of some cosy evenings spent doing spa treatments on each other, face masks and shoulder massages. I would settle for a couple days but then I would become restless and need to be free again.

In school, Amy and I plotted daily for that night's escape. A contrast to the timid child I had been when I had first gone into care the previous year, I now had a good deal of control over a lot of the girls, all of whom were older than me. I ordered who would fight with whom in George House when arranging my decoy. George House girls were my main way of escape due to the fact that when their alarms went off, the power hungry senior care-workers would rush over there leaving the downstairs unmanned so we could run. Later, the George House girls would meet us outside as they could literally just walk out of their front door.

I would spend the night chilling with some local lads, Amy and the other girls in the park or fields. I grew to love The Doors and the ambience induced by their music which played steadily through the night on a big portable ghetto blaster. We would drink beer and smoke spliffs, not that they did a thing for me still. At dawn we would return to Blackbrook, bored, cold and tired, sleep all morning, go to school in the afternoon and arrange the escape prank for that night.

The regime at Blackbrook was collapsing. I had an idea my allegations were being investigated as recently I got away with everything I did. We had four cigarettes a day now, and were allowed to use Tampax or slim towels with wings. All our clothes were now washed in the laundry. The care-workers were losing control and had very little power over us now.

My social worker, Jean, paid me a visit to inform me that my parents thought I was prostituting; apparently the fact I stayed out all night meant I must be a prostitute. Immediately I was up in arms, swearing and becoming abusive towards her, insulting her *fuckin' lesbian, a goofy teethed, ugly old dyke, fuckin' get away from me* and becoming so aggressive she had no choice but to leave. I fumed all day after that visit. Could my parents stoop any lower than accusing me of prostitution? It possessed my thoughts which were already racing angrily due to their latest fire and brimstone lecture letter. *Fuck off with your religious mania. You don't want me, so let me go elsewhere.* Later that day, I walked out of my unit's swinging doors in full view of staff. I believed I was untouchable, after all, hadn't I turned the regimes on their heads? The quiet rooms were hardly ever used now so what could they do to me?

I raced down the stairs only to be caught by the strong wiry arms of Mr Bates who wrestled one of my arms so far up my back that I had no choice but to move with him to the quiet room. When I yelled at him to fuck off, he brutally wrenched my arm even higher up my back, making me yelp and go limp in pain. He flung me on to the bed and sat on me for several minutes. Once he'd gone, the pain in my shoulder intensified and I kept pressing the emergency button, convinced that my shoulder was broken.

My arm was put into a sling although luckily nothing was broken. The doctor was concerned enough about my injury that he requested we wait for the duty social worker to come and speak to me. I smiled smugly at the staff member with me (she had warned me not to say anything) when the duty social worker arrived and proceeded to tell her exactly what had happened. *Fuck you, fuck Mr Bates and fuck Blackbrook.*

I was taken very seriously and two police men from St. Helen's child protection team came to see me encouraging me to press charges. They reassured me they could remove me from Blackbrook but I didn't want to be put somewhere else and suffer the horrible, intimidated feelings I always suffered as a new girl. I refused. Much as I hated the bully care-workers and the strict prison like regimes, I was safe amongst the other girls and that mattered more than anything.

The detectives told me they would be arresting Mr Bates in the near future. This, combined with the previous allegations that I had made in June, resulted in the Blackbrook staff asking the social services to find me a new placement. I was sent to Cotsbrook Hall School in Shropshire.

Blackbrook was closed down a few months later.

Chapter 15
Respite in the country

Oct 1991 - Feb 1992

I slept for the two hour journey, leaning into my mum, who, surprisingly, had come to the police station with the social worker and accompanied me all the way to Cotsbrook, an establishment which consisted of three white houses in private fields set amidst miles of countryside. She saw me settled into my new bedroom and even hugged me before she left. *Don't leave me, Mum, I am so far from home.* Another kidney infection hit me within a few days of moving there.

Cotsbrook housed kids from all over the country. There were lots of girls from places like Birmingham and London, huge for their age in comparison to tiny little me. They appeared quite scary to me at first with their strange accents. There were a couple of kids from Wallasey, Roy and Hayley, who befriended me instantly as did Tania, a large, stocky, Caribbean girl from Bristol.

There was a lot more freedom at Cotsbrook than Blackbrook. We could smoke whenever we wanted except during class and had the chance to earn lots of spending money by doing jobs such as setting tables, washing up, and hoovering. Each kid could pick their job contract for the week so everyone got a chance to earn. There were shop runs every night in the minibus as Cotsbrook was about eight miles from the nearest big town and we would buy sweets, chocolate, magazines and cigarettes before returning home in the minibus to take part in bingo games where we could win more ciggies and sweets. We had video nights in as well as lots of outside activities such as cinema trips; ice skating, swimming and in due course, horse riding became part of the school curriculum.

One of the benefits of being in care was that I got to try lots of new activities and saw a fair bit of the country as we went out every weekend in the home's minibus. I also had more clothes now than I had ever owned. My own social services had to provide £150 every six months to clothe the kids in their care and Cotsbrook also gave us clothing grants. Soon I was dressed in Nike from head to foot, preferring sporty boy's clothes to girl's fashions. *Cover up this hated body.*

Despite all the above, I complained regularly that I didn't want to be there, never able to adjust, always wanting to go back to the last place I had been.

Cotsbrook girls were hard but I managed to get on side with the right ones, more so after several of the girls decided to jump another, Chloe, for supposedly making racist comments. Despite this being my worst fear, I joined in as we held Chloe down and painted her face black with boot polish, kicking her, punching her and saying, "Who's the black bitch now?" *Vicki Morgan, I would love for you to be here!* She ran crying to the staff and was removed to the boys unit for a week for her own safety. When we were told we weren't allowed shop runs for a week, a huge riot kicked off that called for several of the care-workers to physically intervene.

I had been locked inside my desert mind again, where I always ended up when new to a home, scared and unsure of myself but now I became the tornado and smashed most of the windows of one of the classrooms which consisted of several small panes of glass in between old fashioned square wooden frames. My new friend Hayley went so crazy attacking staff that extra care-workers had to be called in and that night her social worker turned up to take her to another placement in Derbyshire.

I kicked off a few times but soon met my match in one of the care-workers, a petite blonde named Ellen. "Get out, you fuckin´slut," I shouted at her one morning while she was attempting to get me out of bed and up for school. Ellen left the room as I lay back down and snuggled deep into my cosy pink duvet. Within minutes, she burst back into the room along with Dan, another care-worker who also happened to be her boyfriend. The pair of them sat me up, Ellen swinging my legs to the side of the bed while Dan lifted me by the shoulders, frog marching me between them straight into the shower, still fully clothed in my pyjamas. I shrieked when the water hit me but actually saw the funny side of it and giggled making Ellen laugh too.

I developed a healthy respect for Ellen from that day forward. She was the first to look beyond the terrible way I was portrayed in my reports from previous homes and understand that my pre-care life at home was not as stable and loving it was made out to be after being in the office one evening during a traumatic phone call from my mum. Ellen hadn't been able to help over hearing the recriminations coming from the other end of the phone. She was shocked at the religious intonations that warned of my certain damnation and eventually snatched the phone from me and slamming it down.

My left ear still burning from the hell fires coming

from ninety miles away, I looked at her in amazement. "What did you do that for?"

"No child should have to hear that! If I'd heard any more I would've said something to your mother that I may have lost my job for."

I was shocked. Never had anyone sided with me against my formidable mother. I hated her religious lectures but assumed somewhere deep down that they were well deserved and that my anger on hearing them was the devil in me rejecting the lessons of the God I had angered. Up until that point I had complained daily about being sent to live so far away, about how much I hated Cotsbrook but after Ellen had seen a different side to my situation I began to develop positive relationships with the care-workers and although I wouldn't admit it, I felt happier and more settled at Cotsbrook than I had anywhere else.

I was hassled so much by some of the other girls to get a boyfriend that I got with Roy. I didn't fancy him but could have done worse. He kissed nicely and never forced me into anything, satisfied after being allowed to let his fingers explore inside my knickers. It was a novelty living with boys again after Blackbrook although lots of them teased me about my looks, laughing at my ruined hair and my skin, which constantly erupted in angry, red spots with yellow pustules.

There were lots of lovely adults who worked at Cotsbrook. Elaine, a motherly woman who I adored, did beauty treatments every week consisting of face packs and face steaming, thus helping my troubled skin. She sorted my hair out, buying me a dark hair dye and helping me apply it, improving my appearance dramatically. She also got a very competitive scrabble club together in which I excelled, taking pride in my high word scores and often winning the prizes.

There were innovative, alternative approaches to dealing with the behaviours we'd commonly exhibited before being admitted to Cotsbrook. We were allowed to keep small pets. We had incentive to earn money. Dan did mechanics with the lads every day. They went to scrap yards, picked up old cars and parts and after fixing up the cars they were allowed to rag them round the fields, satisfying the thirst for adrenalin derived previously from joy riding. The fact was it worked. Rarely did the lads run away or have their previous urge to steal cars. There was also a boxing ring and any bullying or fighting was usually sent to the ring to be fought out fair and square.

The only real problem I had was Tania, whose roommate I had ended up becoming. She treated me as if I was her personal property, a little doll especially gift wrapped and sent to her. She would make me tell her stories for hours every night of her fantasy that one of the lads, Des, would fall in love with her. Totally obsessed. I had to describe their various happy ever afters, sometimes until three in the morning meaning I was always tired when we were called at seven for school.

She controlled certain staff members as much as me. Her key worker was even paying her to quit smoking, a fiver a week for every week she didn't smoke. Tania would sit with me while I smoked; demanding I put the cigarettes to her lips while she toked on them but never offered me any share of her ill-gotten gains. She wanted me with her every minute, which I hated but Tania was not a girl you argued with.

I missed Amy and ran away, desperate to escape suffocating Tania for a couple of days. Amy sneaked me into the Manchester children's home where she'd been sent after I'd been kicked out and introduced me to her new mate, Ron, a good looking fifteen year old who constantly yet good-naturedly took the piss out of us both in his weird Liverpool/London mixed accent. She told me he was our brother now. After I'd been returned to Cotsbrook, they both wrote to me regularly. Tania had been fuming when I returned and wouldn't let any of the girls speak to me for two days, until her need for her bed time stories got the better of her...

My parents decided I wasn't welcome there for Christmas after a home leave that had gone horribly wrong - I'd refused to leave when the minibus had come for me, begging my parents to let me stay. My dad had called the police to remove me and I'd been handcuffed and removed in full view of Teresa and Liam. My brother and sister had cried as much as I had.

I cried even more when told I wasn't going home for Christmas - they still had the power to hurt me through their rejection - but it ended up being one of the best Christmases of my life. *Not all care homes are bad.* Many of the staff turned up on Christmas morning with a present for me bought out of their own money. One brought me a baby budgie in a cage. I received life size pictures and posters of Jim Morrison, now my absolute idol, videos and tapes by The Doors and Pink Floyd, new clothes, makeup and a ghetto blaster and also some spending money for the sales. Elaine took me home with her the next day to enjoy a Boxing Day dinner with her husband and two young children. I wished Elaine was my mum.

By the middle of January, although all the boys were still in residence, only three of the girls remained, some having run away, others not having returned from their Christmas home leave, *no more Tania, yay.* We moved into Lewis House, which was smaller and cosier, and the boys into Bert House where the girls had been. I'd dumped Roy by this time and begun seeing another boy, Simon Love, who I really fancied. I think he only went out with me at Dan and Ellen's request as he never seemed overly interested in me and the one sexual interlude we did have was in the dark, kept secret and never referred to again.

I began sharing a room with a nice girl called Alice. We spent hours together playing with our new pets. We went horse riding every Wednesday for our P.E. lesson. I got on well with the care-workers, earned good house work money and had managed to get a nice little music collection going. I began to feel really settled at Cotsbrook. I showed avid interest in my school work once more, even making a concentrated effort on the finer details such as handwriting and presentation. Some friendly competition went on between Alice and me as we were both doing our key stages in Math and English, working towards some in-house exams that were the equivalent of the mainstream schools' G.C.S.E.s. My turbulent emotions settled down for the first time in years.

One night, during an extra study session, I nipped back to Lewis House to collect something and ran

into the dark front room where I heard someone
giggling. I turned, and could just make out Roy and
Chloe on the couch, obviously up to something.
Chloe smirked and began pulling her knickers up
while Roy looked suitably embarrassed.
I thought no more of it until a couple of days later I
saw Chloe with the police and her key worker going
into one of the offices at the back of Lewis House.
"What's going on?" I asked Elaine.
"It's confidential sweetheart. I can't say. But the police
will want to speak to you soon enough."
They came for me an hour later.
"Chloe has reported a serious occurrence that she says
you were witness to."
"What? I haven't witnessed anything."
"Think, Marie, cast your mind back to two nights ago,
to something you may have walked in on."
The incident from the other night couldn't be what
they were referring to so I said nothing.
"There has been a rape allegation Marie, you need to
think hard."
I was astounded. Even though I wasn't sure that what
I had been through constituted as rape, in my opinion,
what I had witnessed with Roy and Chloe wasn't
even close. I told them what I'd seen and even went
on to explain that I had used to go out with Roy
myself and although I'd refused to have sex with him,
he'd certainly never come close to forcing me.
"Thank you for your help, Marie. We have a couple
more questions, not regarding Chloe or Roy. We
understand you may find it hard to answer them but
we really need you to be truthful. Have any of the
male care-workers here ever hurt you in any way?"
"No."

"So they have never restrained you or held you in any way?" The detective woman looked disbelieving.
"Well, yeah, there were a couple of times when I proper kicked off, smashed windows and stuff and two of them had to hold me still. But they never hurt me, not like in the other homes."
"Marie, you can tell us the truth you know, love. We can remove you today if you give us a statement."
"Nothing bad happens here."
"We have heard otherwise. You can tell us you know."
Though there had been a couple of incidents in my first month, that was the past; I loved Cotsbrook now. Pissed off with their patronising voices, I walked out of the room.
Chloe was removed later that day and taken back to her home town to a home there. *Poor Chloe, I think as I look back now, she was only twelve; confused, damaged and naïve. No one should have been having sex with her.* Roy was taken to BrynAlyn in North Wales for his own safety as the lads were going to beat him up. It was only after he had gone they decided he wasn't guilty, not of rape in its true sense.
A week later, both Alice and I were called to the office by Dan to be told that our social workers were looking for new placements for us. Apparently, Tania had made loads of allegations of physical abuse against certain male members of staff and had been backed up by the other girls, hence why none of them had come back.
Despite calling our social workers daily to convince them that we were happy at Cotsbrook, two weeks later Alice's social worker came and took her to her new placement in Rugeley, her home town. My last

memory of her was her tiny heart shaped face obscured by her mass of hair, smiling sadly and waving at Elaine and me as the car pulled off down the country driveway.

I was going to Taxal Edge, where Hayley had gone after Cotsbrook. I had the same social worker as Hayley now, a pretty young woman with a dry sense of humour called Bryony Black who, despite myself, I grudgingly liked. I was angry and sadly devastated about having to move to Taxal even though Ron, my new 'brother' now lived there and Amy also lived in a hostel near there.

Bryony arrived at tea time and I subjected her to a load of tearful abuse before I suddenly made a break for it and ran. I managed to hitch a lift into Telford where I wondered round miserably before resigning myself to the inevitable. Elaine picked me up in the minibus after taking my call. Her eyes were wet as she hugged me and shoved a present into my hands, gently pushing me into the back of the car already loaded with the five bin bags that contained my life. I was inconsolable. I wasn't even allowed to take my budgie with me. I hated Taxal Edge before I'd even arrived.

Chapter 16
Juvenile Delinquent

Feb - June 1992

Taxal Edge was in a little village about fifteen miles outside of Stockport and all its rules comprised of a 'group system.' Anyone, kids or staff, could call a group meeting at any time. Punishments or 'consequences' involved being put out of the group meaning that all privileges were stopped, no going out, no phone time, not even paid calls on the kids' payphone and although people weren't supposed to ignore a time outer, they were not allowed to play pool or do anything specific with them. Sometimes the group was lenient depending on the crime and either verbal or written apologies or cups of teas were to be made by the culprit to the care-worker or child who had complained.

Kids who refused to attend the school that was part of Taxal were automatically classed as out of the group until they'd made up the time they'd missed at school, usually through writing pages and pages of irrelevant information copied out from various text books - two sides of an A4 counted as one hour's school work. I resented the fact that the other kids had jurisdiction over me although at first I abided by the rules.

In addition to the several-times-a-day group meetings, we had an official weekly group meeting where we looked at our life plans, symbolised by triangles drawn on cardboard, the top point being our dream placement, the bottom two points being Taxal at one side and a secure unit at the other, the worst threat to care kids. Depending on our progress we would be placed on the triangle nearest to the point where we were at that moment. A bit like my mother's ladder but without the Hell factor. *I don't want a fuckin' triangle!* Cotsbrook or foster parents, my only choices, weren't options apparently and I refused to take on any suggestions from my key worker Abby who I was determined not to trust in any way no matter how nice she appeared.

She tried hard to gain my confidence, taking me to Little Chef for chocolate sundaes every week to conduct the obligatory key worker sessions - I would have been put out of the group if I hadn't attended them so this was really nice of her. However, previous experiences of being betrayed by the ones I was supposed to be able to trust prevented me from ever opening up and Abby would end the session despairingly, unable break through my barriers.

My heart ached for Cotsbrook and the surrealism I'd experienced while living there, safe from the world. Now I was back to a shit reality where I felt the need to play up in front of my peers.

However, it was great to be able to see Amy again, by this time sixteen and living in an independent hostel for care-leavers. A few times a week the care-workers would drop Ron and me off in the minibus to meet up with her and we would hang around Stockport town centre for a couple of hours, amusing ourselves by being needlessly abusive to passers-by.

Stephanie from Wimbrick was also at Taxal and we became close again. We spent hours listening to The Doors, having discovered we both loved Jim Morrison. We had pictures of him all over our room and obtained a tape of his poetry which we would write and try to memorise.

We read books about him and watched his videos, not caring that the other kids laughed at us for our musical tastes. Jim Morrison was my total idol in every way and I would have loved to have been alive in his time.

I also adored Pink Floyd and listened to Bob Marley and UB40. I never listened to chart music anymore, preferring music that had lyrics that actually meant something.

School work was too easy, boring. I wasn't allowed to continue my key stage preparations for my G.C.S.E.s. They told me if I did well at Taxal School they would work on getting me back into mainstream school instead. *No, I wanna go back to Cotsbrook.*

Taxal School also took part in a disabled horse riding scheme offered by a riding school near Derby, which involved us helping out with disabled kids and then being able to go on the horses ourselves. The first time I went, I refused to go near the disabled kids, remembering what I had been accused of when kicked out of Othona but I gave in when I realised that if I didn't help, one of the disabled kids wouldn't have his ride. I was praised by everyone when I helped and found I really enjoyed looking after the little boy while he was on his horse. I loved my ride afterwards; liberated and exhilarated by the sensation of the wind through my hair while my horse galloped freely.

I got on well with most of the kids and for a while I was an active member of the group. I surprised myself sometimes by taking part in the kangaroo courts and offering good advice to the meeting. All of us took our turns being an enthusiastic group member. Hayley was well into the group at times but, damaged and highly strung like me, she sometimes kicked off big time. Once when some girl started a fight with me, Hayley kicked her right in the nose. Splat! Blood everywhere. Hayley was sent to live in the same hostel as Amy when she turned sixteen.

I had to attend the magistrate's court for the committal of my rape case to crown court. My parents were there to support me along with Abby and Bryony and the police from the child protection team. After giving evidence in a shaky voice and being brutally cross examined by Paul's solicitor the case was committed to crown court.

The experience of court was so horrible I didn't want to take it further and was plagued with doubts that what had taken place was even rape. *If I had been stronger in saying no I would know it was rape. It was my fault. I should have yelled out NO, NO, NO. But I didn't. Why did I want him to care about me afterwards? It isn't clear cut rape.* My nightmares started up again, subconscious confusion amplifying my dark dreams.

After court, I got properly stoned for the first time in my life. Danny and Bobby, two guys around my age, came up to my room when I returned home subdued and tearful, all proud of themselves because they'd burgled a dealer's house and had two big chunks of weed. After several bongs I found myself pleasantly drifting off as I lay back on my purple quilted bed. I lost track of myself several times, falling back into the reality of my bedroom with peals of laughter I had no control over. Everything was funny; Bobby as he spluttered the smoke back into Danny's face, Danny's unimpressed expression; my own laughter made me laugh more. I felt carefree and delicious. Pink Floyd had never sounded so good; everything was more colourful, brighter. Finally I saw what the fuss was about. *I love being stoned. I am a happy, giggly child.* I still don't understand to this day why it affected me so much that day whereas it never had before but from then on I got stoned regularly, craving that carefree, giggly feeling. It switched me off to emotional pain, lit up the dark tunnels of my mind, filling the empty spaces while emptying the angry places. Ron often had a supply which he willingly shared with Katya and me. Katya was a pretty girl from Toxteth, who had also been at Cotsbrook before my time there. She was currently one of Taxal's success stories, going to mainstream school and never robbing anymore, a great achievement as most of her childhood had been spent shoplifting.

I often went to school stoned out of my face if I bothered to go at all. *What's that? I'm out of the group again? Do I give a fuck!* Weed enhanced the drowsiness caused by my hay fever tablets and I often dozed off in class. The only subject I enjoyed apart from horse riding was some social services version of social studies. We could do a project of our own choice and I'd chosen drugs. Stoned out of my face I would cut and glue pictures of crack pipes and heroin syringes, fascinated by them.

I developed a taste for strong lagers, namely Special Brew. The combination of alcohol and weed brought a different buzz, however, only Amy could get served and she wasn't always with us. My need for the escape I found in the bottom of a can led to my first time in court, up on a charge of aggravated robbery. We were hanging round Taxal bored, no weed, out of the group and nothing to do. I needed to get high. Katya suggested we go into the village to rob some lager. There were five of us in all and our plan was simple, we would pick up what we wanted and then just simply leave. We grabbed a pack of lager each and ran back out but Stephanie wasn't quick enough in getting the wine she wanted and was hauled back by the shop woman.

"Fuckin' let her go!" I demanded, having run back in to save her.

"Put the stuff back then," she countered.

I picked up a bar of chocolate, opened it, took a bite, chewed for a couple of seconds then spat it out on the floor, "there you go, you got it back, happy now?" *I was a brat!* I thought I was solid, threatening the terrified shopkeeper. Stephanie finally kicked her and yanked her arm from her grasp. Again, we left the shop, this time deliberately knocking over the wine displays, shouting abuse and laughing at the woman. *I later found out she suffered a breakdown and early retirement due to the incident that had just taken place.*

We returned to Taxal pissed out of our faces, all belligerent when they questioned us on our inebriated states. The next morning, the police arrived and took us to the village police station if you could call two town houses joined together an actual police station. We were questioned separately, subsequently charged with aggravated robbery and then bailed with conditions to return to court a few weeks later.

I began seeing a slightly older lad called Barry Hines,

a previous resident of Taxal Edge who was now living in an open remand centre in Cheadle Hulme. Good looking and popular with the girls, he was infamous in all the surrounding care homes as well as respected in Manchester by the up and coming gangsters. According to him, he was paid to steal cars and drive up to Scotland to do huge coke drops for them. Together we went to Macdonald's, walked in Disley Park and he would take me in various robbed cars around to his old children homes to show me off. He would get me stoned then kiss me gently. *Romantic juvenile gangster love, I adored it.* He told me he loved my cute voice and innocent face. Looking back I think it was my shy innocence, the true essence of me, buried beneath the tough care girl act, which he'd been attracted to.

Everyone was impressed after a few weeks when we were still together as he had a track record of dumping girls after just a couple of nights. One afternoon, drunk on White Lightning cider in a graveyard, I instigated sex with him; acting up to my own perceived expectations. It was awkward for both of us, jeans around our ankles, my bare bum chaffing on the stones and dirt during the two minutes it took him to cum. His interest waned rapidly afterwards and he finished with me just a couple days later after one of the Taxal care-workers saw him with another girl. I was devastated.

I spent days crying over him and reliving our romantic moments *steal me a car, sort me a spliff and I'm yours.* I berated myself bitterly. *If I was prettier he would never have left me. Why would he need anyone else if I'd been enough?* I obsessed over him for weeks. My familiar insecurities returned and I began seeking out the highs of marijuana and alcohol more than ever before.

I was lucky in the way I wasn't sexually abused by adults while in care, something I used to put down to the fact that I was rebellious. I now know it was because I was never a child victim of sexual abuse and therefore not such a likely target and also that my religious parents never completely gave up on me. They attended all my reviews and maintained regular contact, even when I told them where to fucking go, which I did often. The paedophile staff that got found out years later tended to target the kids who came from backgrounds of sexual abuse or who had no one on the outside. There are always exceptions to every rule though.

While driving through the Peak District one afternoon, Neil, a large and seemingly pleasant male carer who I'd always respected suddenly stopped the car and put his hand on my bare thigh, looking at me questioningly. I stiffened in panic but my natural anger came to my rescue and I told him to fuck off as I shoved his hand off my leg. He tried again, this time putting my hand onto his leg. *What part of fuck off did he not understand?* I became really abusive. Luckily for me, he left it.

I wondered silently about Stephanie, who was his key kid and always out with him alone. She'd always been a naturally gentle girl but her behaviour had gone mental recently and she was constantly drinking, tattooing herself and cutting up her arms with razors, (sometimes I copied this behaviour and cut myself but only superficially, the sting relieves the emotions somewhat). She even resorted to trying to poison herself by pouring ink on to the cuts. I used to drag her upstairs shoving her arm under the tap to get the ink out. During a drunken outburst she'd told me that she'd been sexually abused by her stepdad and that was why she'd still been a bed wetter by the time she'd been admitted to Wimbrick.

It was more than possible that Neil was abusing her if what he'd tried with me was anything to go by. But what could I do? No one would have believed me anyway; I was a known trouble maker.

It was around that time that I began suffering waking night terrors. The first time it happened I was just drifting off when suddenly I felt something on top of me, *I'm still awake. THIS IS NOT A DREAM!* Completely paralysed, the sensation of a malevolent presence was overwhelming. The first time was so frightening that I ran downstairs to tell the staff I was being haunted but they just sent me back to bed. These episodes continued frequently and intensely for a few weeks but the frequency eventually died down to just a couple of times a month.

Katya, maybe due to the weed we were smoking or perhaps the fact her six month deferred sentence had just ended in a conditional discharge, reverted to her old ways and got kicked out of mainstream school for robbing a teacher's handbag. Back in Taxal School, she was every teacher's worst nightmare, putting salt in their drinks, hiding their milk, even putting her own shit in the teacher's kettle, making us all want to vomit as the fumes filled the prefab school during break time. The shit trick was her trademark and her name had been infamous in Cotsbrook for exactly the same prank.

She also put salt in my drinks, painted my eye lids with nail varnish while pretending she was giving me a make-over and smeared her African hair oil throughout my hair leaving it oily for days. She always laughed wickedly but without malice at my reaction. In turn, she let me paint her eye lids with nail polish then ran to care-workers pretending I'd bullied her, falling about laughing when I got pulled for it in a group meeting.

The care-workers were at their wit's end with her but we became close, planning and carrying out various schemes to obtain money for weed and alcohol. We tried robbing the video camera from school a few times but always got caught. We would go mooching in the surrounding villages for hours until we found something of value to steal. Ron accompanied us sometimes when we went 'on the rob' as Katya referred to it.

One afternoon, after hours of traipsing in and out of doctor's surgeries, shops and offices pretending to be looking for my mum, we came upon a handbag in the dentist's, left on the seat by its owner while she had gone to the toilet. *Thanks very much Miss Trusting Citizen, now we can get wrecked.* Although there was no money in the purse, there was a credit card for the NatWest Bank.

"Who's goin' the bank then?" Katya looked at us conspiratorially. "I reckon Marie."

"I wouldn't know what to say," I protested, not wanting to go into the bank with the stolen card at all. "Easy, just say yer sister's ill and that yer need money for shopping. Loadsa me mates from Tocky do it."

"Well, why can't you do it then, seein' as you know so

much about it?"

"Dur, 'cos am black, divvy, and me accent is way stronger than yours. They'll know I'm not from round here and get on it straight away. And Ron looks like a scally. You look innocent."

Ron pulled a face at me, smirking as I reluctantly went into the bank and presented the card to the counter clerk explaining to her in tones that my Upton teachers would have been proud of that my sister was ill and needed me to get some money out. After an agonising pause she conceded that I'd need to bring a signed letter from my sister authorising the withdrawal.

Ten minutes later, I re-entered the bank and asked for the eighty pounds Katya had requested in the letter. I couldn't believe it when the woman handed over eight crisp ten pound notes and after managing to forge another exact replica of the signature, I left the bank triumphantly. The receipt said the balance was now one hundred and twenty pounds and six pence in total.

After seeing the amount of money still in the account, Katya wrote another letter asking for the account to be closed and for the balance to be withdrawn there and then. Against my better judgement, I went back into the bank for the third time. The cashier took the card then requested that I remain in the bank while they called my sister. I flew out of the door.
"RUN!"

We didn't stop until we got to a quiet field on the outskirts of the village. Katya reassured me that they'd have just thought I was ripping off my sister and not that I'd stolen the card. I wasn't convinced but half a bottle of cider and a few spliffs later it didn't matter anymore.

We were in trouble and out of the group when we returned to Taxal totally wasted late that night but nothing was mentioned about the bank. By the time the police eventually did catch up with us a few weeks later, we'd committed a string of several petty thefts and robberies.

I ended up being arrested because I'd written a letter to Madeleine, my old childhood friend, boasting of all our illegal activities and stupidly left it in the school where it was read by one of the teachers who immediately alerted the carers and the police. This, coupled with the conditional discharge and fine I had just received in court for the aggravated robbery, did not leave things looking hopeful.

"But it's all written down," I whispered miserably to the duty solicitor.

"Have you admitted anything to the police?"

"No, I just called for you."

"And did anyone warn you in any way, shape or form before you wrote it that the letter you were writing could be used in evidence against you?"

"Er, no."

Was he stupid?

"Well, in that case unless they have photographic evidence, fingerprints or an eye witness there's not a thing they can do."

"Really? How come?"

"Anything that is committed for evidence, even a confession, requires that the defendant is warned that whatever they say will be used as evidence. This won't stand up in court."

Far from stupid! Total genius!

For once I had beaten the system I hated. I told the

interviewing officer that I'd just been trying to big myself up to my friend. His dubious expression made me laugh. *Fuck you, Sergeant Pepper.*

After only being charged with the burglary and theft of the handbag, although I didn't see how walking into a surgery in the middle of the day constituted as burglary, and the forgery and deception inside NatWest, for which I had been duly caught on camera, I was released without charge for about ten other offences. Katya and Ron got away with everything. Our little crime trio broke up shortly afterwards when Ron was sent to live on a new-initiative remand boat for repetitive offenders.

My behaviour grew ever more violent when I was without weed. I ended up banned from the dentists and shops in all the local villages and our GP surgery after we'd caused a riot one afternoon terrorising the local pensioners in the waiting room, determined to steal the drugs we imagined would be in the doctor's rooms. This incident made the local paper.

I frequently assaulted care-workers and several times dared Lynda, the manager, to kick me out. One care-worker had me charged for ABH (actual bodily harm) – really, her arm suffered a tiny two inch scratch after I'd battered her with an empty can of Special Brew. She'd asked for it, in my drunken opinion, as she'd taken my can from me, thrown its contents down the toilet then thrust it back at me, taunting me, "You want your beer, here it is."

I flipped - Special Brew made me even more aggressive than usual - launched an angry attack on her and had to be pulled off by several kids as well as staff.

Nothing could rein me in. I lived my entire life

outlawed from the group. Katya and I were always on the rob and by now on conditional bail with a court curfew that forbade me from leaving the home between the hours of five pm and eight am; Katya's, for some reason slightly milder, ruled that she had to be home for eight.

Chapter 17
Remand

June/July 1992

It wasn't long before I broke my curfew. The police picked me up one Saturday night in the neighbouring village sprawled on the side of the pavement, an empty bottle of Thunderbirds still in my hand, a half smoked spliff hanging out of my mouth, drunk on the proceeds of our latest little theft - we had robbed the money bag from a bus while the driver had gone to change drivers, obviously not realising we were upstairs.

"Looks as if someone can't tell the time," they joked as they hauled me up into the back of the police car. "You're locked up til Monday."

I cried and wailed, hideously drunk, for some reason begging for Elaine my Cotsbrook staff until I blacked out. They had to get a doctor to see to me during the night. I didn't remember any of this but Katya told me I'd been out cold and she'd thought I was dead.

The next day we were transferred to Chesterfield where there was a police matron. As we were juveniles it was the law that if in custody for more than one night, a female had to supervise and there were none in Buxton that weekend. They left Amy and Katya together but I was kept in solitary custody. Boredom pervaded me and I spent hours twisting my hair into countless little knots before pulling them free, a habit I'd developed during many long hours in the cells.

On the Monday, we were escorted in a sweat van to Buxton Magistrate's Court where we were locked in a secure room with windows making us visible to the entire waiting room of the court. Shameful! Coincidentally, Ron was in court that morning too, answering to previous charges and we shouted to him from our cell.

He was with a man who he introduced as Keith, the manager of William House of which Ron's boat, Cruise Challenge, was an outreach placement. Keith, who was good looking in a dark, broody Italian way, seemed amused by our antics even though he told Ron we were bad influences. Although he spoke seriously there was a twinkle in his eye. He reminded me in a way of my Uncle Paul. I liked him immediately and I wanted him to notice me.

"Nah, he was the bad influence," I joked and was rewarded with him replying that I looked far too innocent to be locked up.

We didn't help ourselves in the court room by breaking into hysterics when the judge read out our names. The fact that he said Stella Maria McClure instead of just Marie caused the first explosion of giggles, Stephanie Shirley Jackson made us all laugh even harder, but when the stern faced magistrate read out Katya Amona Abubu Ramona Geraldine Ray, stumbling over their correct pronunciation, we all cracked up, laughing helplessly until we were arrested again; contempt of court.

Soon after this, Katya got moved to Lockhart in Manchester and Stephanie to Bryn Gollen in North Wales, leaving just me at Taxal with the other 'good' kids who were always in the group. I began corrupting their precious group system and on one occasion, I involved several of them in a bomb scare in Stockport, enjoying the power I wielded over them.

Gone was the girl who was scared of her peers, this lot did whatever I told them.

After that little incident, at exactly eight o'clock every morning, the hour I was free from curfew, the police came to arrest me on some jumped up investigation of various local crimes. It was their only way of keeping me off the streets and their frightened villagers reassured that they were safe from the delinquents that had terrorised them recently. I'd be kept in the cells, twisting at my hair all day and then brought home just as my curfew kicked in.

"See you tomorrow," laughed the custody sergeant every day. *Fuck off knobhead.*

Apart from the rigged up daily arrests the care-workers were unable to control me. Lynda still stood firm Taxal wouldn't give up on me. Give in to me more like! It was obviously a battle of wills by then as anyone else would have been sent to another placement after causing half the amount of trouble I had. Something had to give.

Lee, my latest sidekick, bet me I didn't have the nerve to set Taxal on fire. That Saturday, after warning the others to get out if the alarms went off, I tried setting the laundry room on fire in a way that would look accidental. Twenty minutes later, when nothing had happened. I went back and found that the iron had been switched off and put away. Irritated, I went to the meeting room, struck a match and stuck it to the couch. *Light, fuckin' light!* Finally I was rewarded with little flames spurting forth from the couch. Within minutes the alarms sounded and all the kids immediately ran to the safety of the large driveway. Neil the Nonce commented that he had never seen such a quick reaction to a fire drill.

"Almost as if it was planned," he looked at me but I quickly averted my eyes and began a conversation with the girl next to me.

The fire engines came a few minutes later followed by the police who immediately went for me and shoved me none too gently in the back of the car after telling me I was under arrest for arson.

"No point denying it. You were grassed up by your so called mates."

I was taken to the main police station and held until the morning. Before being signed out of the custody suite, Elaine tried to make a deal with me.

"Tell us where you score your drugs from Marie, and we'll help you out. Arson is a severe charge."

Seriously? I smoke weed not heroin and you are not L.A.P.D. my love.

That Sunday was the longest I'd ever known although the police matron took pity on me and gave me a book to read. I spent the night alternatively reading then crying desperately as I'd been told that I was going to be put on remand in the morning. *I wanna take it back, I'm so sorry.* So much remorse, regret; despite having been hell-bent on getting Lynda to kick me out of Taxal, now I wanted nothing more than to go back there.

At the magistrate's court on Monday morning, my social workers rescued me from my young offender's institute predicament when they stated they'd sorted out an emergency placement that was also classed as an official remand placement; my last chance to remain out of custody. Cruise Challenge, which had worked wonders with many juveniles, was described to the court. For a moment I thought the grey-haired lady magistrate was going to refuse and send me to an actual remand prison but her severe face softened momentarily as she looked over at tearful little me. Sighing, she remanded me back into the care of the social services, warning me that if I broke my remand conditions and absconded that it would be a very different case to breaching bail.

I cried for the entire journey down to Gloucestershire despite the fact I'd got off extremely lightly. I was going straight to a campsite - Cruise Challenge consisted of camping from Monday to Thursday and then spending the weekend on a barge that travelled and moored around Staffordshire on the Shropshire Union Canal. It was the same place Ron had been sent to and I tried to comfort myself that at least he'd seemed to like it.

Ron wasn't on the boat anymore, having moved to another part of the home's organisation, Wallace House. Kerry, a girl who'd been at Taxal, was at camp as well as two boys, Richard, a pale, ginger haired lad of sixteen and Calum, a mixed race boy of fifteen. Calum, who desperately needed a shower, lived at Wallace House in one of the tracker placements but had chosen to come camping that week.

I impressed them with my charge sheets, by then having incurred eighteen charges including petty thefts, burglaries, assaults, criminal damage, breaching of bail, and now arson. "Yeah, I was robbin' every day, fuck me curfew, I don't give a fuck about the police, fuckin' pigs. I would've burnt Taxal to the ground if I hadn't got grassed up." *I am so hard; please don't see past this exterior, I'm soft as shite inside.*

After Kerry and I had settled into our tent for the night and the care-workers had retired to theirs, Richard sneaked in to ours and asked me if I wanted to get off with Calum. *Ew, no! Get a shower you sweat.* Kerry, however, sneaked into the boys tent with Richard when he left and came back all of fifteen minutes later - getting off with him had turned into her having it off with him. *Gross.*

The camping trip was actually fun, the care-workers were laid back and relaxed and Golden Virginia rolling tobacco was supplied endlessly. One of the staff, Colin, an outward bounds instructor in his early twenties, bought us all twenty Embassy cigarettes, true luxury, the day we returned to the barge, currently in Stoke.

Deon, a tall slender hippy type woman with huge masses of curly blonde hair dressed in skin tight jeans, was waiting for us on the boat. She was casual in appearance and I could see she demanded respect but, as I was soon to find out, she also possessed a kind, down to earth nature. Her strictest rule appeared to be that we referred to the boat, which was also her home, as a narrow boat, never as a barge and even I dared not break this rule. I was to stay at Cruise Challenge for four weeks and then, depending on my behaviour and whatever sentence I received in court, I would be rehoused in another long term placement. That weekend, Kerry and I absconded after being told off by Colin for messing around by the canal. We hitch hiked to Stockport and then bunked a train to the village as I 'needed' to go back to Taxal to sort out whoever had grassed me up for the fire. After kicking off on the girl responsible, the police arrived and threw the handcuffs on me. Taxal's practically resident constable took great pride in saying the words, 'You're under arrest for being unlawful at large.' *Bad cop movie - Buxton Police Force Hits the Big Time.* However, the fact I had broken remand conditions did make it a lot more serious.

Miraculously, Colin from the boat managed to get them to give me another chance when he came to collect us from the station.

He was stern but caring in the car on the way back to the boat, "Marie, this is your last chance. You'll be remanded into custody next time. Richard has just been sent to a juvenile prison for absconding right after you left. Do you really want to be locked up?"

I didn't answer, not wanting to seem weak in front of Kerry.

"Marie, mate, we aren't like the other homes. If you give us all a chance you might just find you like it. Your mate Ron did."

Kerry's four weeks were up that week and once she'd gone, I was the only one left on the boat. I surprised everyone, including myself by becoming pleasant, cooperative and participating willingly in activities such as rock climbing and canoeing, getting over my initial fears with the constant encouragement of Colin and Sal, another outward bounds instructor who I got on well with. To my delight, Colin also arranged for me to go pony trekking in Llangollen during one of the camping expeditions.

Now free from the oppressive influences of weed, alcohol and my other teenage peers, my mind felt clearer and lighter and I discovered an inner happiness that I hadn't felt since Cotsbrook. I had come out of the shadowy place inside my mind, the one in which I had lived for years, and was experiencing true happiness, not the fake marijuana high but an inner joy that coloured my world. My behaviour was a stark contrast to most of my time in care and my unhappy years before entering the system. I asked about the possibility of staying with Cruise Challenge long term but was told it was impossible as it was only a four week program.

I enjoyed being on the boat as well as camping, loving the feel of the summer breeze on my face as I sat on top of the narrow boat as it made its way through the canals from Stoke to Llangollen. Everyone we passed on the canal would wave and say hi. Deon taught me how to open the locks and most evenings she took us to local village pubs by the canal and we'd play pool and choose songs on the jukebox.

After I'd been on the boat for a couple of weeks, Keith Black, the manager of Wallace House, the man I'd seen with Ron in court, came to visit. I found myself opening up to him, not able to stop talking once I'd started and was pleased that he seemed as impressed with me, despite my past, as my uncle had been when I was a little girl making my first communion.

When he answered my many questions about Wallace House and its tracker placements, separate houses which cared for the individual young person instead of several, I decided there and then that this was the home for me. Wallace House was privately run by Keith and his brother and it cost the social services a fortune to place someone there but he promised to speak to my social worker about it and also to accompany me to court in Buxton later that week.

He picked me up in his Shiroko sports car, which, as far as I was concerned was practically a Porsche. He stopped on the way to treat me to a Macdonald's breakfast also buying me some ciggies, proper ones, not tobacco. I looked and felt healthy and glowed with the tan I had acquired courtesy of the outdoor living.

Keith gave me all his attention during that journey, impressing me with the fact that he'd been friends with Rik Mayall from The Young Ones before he'd become famous - from that day onwards I became Rik Mayall's number one fan. I suppose I was desperate for a father figure, well, an Uncle figure and I fell hard for Keith. I didn't think about him in a sexual way, only really being sexually attracted to scally lads but he did make a huge impression on me. I hadn't felt that way since being a child snug in the love of my Uncle Paul. *I love Keith Black; I wish he was my uncle.*

Despite my recent excellent behaviour and Keith's glowing report of me getting me back off remand and onto bail again I couldn't say no to Katya, Stephanie and Amy when they said we were running away after court. In those days I was never able to stand up for myself to my peers and they put loads of pressure on me to run with them. I didn't want to go but of course I went.

That night, I was picked up from Crewe Police Station by a disappointed Colin who told me I'd let everyone down, most of all myself.

"Marie, those girls are no good for you. No good at all. You nearly ruined your chances with us and you've done so well too. Don't run again or you won't be able to come back."

Keith forgave me immediately when he came to see me the next day. He had a way of making light of a situation while still getting his point across. He also understood me and promised me again he would do whatever it took to get me into Wallace House provided I stopped running.

During the last week of my placement on the boat, I had to go to Liverpool Crown Court for the rape hearing. Jean, a motherly care-worker who worked in the house in Cannock, drove me to Liverpool as Keith wasn't able to make it. My tummy was full of butterflies. I was dreading standing up in front of the crown, Paul, and all of his family and saying what had happened that night. Going to court for my own crimes was nothing like this impending hell.

I had kept my nagging doubts to myself, convinced everyone would say I'd made the whole thing up. The child protection team told me I was almost certain to win. *But I didn't say no enough.* Kate had been called to give evidence for the prosecution. It was the first time we'd seen each other since Othona and she was like a different girl, happy, grown up and sophisticated. Paul's friend was also giving evidence for the prosecution - against his will - apparently he had let something condemning slip in his police statement.

The wait was agonising. My stomach was in knots and I panicked every time an usher came out in case it was my turn. Several hours later we were told the case had been adjourned until February, another six months, for God only knew what reason. Then the usher released Paul from court before us, resulting in him and his family hanging around in the square outside the court looking all threatening so we had to wait until a police escort could be sent to see us safely to our cars.

It was a horrible day and I only felt safe as we left Liverpool behind us. The summer blossoms painting the summer country lanes comforted my soul, helping me feel a million miles from the rough dockland area where I had met Paul that fateful night.

Although I continued to flourish in my boat placement, the social services simply would not agree to such a financial gamble on me given my track record and decided to send me to Bryn Alyn in Wrexham. Bryony told me she'd keep trying for me but not to hold out my hopes. I cried brokenly as I said my goodbyes to Sal, Colin and Deon as Bryony took me away that sunny July morning. Keith had paid me a brief visit the previous evening and urged me to stay safe and out of trouble. I felt like I was being plucked from paradise as familiar shadows began looming in my mind. I hated Bryn Alyn before I'd even arrived.

Chapter 18
My Own Way For Once

August 1992

Lonely, hopeless, self-destructive, back inside my desert mind; Bryn Alyn was a hostile place although Stephanie was also resident there "Don't try your tricks here, little girl." The manager's easy smile hid something sinister. The care-workers on my unit were unfriendly and another resident, Simone, scared me, *where had all my bravado gone?* She saw beyond my hard act, reached in and found my weak points. The care-workers encouraged her bullying.

For a couple of weeks, I ran away; hitch hiking here and there, getting caught, taken back, then running again. If I was lonely on the run, with nothing but my reflection in the glass doors of the phone boxes in which I took shelter from the summer rain storms to keep me company, I was desolate back at Bryn Alyn under the threat of Simone. Only when ensconced in my room with my novels for company, safely alone, I would cry. I only ever cried alone.

Simone was told to make sure I didn't go anywhere, a job she was more than happy to take on. She was the most effective as, although I would attack care-workers without thinking twice, I wouldn't have dared hit her. I was intimidated by her presence, all my previous fight having deserted me. *Totally aggressive or completely terrified; one extreme to the other.* Much to my relief, after I had been there for two weeks, most of the kids, including Simone, went away on holiday for two weeks to Spain. Stephanie, Roy from Cotsbrook and a couple of other kids hadn't been at Bryn Alyn long enough to qualify for the foreign holiday stayed back with me. We absconded regularly, got drunk and brought home by the police, sometimes fighting with the police and collecting more assault charges. The care-workers on our unit, cold-hearted young women most of them, blamed me for Stephanie's behaviour and sent me to some sort of Coventry, refusing to even speak to me. *Nice and professional! You are paid to look after me.*

When the other kids were due back from Spain, I ran away again, managing to thumb a lift from a man who took me to Chester. I'd decided to go back to Taxal Edge - I didn't have many options - and caught another ride at the slip road of the M53. I was picked up by a man who looked about fifty. When we got on the motorway he reached his hand out and rested it on my leg, putting my hand on his hairy one.

I snatched my back and called him a dirty bastard. The man removed his hand but smirked that he knew I was up for it, my type always were!

"Come on, you might enjoy it."

He put his hand back on my leg.

"Get the fuck off me, you dirty fuckin´ paedo! Let me out this fucking car NOW."

The man removed his hand but carried on driving, smirking knowingly. Fear made me crazy.

This is so not gonna happen to me!

"Stop the fucking car or I'm gonna open the door. STOP THE FUCKIN CAR!" I rattled at the door handle, "Fuckin' open it."

Why won't it open?

"It's child locked," he sneered, foul breath hitting me through his yellow teeth.

I wound down the window and put my hand on the outside door handle not caring that we were on a motorway.

"Stop this fucking car now or I'll open the door and jump out," I was punching him in the head with my other hand and kicking hard at him.

He pulled up on to the hard shoulder.

"Little prick tease. I thought you were older when I picked you up."

Skinny little me hadn't even reached five feet tall. "I don't even look fourteen, you sick fuck!"

I caught another ride, this time from a decent man who took me to Stockport and gave me a tenner to get some food. I thanked him, bought a portion of chips and gravy and ten ciggies then caught the train back to Taxal making it to my destination only to be discovered in Lee's room after about an hour and once again the familiar Buxton police, friendly in comparison to the Wrexham police, came for me.

I was taken to a children's home in Buxton where I was given some supper and a glass of milk. The emergency social workers arrived after a few hours and took me to a secure unit in Chesterfield. I arrived in the middle of the night and was shown to a room with a sodden carpet - the last kid had flooded the room - and a bed nailed to the floor with absolutely no way of escape.

The windows, like those of Blackbrook, were of strong plastic and had sturdy locks holding them down. All the mirrors were plastic too and the water logged carpet squelched when I walked on it. The room looked out onto a playground made secure by the other buildings, other parts of the home which, like Blackbrook, were only semi secure. There was a perimeter of high railings and wire meshing surrounding all of the buildings and I knew running away would be impossible. I was stuck there, until Monday at least.

I missed Keith, the happy, healthy version of me from the boat and all the positive care-workers. Ever since leaving the boat, I woke with the words 'Wallace House' flying round my head every morning continuing an obsessive replay throughout the day. My solar plexus was nervous and unsettled, suffering with the strain of so much nervous energy festering there. I couldn't sleep properly and when I did it was all nightmares. *Just let me live in Wallace House and I'll behave.* There I wouldn't have to mix with anyone, wouldn't have put this act on anymore. Why couldn't the stupid social services see that?

The kids in the secure unit were quite friendly. After the knife count was completed, they told me we were allowed to smoke six times a day and got enough pocket money to cover this. They each donated a couple of cigarettes so I could smoke with them at the designated times.

Secure unit teenagers were less likely to bully or start a fight under the constant watchful eyes of the care-workers than teenagers in assessment centres such as Wimbrick or a big home like Bryn Alyn. I felt safe and associated the feeling with my early days at Blackbrook when I'd conformed to the rules temporarily and decided that if Wallace House really wasn't an option then I'd opt to stay here instead. Anything was better than going back to Bryn Alyn.

On the Monday, Bryony, who had been on annual leave since I'd been sent to Bryn Alyn, arrived to sign me out of the secure unit. She grinned at me in mock despair as she asked me what on earth she was going to do with me.

"Well…"

She interrupted me, "Your mum has agreed that you can go to her for a couple of days while I try and sort Wallace House."

"Oh my God! Really? Why?"

"They're worried about you and your constant running. I've managed to convince them that you could do really well at Wallace House, that you were happy and well behaved on the boat and that you really want to make a fresh start. They've agreed you can stay while I negotiate with my team leader about getting you into Wallace House. I've had lengthy talks with Keith who has written a proposal both to my boss and to the courts. Your parents are quite impressed with him."

"Bryony, thank you so much. I can't believe they're letting me stay overnight at home. I've not been home in ages. I promise you if I go to Wallace House, I'll never run again."

"I hope not, girl," she smiled archly. "Are you hungry?"

"Starving, can we go Macdonald's?"

It turned out that Bryony had threatened her resignation if they didn't do what she believed to be right by me. No one had ever put themselves out for me to that extent. After I had been at my parents' for a couple of days, Keith called to confirm that my place at Wallace House would begin the following week. I was so excited and readily agreed when they told me I had to go to Wimbrick that night before going to this temporary placement, Clifford House in Hereford, that Keith had arranged for me as I'd been at my parents for two days by then and they were worried that too much time with them may upset the proverbial apple cart.

It was a good thing really as my mum let slip that she and my dad had been paying a solicitor with the money from my savings account to try and get me issued with a secure order. Apparently Bryony's team leader, Paul Burns, wasn't in agreement with secure units as being the answer for everything. *Well thank you God for Paul Burns but why did you give me these shit parents*? Normally I would have gone mental but I was happier than I'd been in a while and I managed to stay calm when she tartly informed me that she and my dad had been left with no choice as I was so out of control. For some reason she let me have the bank book to take with me but told me she expected it to be kept in the office. It had just over two hundred pounds left in it and I knew she was giving me some sort of trust again.

Chapter 19
Wallace House
A Temporary Paradise

Aug-Dec 1992

A week later, Bryony and Keith came to collect me from Clifford House. Keith had bought me a little portable tape player ghetto blaster for my fifteenth birthday which had been two days earlier. I was to live in 'the bungalow' for a week until my place was ready. My temporary care-worker, Jean, took me shopping and explained to me that I was allowed fifty pounds a week for food and I could devise the shopping list myself, as, given my age I would be preparing for independent living.

My sixteenth birthday seemed so far away and it goes without saying I picked all the junk food I could, crisps, chocolate biscuits, pizza and chips although Jean managed to persuade me to pick up some salad pieces too. I felt so happy I could hardly sleep that night for excitement that I was finally at Wallace House, my dream home.

The next day, Jean took me up the 'flats' to show me where I'd be living and to meet one of my soon to be permanent key workers, Ellie. The flats were two semidetached houses, one of which was all mine, the one next door had the main office downstairs where Keith worked and a flat upstairs. The three Sheffield kids currently staying there, on emergency placement due to the fact their own children´s home had been burnt down, stared at me with undisguised hostility on their faces.

"Slag," spat the ginger haired one, while the other

two sniggered.

"Adele! Enough!" Ellie was sharp.

I felt uncomfortable and felt the familiar retreat inside myself begin.

"Someone's just jealous that's all," Ellie explained in her Cannock accent, looking at Adele pointedly as she escorted Jean and me back out of the front door. Apparently, the Sheffield kids didn't want to go back to Sheffield and blamed me for the fact they had to go. Also, Adele was quite possessive over Ellie and was fuming that she was to be my key-worker.

Within a week they'd gone and I moved into the flats. I liked Ellie; she was tough and down to earth but kind with a sense of humour. She had dark hair and her face softened prettily when she smiled. She was only twenty five and we clicked immediately. I could see why Adele had liked her so much. My other key worker, Sarah, was twenty-two, tall, blonde haired, and had recently graduated from university. She was very clever and had written a book, something which I thought was amazing. Her downfall was she was shy and after I had got over my awe of being at Wallace House, I was sometimes vicious with her, making cruel comments if she had an acne outbreak as I knew she was conscious of it. I'm not sure why I did this especially as I had suffered badly with my own skin since hitting puberty.

Life at Wallace House was idyllic, no demands, no routine and no structure. I could get up when I felt like and go where I liked each day with my key-workers. Keith took Sarah and me to Alton Towers one day and I fantasised that he and Sarah had actually fallen in love, got together and adopted me. Needless to say, Keith's wife and children didn't exist in my fantasy world. He also arranged for us to go and see Rik Mayall in Bottom Live in Wolverhampton, another memorable occasion. I started with a private tutor three times a week and had a clarinet rented for me and private lessons paid for. My sentencing date arrived and I was chaperoned to court by Keith, who assured me I had nothing to worry about as my reports were excellent. I was given a six month deferred sentence which meant that if I stayed out of trouble for six months I would receive a very light sentence such as a conditional discharge, but if I offended again within those six months I would receive a custodial sentence.

"You have a chance Marie, take it," the grey haired lady magistrate told me emphatically and I sincerely meant to.

There was no question of me running away from court that time and I laughed outright at the suggestion from Katya.

My parents came to my first review meeting and were pleased with my progress. My mum even offered me a cigarette to smoke with her after the meeting. A huge olive branch! After that meeting, my parents began to visit every few weeks, taking me out to Stafford along with my brother and sister for a meal out and a look round the shops, often buying me a new music tape of my choice, which was always Pink Floyd or The Doors. For the first time in years I began to welcome my parents' visits.

Teresa, after regarding me sulkily for the first couple of visits, began to warm up a little and I asked my mum if I could take her round to Ron's while they took Liam to get his present that was part and parcel of their visits to me. I was shocked when my sister, now thirteen, produced a packet of cigarettes and offered me one. That simple gesture, which we both conspired to keep from our parents, brought us closer than we had been in years.

Calum, the boy I had met at the campsite moved into the flats for a couple of weeks as the bungalow where he now lived was having work done on it. I didn't take kindly to having this boy in my space. His stench and his Dudley accent irritated me. Whenever Ron came to see me, he never failed to call Calum a sweaty cunt and Callum was too scared of Ron to say a word back. He was never so passive when Ron wasn't there though and went out of his way to wind me up about everything and anything. This, coupled with my explosive temper, caused huge fights between us, which often became physical. I was happy when he had to go back to the bungalow.
As I lived next door to the office, the boat kids came to mine every Monday while all the staff had their team meeting. Frankie was a sixteen year old bad boy from Gloucester, irresistible with his dark brooding good looks. After he'd been to the flats a couple of times and we had exchanged long brooding looks, I requested permission to go camping with the outreach team and we spent the journey in the transit van kissing passionately and fumbling in the dark under the blankets of the cold van.
That night, I sneaked into his tent where he took me quickly, urgently; giving me pleasure I'd never before derived from sex. He asked me for a blow job but I hadn't a clue how so I made out there was some dark secret in my past that prevented me from doing so.

We fucked several times until I was dripping with our lust. I couldn't wait for the next time but I was in for a disappointment as Frankie refused to make eye contact with me the next day and went off somewhere every time he saw me approaching.

Rejection danced in my stomach, killing my appetite, nervous energy making a big empty hole in my belly. Worst of all, the care-workers were constantly calling him to receive calls from various girls on the boat's huge mobile phone. When I heard him tell the one of them he loved her, I took refuge in my tent not wanting anyone to see my tears.

I couldn't believe he had girlfriends already, especially from home. I thought I should take precedence over boring normal girls who lived at home and bitterly resented the girls on the other end of the phone. *How could he sleep with me then ignore me the next day?* I couldn't deal with the camping trip any longer and told Sal that I was ill and needed to go back to Wallace House.

Back home, my brain wouldn't let me switch off from the humiliating events of the last twenty-four hours. Play, rewind, repeat. I was plagued with self-doubt. *Why would any good looking lad want you? Sad, ugly bitch!* I chain-smoked tobacco until I was sick. Desperate to escape the prison of my own emotions, I took an overdose of several ibuprofen but soon admitted to Ellie what I'd done.

After a dose of foul brown medicine that made me puke violently, Keith arrived at the hospital and enfolded me in a deep hug. I cried my heart out, comforted within his strong arms. Once again I was reminded of the love of my childhood hero and never wanted Keith to let me go. *Be my daddy, Keith, make*

it okay again or better still, be my Uncle Paul. The
searing, humiliating pain of being used and rejected
eased slightly as he held me.
"Why did he do that though? How could he do that?"
"Marie, most boys of his age are like that. It's not you.
You're beautiful, funny and smart. He isn't worth your
tears and certainly not your life! Promise me you will
never do anything like this again."
I wished I could erase the last twenty-four hours of
my life but began to cheer up as Keith told me some
funny stories, laughing me out of my despair.
I didn't see Frankie again. I think Keith made sure he
wasn't allowed to come to the flats anymore.

With the staff's encouragement I started visiting Ron
in his flat. He was sixteen now and lived alone in his
flat in Stafford. They believed I'd do him good as he
was starting to get in with some rough local people.
Despite my recent good intentions, the lure of his
cannabis was too strong to resist and I looked forward
to our sessions. If my key workers suspected
anything, they never mentioned it and I would come
home and pig out on whatever was in the cupboards. I
loved going to Ron's and we began tripping off gas
again while we were stoned.
Amy and Katya came up one night but Ron didn't
seem overly happy to see Amy again, and I wasn't
happy to see Katya. She was still into going on the
rob, and I was relieved when they caught the last train
back after much persuasion from Ron that if they
caused problems this time then I wouldn't be allowed
out next time. I liked having Ron to myself anyway,
the girls made me look stupid at times and I knew
they did it on purpose. That was the last time I saw

Katya.

I had everything I wanted but smoking weed and taking gas awoke the self-destructive streak within me and my behaviour began to deteriorate. I refused to get up on the mornings of my tutor sessions. I lost interest rapidly in the clarinet. There was no structure to my life apart from going to Quasar and bowling in Stafford very evening. I lived on junk food, smoked twenty cigarettes a day and stayed up into the early hours watching MTV and playing Sonic the Hedgehog on the Sega. I didn't run away anymore or break the rules as such but I had no need to, there was nothing to rebel against, I could do as I pleased.

I grew more attached to Keith, brightening whenever he visited and insisted one day on showing him my recently acquired cooking skills that Ellie had taught me. Although they consisted only of heating up frozen chicken drumsticks in bread crumbs, frying curly chips in the deep fat fryer and preparing a little salad, I was proud of the fact I could cook at all and was really looking forward to having Keith's undivided attention for the evening. I was devastated when he called at the last minute to say he'd been held up at home and I felt very resentful of his wife and sons who had him when I needed him. After complaining bitterly and crying, I spent the rest of the evening in my room refusing to be consoled in any way. My feelings for Keith absorbed me. Although my feelings were platonic, I was totally attached to him.

Dec 1992

"But why do I have to spend Christmas on the boat? It'll be freezing. Why can't you or Ellie stay with me?" I argued with Sarah.

Apparently she had "plans" and so did Ellie. Obviously they didn't care at all and the rejection hit me hard. They were MY staff but they would leave me at Christmas. All adults were the same, shit. Keith didn't even come to see me anymore and whenever I went to the office, hoping for a couple of minutes of his light hearted humour that always cheered me up no matter what, I was told he was busy. Even when I did see him, he seemed distant and distracted and his withdrawal from me hurt, big time. My obsessive thoughts tortured me and my self-destructive behaviour was getting worse every day.

Boat life in December was freezing. Even when Deon had the portable gas fire burning which made the inner cabin all warm and cosy as we watched videos, the snow covered canal banks assaulted us with their minus zero temperatures as soon as we stepped on deck. The cabins were so cold the bedding felt wet when I first climbed into bed and it took at least half an hour before my body temperature warmed it up and it felt dry.

On my last night there, I dreamt the flats had been robbed. It was so vivid I woke up screaming. When I returned home the next day, it turned out that an ex-Wallace House kid had robbed the flats, taking the Sega and video recorder as well as my Christmas presents that I'd opened the day before Christmas Eve and left there, thinking that gold earrings and a bracelet wouldn't serve much purpose on an icy canal in the middle of nowhere. Thankfully, my new budgie had been left undisturbed. Everything was replaced within days but I still felt angry, invaded and even more justified in my bitterness at having been sent away at Christmas.

After Christmas, Ron got sent down for four months.
The young offender's institute was horrible. When I
visited, a very subdued version of my piss-taking
mate urgently whispered at me not to put my hands
on the table as the others would think I was passing
him stuff, stuff they would expect a share of later on.
Some visits I saw him with black eyes and it made me
miserable. I loved Ron like a brother and hated to
think of him going through this. He'd been told he
would have to go back to his mum's in Liverpool
after his release and I missed him badly. Another care
sibling lost and never to be seen by me again.

Chapter 20
Spiralling

Feb-March 1993

Leah, one of the boat kids I had met at Christmas moved into the flat next door to me, making up slightly for the loss of Ron. She was a few months older than me, pretty and funny with a wickedly dirty laugh. We went with our staff to bowling and Quasar in Stafford most nights and developed huge crushes on two of the young men that worked there. Although amused by us and our antics and even slightly impressed that we always came out with top quasar scores they were not remotely interested in us, both having girlfriends who were older and definitely more sophisticated than us.

We spent all our activity money on large cokes and salty fries. Our diets were ludicrously unhealthy but no one ever advised us otherwise. I think the key-workers, although lovely, were employed just to keep us happy and crime free, not to actually change us for the better.

Calum sometimes came along to the bowling alley with us and Leah and I vied for his attention and I got really jealous when she told me she liked him, which was crazy as I'd always hated him. I called him up one night and asked him how he felt about Leah and when he said she was fit, I asked him what he felt about me. He paused but then admitted he'd always liked me, ever since the campsite, a fact I was counting on. From then on we were together.

It wasn't long before I was sleeping with Calum and we were sneaking to each other's houses in the middle of the night for sex. I got used to his Barely

Disguised with Lynx body odour, even craved his pungent smell. Leah was a little pissed off but didn't say much. If Ron had still been around he'd have ripped me to death for shagging 'sweaty cunt' Calum. A few weeks into this relationship, Ellie took me to the family planning clinic to put me on the pill after a pregnancy scare, one that was totally made up inside my head. Calum's key-worker, Masudi, bollocked him and Calum wouldn't sleep with me again until I'd been on the pill for a week. My insecurity over this made me ridiculous. I became his stalker, calling him all the time, begging him to say he loved me, flipping out if he didn't give me the attention I craved. The further he withdrew, the worse I became, losing all self-respect and sense of pride.

I felt physically sick, just like I had in the aftermath of Frankie and thought about running away to Amy in Manchester and injecting myself with a lethal amount of cocaine. Amy had recently told me that she had tried injecting coke and it was an amazing rush so I figured it wouldn't be a painful way to die. All sorts rushed through my head in the face of any rejection, life felt too painful to withstand and any upper hand I had once had with Callum was totally lost.

My return to court to stand witness in the rape proceedings was imminent and probably due to the inner turmoil caused by this along with Calum's rapidly growing indifference to our relationship, I fell ill a couple of days before the hearing.

Colin, who was now manager in place of Keith who had become the director and had less to do with any of the kids, especially me, was extremely unsympathetic to my illness. He told me I was faking *but I have a temperature and everything* and threatened me that the police would come for me with a warrant for my arrest if I did not stand witness in court. He had changed remarkably from the easy-going outward bounds instructor he had been the previous summer on the boat.

I was extremely confused as well as angry. I was the victim for fuck's sake. How could I be arrested for not going through with it? I rang the officers from the child protection team and pleaded my case with them, crying hysterically. The charges were dropped after the local police came to collect a signed statement from me and I no longer had to worry about it. *Fuck you Colin, you fuckin' dictator.*

I returned to the desert world inside my mind, the hot, empty place of anger and rejection-induced sadness. Shadows clouded my brain and I forgot what colour was apart from the scarlet rages that went from zero to sixty in a matter of seconds. Some called it self-destruction, others called it ungrateful stupidity, some even called it devil possession; I look back now and realise my Borderline Personality Disorder was spiralling again and wonder how no one ever realised that I had psychological problems?

The next time we went to the quasar in Stafford, Leah robbed the keys to her key-worker's car and I went along with her. Despite the fact we were only in the car five minutes, we were arrested in front of everyone at the bowling alley, including the two lads we crushed on. I was remorseful when they released me, genuinely regretting being so stupid but Ellie wouldn't even speak to me - her cold rejection on top of everything else - I couldn't stand anymore. I kicked off big time, throwing cups at her, screaming, cursing, and hitting her.

She held my hands away from her until I weakened. I cried myself to sleep, begging her to forgive me but the next day, another member of staff was sent to mind me as Ellie walked out on me. I turned a table upside down and began smashing things up, throwing all sorts of objects and my fists at the woman who happened to be Keith's sister. I was packed off to the boat that same afternoon.

Despite my behaviour and my suspension from my tracker placement, I was welcomed back on board by Sal and Deon. A man called Jim had replaced Colin. There were two other lads on the boat this time. One of them, Kev, had developed a huge crush on me during his last Monday visit and now spent his pocket money on little presents for me even though I told him repeatedly I was with Calum. He bought me a tape cassette, 'Bad Girl' by Madonna and I played it every time we were in the van, fantasising I was the one kissing a stranger's lips, not Calum as I strongly suspected he would be with me out of the picture. My fears were confirmed on the Monday when we went back to the flats for the staff team meeting. Calum was in the flat above the office with Leah and I could tell something was up. *Are you smirking Leah? Are you blushing?* Even though Kev constantly tried to flirt with me, looking at Calum defiantly, I could only feel their betrayal

Although deep down I knew it was over, I still hung on doggedly and asked Calum to come with me to talk. I cringe now at my desperation. He followed me and I tried to kiss him and he opened his mouth a touch before breaking away. The words "let's just leave it," left me empty and numb for a couple of hours.

We went to the bowling alley in Stafford that afternoon before returning to the boat and I saw them the second we walked in. Leah was on Calum's knee kissing him, looking altogether sweet and cuddly. *Treacherous little bitch!* I ran towards them but Calum saw me and jumped in front of Leah, shielding her, just as Jim managed to catch hold of me. He pinned my arms to my sides, urging me to calm down.

"Be a good idea to get these two out of here'" he addressed Leah's key-worker who, just to rub my nose in the shit even more, was my very own Sarah. Leah turned around, grinning slyly as she left the building. Jim had turned away to start setting up our bowls and I bounced out after her, catching up just as she was getting in the car. I grabbed her hair screaming abuse at her. I was kicking her, still punching at fresh air as the staff managed to pull me off and get a tearful Leah inside the car. I turned on Sarah who was stood outside the car looking helpless. "You're a fucking traitor too Sarah. How can you look after that bitch? You were my key-worker."
I cried wretchedly all the way back to the boat. I felt humiliated beyond belief. I knew I'd behaved shamefully in clinging so hard to Calum, a boy who had meant nothing to me at first. *I mean, where the fuck was my head at?* Sal did her best to comfort me and even Jim usually a bad piss-taker, told me that they were both low for having done that to me. After crying for no less than five hours straight, I vowed to forget Calum - this was made easier with having the

amorous Kev around - but that I would have Leah once and for all if I ever got back to tracker.

Colin rang me the next morning, surprising me by saying he knew how upsetting that incident must have been for me. He reassured me I still had a chance, that he'd said four weeks on the boat and that he'd stick to that if I proved myself by coming good again.

Apart from one incident where I became very violent towards Sal whilst on a camping trip, lashing out at her time and again until Jim and she had to sit on me, I really did settle for those few weeks. I had woken up in a foul mood overtaken by the restless, irritated feeling that wouldn't let me rest until I'd let rip. After the tantrum I cried remorsefully for hours and begged Sal and Jim not to tell Colin as I knew my last chance would be blown. Jim begrudgingly agreed to Sal's request though he was angry with me for causing the exuberant young woman to have red eyes all that evening. I came on my period the next day. My hormones definitely worsened what was already inside.

The rest of my time on outreach passed without any further problems. When the four weeks were nearly up, Colin came to visit me, all for my rehabilitation back to tracker but told me he needed my word that I wouldn't start any more trouble with Leah or he would have to reconsider. He also informed me that the Sheffield girl, Adele, had been placed at the flats and that I would be going to the bungalow with different key-workers as Ellie was with Adele and Sarah with Leah. I wasn't in much of a position to argue.

"You have to make amends with Leah, by phone."

I nodded, not really that mad with her anymore especially as Colin told me she and Calum were no longer together. Calum had gone back to Dudley to his mum and taken up with another girl there. I still don't get it how he got all the girls.

"What about Adele?"

"She has to phone you to apologise. She's the one with the problem so it's only fair. She's been warned, like you, not to make trouble."

I hated to admit it but Colin was fair. I spoke to both girls on the phone that night and Leah apologised in a small voice. Adele then called me and spoke to me in her clipped Sheffield tones admitting that she'd been jealous but now that she was back in the flats with Ellie she had no problem with me. She then confided she was glad we were making up as Ellie had warned her despite my tiny size I was a "force to be reckoned with" and had been done for several ABH offences before arriving at Wallace House. I looked forward to returning to tracker and was full of good intentions.

Back on tracker, I was assigned one key-worker called Faith. While she had her two days off I was looked after by various temp workers. One of them, an older woman, Mary, who was into the occult showed me how to douse with an object on a chain to get yes and no answers to my endless questions. She told me I was psychic but had to hone my gift. Fascinated, I spent hours in my room dousing. The horrible night terrors I'd suffered while at Taxal returned, always accompanied by the intense feeling of a malevolent presence in my room. Ellie, who by now had now forgiven me, told me of a condition called sleep paralysis, a scientific explanation to what

I was suffering but Mary told me I had an evil spirit haunting me - *where did they get this care-worker from, the local nuthouse?* I preferred her evil spirit theory, it made me feel special.

Spring 1993
Spring came early that year and Leah, Adele and I enjoyed many sunny, drunken afternoons hanging round Hednesford. The woman in the local shop was happy to write receipts made out for sandwiches and soft drinks when in truth we spent our activity money on cider, wine and cigarettes. We had too much freedom and no structure whatsoever. We went on the local sunbeds nearly every day, something that was potentially hazardous to our young skin yet no one tried to stop us. As long as we produced legitimate receipts we could do pretty much as we liked. I actually believed the sun beds to be healthy as they helped clear my skin and gave me a rosy glow.
All of us were of school age yet none of us went at all. The tutor sessions soon fell by the wayside but no one did anything about it. We were supposed to be preparing for independent living but apart from learning how to boil broccoli and potatoes and grill lamb chops, I didn't really make much progress in that area.

I met Kenny, a rough looking yet handsome nineteen year old from the local bail hostel, which was down the road from the flats. I was excited when he asked me out, smiling his lazy, sexy smile at me. He took me for a drive that first night in a car so battered I could see the road beneath us as we raced down the country lanes. My heart was in my mouth but I loved every minute of it. He had ready-made spliffs in the glove compartment and I was smashed by the time we got back to Hednesford.

His hostel was a house, similar to Wallace House, run by a middle aged husband and wife who were out that evening. I'd left Leah and Adele with his mates and when Kenny and I got back, we all got wrecked in the kitchen drinking cider and smoking hot knives. It was way past our ten pm curfew but none of us really cared.

By the time Kenny took me into the front room, I was luxuriously hazy and felt no inhibitions as he kissed me. I responded enthusiastically. We soon had each other's jeans off and my legs parted in anticipation as he fingered me. I pushed myself down on his fingers and he caught my hand, placing it on his dick. I wanked him until he pushed me back onto the couch and the next thing I felt was his tongue probing me down below. Pleasure flooded through me, physical and mental - no one had ever gone down on me before.

"Shh," he admonished mock sternly as I began to moan involuntarily.

I felt sensations all over me as the heat began to spread inside out but he moved off me and gently pushed my head down to him. I had never sucked anyone's dick before but I tentatively opened my mouth licked around the end. "You haven't done this before have you?" he asked me, laughing when I shook my head. "I'll help you."

He moved my head; gently pulling on my hair. We then fucked for hours, all positions. I'd never had sex like this before and every time he came, we rested a few minutes and immediately began again. I was sticky, inside and out, his cum running down my legs but I didn't care. I just wanted more of him.

Loud banging at the front door made us jump. "Shit!" he hissed, shoving me away from him. I yanked my jeans on just as the door swung open. A livid Colin stood there like an angry superhero flanked by two police officers. I was marched out of the house along with Leah and Adele while the police warned Kenny and his mates to stay away from us; 'jailbait' they called us, who wouldn't look good on any of their probation reports. Colin told us in no uncertain terms we were all grounded and he would be round the next day to tell us the exact terms and conditions of that.

I dreamt all night of Kenny, waking at midday with my stomach in knots wondering when I would see him again. I felt sick and nervous all day, like I had after Frankie - sex triggered strong attachments for me a pattern that was getting stronger but I was sure this wasn't just sex; he'd seemed really into me. Faith, my key worker was surprisingly sympathetic and made me hot, sweet cups of tea and gave me ciggies all day.

The hours dragged, broken only by Colin paying me the promised visit. I wasn't allowed out for an entire week and after that week was up, Adele, Leah and I would only be allowed out in twos in the evening, alternating who went out with whom. The three of us wouldn't be allowed out together again. I was totally forbidden from seeing Kenny ever again. I was fuming but he took no notice of my angry arguments. My anger at Colin somewhat relieved the chronic emptiness I had suffered all day.

That evening, I heard a loud engine chugging and

blaring music outside the bungalow. My heart lifted as I saw Kenny with his mate in his battered Escort and I ran out to him joyfully. He kissed me, told me I was his girl and that he'd make sure he saw me, no matter what. Hyper with excitement, I ran back in after he'd gone and hid his phone number in my drawer. *Colin would not stop me from seeing him.*

Leah went into independent living in another town shortly after this incident. Colin's rules weren't adhered to for long and he didn't have the time to enforce them constantly. Adele and I spent every afternoon on the fields with Kenny and his friends, smoking weed, drinking cider and listening to rave music. Kenny was constantly stoned and kept me in a free supply. He dropped acid and E's, went to raves, robbed and burgled and had a hard reputation and a lot of respect from the local in Hednesford and the surrounding areas; they now respected me just for being his girlfriend.

Some nights I would sneak out of the bungalow and walk the half mile to Kenny's and we'd spend hours in the caravan outside the hostel. Some nights he came to me but that was riskier. I would set my alarm for two am, get up and shower, lathering myself down below with Impulse shower gel to ensure I smelt edible and gorgeous for him. Delicious oral sex, affectionate fucks, loads of weed; life was a blissful haze.

I was devastated one afternoon when his friend Rob, who despite being twenty-five still lived with his foster parents on the same road as the flats and the hostel, blurted out the fact that Kenny already had a girlfriend, a 'regular' girl who was in the sixth form at the local high school. He shot a disapproving glance at Kenny, saying he had warned him either to finish with one of us or tell me the truth. Rob was a decent guy, like a big brother to Kenny and his mates and now to Adele and me. Kenny just laughed, watching my reaction through hooded eyes.

I ran back home, only crying after I was out of sight. I loved him so much I couldn't even imagine myself with another guy, how could he have another girl at the same time as me? He phoned me later, convincing me that he cared for me more than her and I believed him when he said he would finish with her. That night I was back at the caravan, ignoring my heartache as he licked me softly then fucked me hard.

I spent all my time thinking about Kenny when I wasn't with him. On the days when he let me down, my emotions were unbearable - partly due to not having any weed - and the care-workers looking after me suffered so much that Colin warned me that my placement at Wallace House would be in severe jeopardy if I continued seeing Kenny. I didn't want to lose my placement but I was too addicted to Kenny and the marijuana soaked days splattered with cheap fizzy alcohol. I was also defiant as I would be sixteen in a few months. No one could tell ME what to do.

I learnt ever new techniques to please Kenny in bed believing that if I was sexy enough, dirty enough, bad enough, then it would secure his commitment to me. I lost all pride where he was concerned and on the days when he stood me up, I'd get Adele to phone him for me to find out why. Even she told me Kenny was a laugh but not worth this sickness and heartache.

I hung on doggedly and ignored his obvious lack of care for my feelings. If I got a spot he would order I get rid of it, like it was a reflection on him but if I got angry and refused to speak to him or answer his calls he would get all interested again and hook me back in. He carried on with his other girlfriend, telling me I was his dirty little secret.

He feels more for me than his stupid posh girlfriend.
Bullshit!
He does, I excite him more.
Why doesn't he leave her then?
Shut up! I don't wanna think about that.

My mind was playing on constant Kenny FM and I made him the high point of every day.

Chapter 21
Tripping and falling.

Adele wanted us to drop a trip and it didn't take much convincing for me to try LSD. Ron had always raved about it, *'the trees, the trailers, the peak, fackkin' unreal...'* in his cockney scouse accent. Kenny was out with his posh bitch that night, something I'd reluctantly got used to. He had scored me two trips before he went, 'Black Lightning' which was notorious for being extremely strong - *the stronger the better.*

We dropped the trip at about seven pm and then smoked a few weed pipes with Rob in the park. After about twenty minutes I noticed everything seemed to have an edge to it, auric bubbles that wobbled slightly. Rob and Adele showed me how to move my hands in front of my face quickly to provoke 'trailers' to fly from my fingers, streamers that became more colourful with every passing minute.

Rob had his stereo with him and put on a tape of DJ Ratty at Kinetic and began rave dancing, encouraging us to do the same with our hands to create ever more beautiful colours. I felt completely at one with the other two and also as if I'd been given great enlightenment as to why the ravers danced the way they did. The higher we got, the more the park changed, the grass blending together and then merging into different patterns that made some kind of logical sense to me. I was unlocking the secrets of the universe.

"I need chocolate," stated Adele her face lit up and glowing.

"Wow, yeah, me too!" I answered, not able to help

grinning as I spoke.

How amazing that Adele has suggested something that I really wanted to do too, our minds are in perfect sync. When I smiled it felt like my face was lit up from within, the sensations all over it making me aware of how a smile changed my appearance. The shop was a mental experience altogether. *The chocolate bars are alive. They're breathing, going bigger and smaller with each breath. So brightly coloured, luminous in their perfect packaging. Incredible!*

"Adele, look at the chocolate!" I whispered in awe. Adele burst out laughing making me giggle uncontrollably. We held each other, stuck in manic laughter, almost wetting ourselves, tripping off each other's' teeth, our laughter echoing inside and outside our trippy little brains until Rob told us we were behaving like lunatics on acid. I marvelled at how clever he was to state the truth but make it sound as if nothing could have been further from it and finally managed to pick up a bar of chocolate and pay for it. It tasted like cardboard and the sensation of it in my mouth was so intensely awful that it felt like I was chewing sawdust. Disgustedly, I spat it all out, causing Adele to crack up laughing again. *My neck feels weird. My body is melting. I don't like this.* Then I remembered Ron telling me about "melting" on acid and calmed again, realising I had tapped into the world consciousness of trippers everywhere. *Melting means I am part of another consciousness.*

It was dark now and the street lamps were throwing out colourful ribbons; *everything is simmering.* The music sounded extraordinary, fantastical, and penetrated something deep within me. Everything I said came out in a voice that wasn't my own. I felt interesting and magical.

"How long will I trip for?"

"At least five hours more. You're not even peaking yet. It gets stronger, Marie." Adele was all knowledge and Rob nodded seriously, backing her up.

"I'll give you some weed Marie, in fact no, I'll roll you some spliffs to help bring you down later. You can take this rave tape too, it will help your trip come up to the best it can be."

"We're gonna have to get home, Marie," stated Adele, "fuckin' Colin, the prick, will have the police out and he's looking for any excuse to get rid of the both of us now. Just act normal when you get in. Ring me if you need me. I'll stay downstairs on the couch by our phone."

The trip began turning bad the second I entered the bungalow.

"Marie, what's wrong with you? Why are you staring at me like that?"

What is wrong with your face, Faith?

I darted into the kitchen but regretted it as soon as I opened the fridge. *Everything is alive!* I slammed it shut, fear overwhelming me. *The whole kitchen, everything, is fuckin' breathing!*

"I'm going to bed, don't disturb me," I muttered at Faith as I ran into my room, my haven.

Nothing was breathing in there. I got into bed, honestly thinking I would be able to sleep but when I closed my eyes I felt like my own mind was caving in on me. *Who are these scary people inside my head?* I jumped up and looked out of the window. At first looking at the trees calmed me but the more I looked, the more the trees' natural swaying motion enhanced

itself. *The trees are alive. They're coming for me.*
The phone rang. I answered it - Faith had gone to bed
- and was surprised to hear Kenny's voice. He knew
I'd be out of my face and started fucking with my
head, saying things then denying he'd said them,
making out I had imagined whatever he had just said.
I put the phone down on him, ignoring it when it rang
back. *Fuck off Kenny, you're a head fuck when
tripping.* Ring, ring. *Fuck off!* Ring, ring. I spent a
few minutes trying to pull the plug out. *Stay still!
You're a wire, not a worm. Oh the worm is growing.
Aaagh, help me, it's a snake. Snake! SNAKE! Echoes
in my head. Oh my God! Get away from me.*
The trip had become a nightmare of terrifying
hallucinations. It was too strong for me. I put Rob's
rave tape on and smoked a spliff. *Yes that's better.* I
gradually settled into my trip, controlling my terror.
*Dancing curtains, coloured streamers, melting walls
and breathing trees. I embrace you all. I am part of a
vast consciousness, far bigger than this person who
contains me. Snakes aren't real, not on my trip. Trip,
trip, tripping, roller coaster of colours and light. I am
euphoric. I love you, LSD.*

Another girl moved into the tracker placement around
that time. Much to my jealous disgust, I often saw
Keith with her and her key worker, going out on
various day trips. I hated her for it and shouted abuse
at her regularly, threatening to knock her out if I ever
saw her on her own. Colin warned me that I was on a
slippery slope but my jealousy made me mad. I felt as
if I'd lost a lover to another woman, my Uncle to
another niece.
Amy turned up out of the blue but I was sickened by

her gaunt appearance and the bruises up and down her arms that she flashed at me proudly, informing me that speed was great to inject, self-importantly showing off her needle kit to me. *Gross*. I wasn't into needles although I did accept the wrap of speed she offered me to swallow. She stayed in the bed and breakfast down the road as she'd just done a little earner and was flush for once and I went back home and proceeded to stay awake all night on the speed which made me vomit several times.

Adele didn't like Amy and wasn't impressed by her track marks, telling me hers had been much worse when she'd been an addict. *Bullshit Adele, when were you an addict?*

The final nail in my self-destructive coffin was when Adele and I took Mary's car one night and drove around Stafford until just before dawn, loving the fact that when we had stalled and were unable to get the car started, the police had stopped and jump started the car for us. Unluckily for us, the staff kept their mileage strictly recorded in order to claim expenses and I was questioned about it almost immediately after I got up the following lunchtime, having refused to attend my quarterly review meeting

"I can't even fuckin' drive," I denied vehemently to Colin who then coolly informed me that my placement had been terminated during the review meeting. The previous night's events had been the tip of a very large iceberg and I would be moving to Clifford House where I had been for a week the previous summer. I was devastated and spent my last week begging and pleading but Colin was adamant I was going. I even resorted to begging Keith who told me there was nothing he could do as Colin was the manager and all decisions were ultimately his. He also told me that I had done it to myself. *I hate you Keith, you and your stupid, fuckin' new girl.*

On day before I was due to move, Amy turned up again, on the run from drug dealers in Manchester. I wasn't happy to see her and couldn't care less about her plight, so wrapped up was I in my own. Reluctantly I let her come in for an hour and she begged me to go on the run with her. I didn't need Amy's problems and didn't respect her anymore. From that day on, I never saw her again.

Adele and I scored an acid tab between us that evening and went to the quasar centre with our care-workers. Quasar was something else on acid. At two in the morning, I ran to Kenny's, still slightly high on the half trip. However, Colin had been on red alert for a runaway attempt. He turned up with the police minutes after I arrived. Kenny looked at me coldly telling me, 'I don't need this shit, Marie.'

I went home and overdosed on my contraceptive pill, taking about three months' worth in one go.

"Take her to hospital," sighed Colin, "another typical attention seeking stunt, Marie. Well, I will NOT budge on this decision. You will leave for Clifford House as soon as you are discharged from hospital."

No medicine was needed that time as the vomiting was naturally induced by the excessive amount of hormones I'd put into my system. I sobbed for the twenty-four hours I was kept in Stafford Infirmary, the only form of consolation being Adele who visited me and arranged to meet me at Stafford train station the next day where we would run away to Sheffield. Although the thought of going on the run again after so many months of security didn't really appeal to me, it was better than to going to Hereford.

I lasted in Sheffield two days before my longing for Kenny took over but I was picked up by the police at Stafford train station as soon as I got off the train from Sheffield. They held me in the cells until an emergency social worker arrived to take me to Hereford. Clifford House was a large house in the middle of a residential area and I was the only kid there. Although my new key worker seemed nice enough, I left immediately after showering and eating and easily hitchhiked the ninety miles north back to Hednesford. I'd told Kenny on the phone I'd be outside the caravan at ten o'clock that night and miraculously I was there dead on ten.

"Wow, Marie, how the fuck did you manage to get here in just three hours?"

He was impressed me with me once more and we fucked all night. *I love the pleasure your sex gives me but I desperately crave your affection and love.* The next day he took me on the rob with him and made my day when he presented me with four gold rings from a house he burgled in broad daylight and gave me sixty quid to pay for the local bed and breakfast as we knew it was too risky for me to stay in the caravan again.

It was luxury being able to order and pay for a room which had a colour TV, comfy bed and a shower while being on the run although Kenny never came back during the night as promised.

He doesn't love you.

Yes he does! He's given me money and rings. He paid for a bed for me. That's proof.

I spent the next couple of days suffering with my

boyfriend's rapidly increasing irritation with me but never one to take a hint, I hung on until Kenny finally tired of me. He gave me a half eighth of weed as some kind of consolation prize and told me to go hand myself in as the police were calling at the hostel frequently for me. "I don't need your shit, Marie." I was so stoned on my arrival back from Stafford, having eaten the consolation prize, that I fell asleep immediately. The next day I needed weed to kill the empty emotional ache and managed to beg a spliff off some guy I saw smoking outside his house.

Now stuck in Hereford, I made friends with a couple of the local lads. One had lived in Clifford house a year before but had his own place around the corner and did odd bits of work on the side for the home such as painting the house, which was how I came to meet him. He invited me to his flat to smoke weed, telling me he was also a DJ at the raves in Milton Keynes which impressed me somewhat. However, his little pencil dick filled me with nothing but shame and yeast which gave me such a nasty case of thrush, I thought I'd caught chlamydia again. Needless to say that was the end of that. *Dirty bastard.*

I still had a couple of hundred left in the savings account after the Sheffield runner and began to withdraw this regularly, fifteen pounds a time in order to buy an eighth of weed. Since I'd dropped that first trip, being stoned brought on flashbacks and the room would flood with colour causing the shadows to dance to the incessant drum beat of my rave tapes. I spent hours in my room, listening to rave music, smoking weed and re-inducing tripped out flashbacks. Being permanently stoned was the only thing that made life bearable.

I missed Wallace House crazily and dreamt of Hednesford, Kenny and Adele almost every night. Deep down I knew I'd fucked that placement up myself, that I'd been given a fantastic opportunity there and blown it. *Stupid, stupid cow!* On the days when there was no one to score from, sick emptiness would collide with agitation and my moods would swing alarmingly. I often picked fights with the staff then smashed up furniture and tore up the house. Two members of staff left because of me.

Bryony had also refused to work with me since getting kicked out of Wallace House and it was decided that as soon as I turned sixteen the following month I would live alone with just weekly visits from outreach care-workers. I was completely unprepared in any way for independent living and had no clue how to look after myself. No one ever suggested college to me, counselling or support groups. I couldn't even cook, let alone take full responsibility for myself.

The staff must have known how addicted I was to weed too as it was impossible to miss the stench coming from my room from the second I woke in the morning. All I wanted to do was seek escape. I had no ambition, no plans for my future; I couldn't see any future apart from my next spliff. I resorted to begging local boys for it, all pride abandoning me as I let one of them finger me in return for spliffs. *No kisses though.*

I was terrified at the thought of living alone. Despite hating the system and having spent the last three years rebelling from it, I needed the security it offered me. My sleep paralysis attacks returned, when I got to sleep that was. Without being stoned I would spend hours tossing and turning.

I begged them not to put me out alone but the social services had decided to wash their hands of me and a week before I turned sixteen I was unceremoniously dumped in a dingy little flat on the other side of Hereford, alone in the big wide world, my care years and childhood over for good. I had been the property of social services for over three years, now I belonged to no one.

Borderline

Part 3

Hell

Chapter 22
Beautiful Amphetamine

Aug – Nov 1993

The flat was in a large old house in a tree lined street, basic and tidy but very rundown with mismatched furniture. At first, my key-workers from Clifford House visited every couple of days. I knew they weren't paid to do so and that these visits were in their own time. The outreach worker, Lily, a blonde woman with a patronising smile came each week to deliver the thirty-five pounds I was supposed to live on now that I was independent. She was sometimes accompanied by Pete, a small dark man with a handlebar moustache who I disliked intensely due to his arrogance and the fact he always acted like he was in competition with me or something, making out like my criminal record was nothing compared to his past. He was always trying to prove something to me.

I liked him even less after one evening when I'd come home half-drunk to find him sitting in the armchair of my tiny lounge. He sat me on his knee and told me he cared about me, which made me feel sick to the stomach. I pretended to be far drunker than I was and luckily, my fake retches saw him off.

I was so lonely in those first weeks after leaving care. For the first time in my life I was completely alone. I had no confidence to go out and meet people. I slept with the radio on, or the cassette player wedged down on automatic reverse playing a rave tape incessantly. Anything was better than the still darkness, the eerie silence that accompanied me after dark and brought on the increasing and terrifying bouts of sleep paralysis.

My sixteenth birthday was the loneliest I'd ever experienced despite Julie coming round and taking me to Macdonald's. Despite begging to be taken back into Clifford House, I was left to live alone. Being alone with my thoughts, with no barrier, was not a nice place to be. I hadn't had any weed for almost two weeks and I was restless, irritable and insecure. I walked down the park river path one evening and approached a group of lads at the other side of the park on the Hunderton estate about a mile from where I lived, boldly asking them if they knew where I could score. I used as strong an accent as I could manage, as if that would give me some sort of street cred with these lads who looked a couple of years older than me. They were interested to know where I was from and looked impressed as they received the news that I was from Liverpool (The Wirral doesn't sound so good) and had moved around various children's homes, recently having ended up in Hereford.

As well as the eighth of weed, I bought a trip and swallowed it immediately, excited in the anticipation of the dancing colours and roller coaster ride that LSD promised. It was a dud. Fuming, I marched back down to their estate and demanded my money back. Pretty soon I'd gained their respect and they became regular visitors to my flat.

I slept with one of them from the gang while drunk, a disappointing fumble that I held no emotional attachment to. I had finally acquired the ability to be cold after sex. A few nights later, they took me to a pub. Wanting to prove I could drink as much as them, I downed pint after pint until I was paralytic on the floor. I don't remember much after the groping of my boobs - obviously the lad I'd slept with thought I was his property despite the fact I'd avoided even making eye contact with him for days. My last memory before I passed out was his leering face above me.

I awoke the next day, fully dressed in my own bed with two girls camped out on the floor next to me. As I sat up and looked groggily around, they awoke and introduced themselves to me as Jodie and Sal. Apparently, they had saved me from being practically gang raped the night before and brought me home after telling my so-called friends what they thought of them. Jodie was seventeen and Sal was fifteen and from that day onwards, we started hanging out together.

The difference between the girls and me were many. They were fashionable, I hadn't a clue. They lived at home; I was an ex-care kid. They had families that made sure they ate and had nice clothes, I had thirty-five pound a week handed over by Pete the Perve but for all the contrasts between us, they liked me for who I was and even invited me to their houses sometimes, a complete novelty for me as I hadn´t been invited to a friend´s house with actual parents since going into care.

Sal's mum actually worked for Clifford House but in another unit outside Hereford. She was sympathetic to my situation, often crashing me cigarettes when I was there much to the annoyance of Sal who, at just eleven months younger than me, was not allowed to smoke and had to spray herself and eat breath mints to hide it from her mum.

My new friends began bringing other lads they knew round to my flat at weekends; lads that dealt speed, lads that needed a place to cut their deals up and to put it into gram wraps, lads that didn´t mind sharing.

The line blasts up my nose and hits me within minutes. Wonder drug! I am beautiful, happy, lively and talkative; on top of the world, aware of myself, my attraction and my ways. I am amazing.
A part of me that has always been missing fits perfectly into place. I feel whole for the first time in my life. I am high and getting more so every few minutes as huge lines are cut and generously offered around. I reverently hold the five pound note tube whenever it's my turn. We are all speeding our heads off, united within the chemical high of amphetamine. I talk endlessly, animatedly, my words racing out of my mouth before I even have time to think about them. Everyone listens, interrupting only to agree with me or to carry on from something I have said. I am fantastic!
I keep getting urges to get up and move, to look in the mirror, to admire my glowing reflection. Why have I never before seen the big, beautiful, sparkling eyes, the wild dark hair? I love how my pupils have dilated, giving my eyes an intriguing gypsy quality. I chew gum and smoke incessantly.
Spliffs are made in quick succession, huge cones passed round. Coffee is made to bring us further up; we mellow off the spliff, snort some more speed and drink more hot sweet coffee. The party inside my head just keeps letting off more stream poppers.
We go out on a moonlight mission. I adore the night; love the way my eyes adjust to the moonlight; like a cat, with my boundless energy and vitality that bounce me through the park. We are all on the same wavelength. I am speeding my tits off and loving it.

Bambi, the one with all the speed, has to drop some off somewhere and then he assures us there will be plenty more for us all. We steal clothes from washing lines, milk and fresh orange juice from the doorsteps on the way home and I revel in the fact that some people actually have loaves of bread delivered, saving my mediocre weekly shopping budget.

The next day, after everyone had gone, I tried to sleep, but my jaw and tongue hurt from hours of ferocious chewing. My eyes kept flicking open and I felt uncomfortable and agitated. I tried masturbating, but was left sweating and frustrated as I kept tensing up and preventing myself from achieving the release I needed.

I lay restlessly for hours then got back up, began cleaning up one ashtray and before I knew it I was scrubbing my flat until it shone, arranging trippy rave flyers all over my bedroom walls and ceilings. I kept going all day, brushing the carpets as I had no hoover. I couldn't stop. I emptied all the cigarette dibs into a box and made rollups from them as I had nothing to smoke and no money. As this thought began to depress me there was a knock on my door. Jodie and Sal were armed with cigarettes and goodies from their mums' fridges.

"The lads are all coming over in a bit, with more speed."

And so the pattern began. Every Friday and Saturday saw us partying all night with lots of fun powder to inhale, surprises such as a bit of coke in with the speed - this was according to Bambi although I don't really think there ever was any coke. I got lots of freebies as it was my flat he was dealing from. My neighbours complained bitterly about the weekend parties, phoning up Clifford House to demand they take me in hand, but I didn't give a fuck. Who could stop me now? I just wanted the speed and my new friends. Sal and Jodie ran wild with me and the three of us often got caught in conversations that went on for hours, rambling on about anything and everything that came into our heads.

When everyone had left, the speed had been exhausted and the comedowns were rife, I just wanted more escape, more feel-good drugs. My comedowns left me achy and cold, my body drained but my mind would be too wired to sleep and I would spend hours in the daytimes when everyone had gone just staring into space somewhere between this world and the land of dreams in a no man's land.

I didn't know the comfort of a cooked meal, the warmth of central heating, a mother's love. I had neither rules nor boundaries. My friends could end the weekend, return to their houses and live normal healthy lives in which their parents took care of them. I had nowhere to escape to; their weekend party house was my life.

I always made use of Bambi's stash at weekends and although he sorted me generously, I wanted more. My thirty-five quid was spent something like this; ten pound on coffee, teabags, milk and sugar and a Friday chippy meal, five on fifty cigarettes, and the rest on speed which only served to postpone Sunday´s comedown to Monday. I washed my clothes in the bath, well able for this task while infused with my party powder.

I never had food in and lost lots of weight but Sal and Jo sometimes came with food or took me to their houses for dinner with them. Liz still came to visit sometimes and took me to Macdonald's and I would wolf everything down, my body craving nourishment and my low sugar levels desperate for a boost. She was concerned about how unhealthy I looked but I actually took pride in the bags under my eyes and felt my drawn cheekbones accentuated my looks, making me appear more interesting in my amphetamine misted mirrors.

During the mad speed weekends I met a lad called Scal. Although he was ginger and freckly he possessed loads of charm which had many girls eating out of his hand. He fucked me hard and fast, taking me roughly in my bedroom while the party crashed along downstairs. I knew he had girls other than me but he I enjoyed the sexual high that he brought with him every Saturday, enhanced by my fluffy white new best friend.

Mushroom season was big in Hereford as there were loads of mushroom fields surrounding the city. Bambi turned up one Monday night with a bag full of them. He told Jo, Sal and me that there were roughly a thousand and proceeded to boil them up in a large pan of water. Eagerly, we drank the disgusting liquid that looked and tasted like pond water.

Magic mushroom trips were nothing like LSD and the hallucinations were strong, fast and fierce. Knocked off our feet on to a magic street bench, we were transported to Cartoon Land, full of bubble cars in moving streets with snakes and ladders swirling round the walls. People kept popping up like Nintendo game characters; we recognised every stranger we saw and then argued crazily about whose hallucination was correct.

For the next few weeks we did mushrooms every weekend, on top of all our speed. I began living in a permanent hallucination. Even when I hadn't taken anything my perceptions were blurred in places, over-heightened in others.

Everything was weird. I didn't see the plane crash I had become. I thought the grey jumper and blue jeans I wore day in, day out to be far more flattering than they were. I washed them as often as I could and spent hours trying to dry them by the bathroom heater. I did have other clothes but had got stuck on this amphetamine induced image of myself looking good in this outfit. In reality I looked scrawny and grubby. My hair was unkempt and wild. I didn't know makeup apart from eyeliner and my skin was breaking out angrily once again.

One weekend my flat was trashed and windows were broken downstairs by three lads I had kicked out for blatantly trying to rob my telly. The next day, a couple of care-workers were sent from Clifford House to help me clear up and to give me a good talking to after I called the office emergency number in the midst of a tearful comedown.

After the staff had left, I sold my telly through a mate of Bambi's, Cuck, a rip off bastard who brought me forty-five quid's worth of flour for my pain. Sal and Jo went mad when they saw I'd sold my TV and told me they were really worried about me. Their worry and concern wasn't helpful to me. I needed speed and couldn't handle my cold, tired, sad and hungry life without it. Speed was the only thing that made life worth living.

During the week, I would rummage through the

battered couch hoping to find pennies, look in the local telephone boxes and even scrounge money from passers-by, just enough to buy a twenty-seven pence toffee crisp bar which would sustain the hunger pains for an hour.

One night, Cuck and I went back to Clifford House and he waited outside while I burgled it. I got away with the video recorder, game console and games and felt no remorse. I knew it would be replaced within days for the boy who lived there. We got enough speed to keep us up for a week and by the time I was coming down, my new social worker paid me a visit, which ended in me attempting to stab her with a pen-knife. I hadn't liked her news of the plans to bring me back to the Wirral and I just lost it. Pete the Perve gallantly came to her rescue and hurled me back inside my front door as they escorted her away.

The following Monday, I had a surprise visit from two support workers from a hostel back on the Wirral. Hayley, my old friend from Taxal and Cotsbrook was currently living at the hostel and had been brought along too, probably because they knew I wouldn't kick off with her there. I couldn't believe they'd turned up unannounced like this although they told me that I'd been informed of their visit. I was in my pyjamas, wrapped up and shivering in my quilt. I had flu – I often had flu like symptoms during the week. Hayley told me I looked awful and the two women agreed. One of them, Margaret, reminded me of my Auntie Tricia, pretty and flamboyant with all her make-up and brightly dyed red hair. The other one, Lizzie was hard, appeared to be a total battle-axe but had something really kind in her eyes as she told me I was more than welcome to move to their hostel but that my drug use would not be tolerated.

"I'm not moving," I stated as belligerently as I dared.

"No choice girl," she smiled

I'm settled here though," I whispered feebly.

Margaret looked around in sympathetic disgust. "It's filthy here queen. You're a mess, you need to come back home."

To get rid of them I agreed and it was arranged I move there the next week. *No way!*

That weekend, after a particularly strong and not so nice trip, I spent the Saturday in bed, cold and miserable in my return to reality. I had no speed as there was a drought on. Sunday evening was spent inhaling gas under the bandstand with Jo and Sal, both of whom were devastated at my pending departure. The next day, I got myself a bedsit, secured housing benefit and took my stuff there. The bedsit was awful but I had attachment issues and a speed habit to think of.

I was picked up by the police later that afternoon as I walked with Sal and Jo through the city centre, taken to the station and detained until the Clifford House staff could arrive. No one listened to my protests that I was sixteen and they had no right. I was escorted to the staff car by the police and driven the two hundred miles back to my hometown.

Chapter 23
Small Time Dealer

Pembroke Court, Birkenhead
Nov 1993 – April 1994

Pembroke Court consisted of three council block buildings containing several flats. I was in 'first block' where everyone was between sixteen and eighteen. Some were ex-care kids like me; some came from broken homes where the parents were alcoholics or drug addicts. The other two blocks were for over eighteens who chose to live away from home but didn't want to be completely without support. The flats were actually quite nice and well equipped; a million times better inside than outside.

I felt so intimidated by everyone. I had no way of scoring and my new found confidence disappeared. Tongue-tied, I could barely utter a word and I hated the common room where we gathered every evening. Back in the shadowy place from which I had been fighting so hard to escape, I had no means of snorting my way out of it.

Every week day, I was sent to AMARC, a youth training scheme placement that paid sixteen and seventeen year olds the grand sum of twenty-nine pounds and fifty pence a week. I did basic Math, English and was supposed to be training for something that would guarantee work yet the only option there was engineering. *Hmm, because engineering always was my first career choice!*

At first, I towed the line and attended the centre every weekday, nine until one along with Hayley and Star. Hayley was popular with boys there because she was hard, Star because she was pretty and sophisticated. I wasn't popular with them at all. In contrast, the Pembroke lads loved me but I wasn't really into any of them.

I went back to visit Hereford on my first weekend, some sort of new person concession but I only brought a one way ticket with the money they gave me. Jo, Sal and I spent the weekend tripping on Bart Simpsons, a light happy trip which was like being inside a fluffy cartoon. On the Sunday when I admitted I hadn't bought a return ticket, Sal's mum let me stay over but telephoned the Pembroke staff who told her to put me on a train home the next day promising her the money would be reimbursed. I was never invited to Hereford again and lost touch with Sal and Jo.

I visited my parents for the first time since I'd stayed there overnight fifteen months previously. They were obviously uncomfortable in my presence and remained tight-lipped the whole time I was in their house. Teresa, now fourteen, and her friend were quite impressed by me though and I played up to my bad girl care kid role. However, I remained abnormally quiet at Pembroke, that is, until I found a new supply of speed.

The brother in law of one of the girls took a shine to me the moment he saw me and on discovering I was after some speed, told me he dealt it. After scoring, Ian and I spent the night speeding our heads off, talking shit and walking round Seacombe, all my confidence restored. Despite the bitter freeze of the Mersey wind there was no need for coats as speed supplies its own central heating system although the comedowns now made my bones shiver inside.

I had a constant supply from then on. I hung out with Ian a lot as he always sorted my ever growing appetite for speed. He asked me more than once to be his girlfriend but his long hair and slight build did not attract me in the slightest, thank GOD as I later found out he had a dark secret in his past to which, none of mine compared.

I glowed in the common room, chatty and animated with everyone, loving their surprise at my apparent personality transplant. I got more confident at AMARC, and attracted one lad, Paul, who I discovered could easily be corrupted by my drug and manipulated to suit my own purposes.

Paul would front the money for a quarter ounce and I would give him maybe two grams telling him they cost far more than they did and keep five for myself, snorting one as soon as I got it in two big fat lines. I spent hours up at night, chopping and sweeping, messing and cutting, smoothing and sectioning to make as many shit deals as I could get away with. I meticulously made paper wraps, taking pride in my neatness. I could spend hours alone in this zone, listening to the same beats and repeating my actions all night. I would save about five crappy little wraps, sell them to idiots who knew no better and make enough to score another quarter.

When dawn broke, I would shower before going to score again, a newly initiated speed freak luxuriates in the act of cleaning and preening. I still thought my eyes looked great with loads of black eyeliner on the inside rim; I thought that leaving conditioner on my hair without rinsing would make my hair as glossy as Star's, never noticing the greasy truth, always seeing myself through falsely confident speed eyes.

The lads at AMARC commented that I was witchy and not in a good way but I ignored them. I didn't care for stupid AMARC boys who still lived at home with Mummy. They were beyond my contempt. I lasted at AMARC until Christmas then refused to go anymore, instead claiming income support hardship allowance for minors who were without income or family to take them in. This gave me five pounds fifty pence a week more than the fruitless training scheme, *so much incentive to better myself.*
I slept with a few of the lads in my hostel, dumping them straight after and swearing them to secrecy, ashamed of myself after deriving my pleasure in the dark, blanking out the face and person it was. On a comedown, needing comfort and pleasure of some sort, it was just sex for me; I didn't get attached anymore. I never touched them back; sometimes I wouldn't even kiss them. I just liked their fingers inside me, their tongues pleasuring me; the thrill of illicit sex; dirty pleasure hidden by a coat of anonymity in the darkness. *Shut up and fuck me.*
I used Paul to buy my speed but I never as much as kissed him, never mind anything else, playing along that I was shy but letting him believe I was his steady girlfriend. I ended up dumping him after Star, my flatmate sent him into my room dressed up and painted like a woman while I was on a horrific comedown after being up for days. He still continued to buy my skinny cut deals though.

When Hayley, by then seventeen, moved to her own flat in Wallasey, I began spending a few days a week there. I convinced her and a couple of lads from Pembroke currently sharing our beds to drop some acid. Stupidly I decided to take three to everyone else's one. By the time I was peaking, more than eight hours into it, they were all asleep, their minds their own once more. It had been fun at first while they'd been coming up and hitting their own peaks but once they were sleeping, their snores became terrifying as my triple dose amped up the hallucinations. A bad trip that lasted for several terrifying hours ensued. The next day, I felt detached from the world all day, surreal, and didn't feel normal again until the following day when I saw Ian. Two gusts up my nose blasted the nastiness of the acid still left in my system. Beautiful speed.

I spent Christmas day at my parent's, trying to appear normal, but the roast turkey and potatoes simply wouldn't be swallowed no matter how much I chewed. My parents didn't say anything about my non-existent appetite, wild staring eyes, dilated pupils or the fact I was sweating despite the cold British winter. Couldn't they see my jerky movements or my contorted, grinding mouth? *Can't you see the state of me, Mum? Dad?*

After Christmas, I was arrested for punching one of the staff while on a violent comedown. I had just come home from Hayley's after becoming paranoid around her and the lads. I felt distant, separated, even agitated when around them. Hayley didn't approve of the amount of speed I was doing and my constant moving round at night irritated her.

For the assault, I was locked up in the Bridewell for the night. Surprisingly, my mum came to the interview to be my appropriate adult and took me back home with her the next morning while my social worker bargained for me to have another chance at

Pembroke. I was charged and had to go to court for assault a couple of months later but got let off with a twelve month supervision order and a small fine after my solicitor pulled the poor little care girl story in court.

I returned and moved into Star's flat with her. She was the only person I never charged for speed but she didn't take it very often anyway. I enjoyed playing the big dealer sorting my friend but the truth was I really had no right to charge her for anything as I never bought any food but still helped myself to whatever was in the fridge when I was on a starving comedown. Star was poised, sophisticated and fashionable, nothing at all like a care girl and I enjoyed having a feminine and somewhat "normal" friend.

By then, I was ruling the kids I'd previously been intimidated by. All the new lads that were admitted loved me and my speed and followed me everywhere; sorting me with ciggies and weed, and cooking for me when I wanted feeding. They also bought my speed at much higher prices than I paid for it.

I was invincible, full of it with them all in first block, staff and residents alike. However, with the second and third block residents, I slammed back into my shadows, even while speeding. Thoughts jamming, synapses not quite connecting thoughts to words, rendered me stuttering; my buzz giving over to a highly alert sense of introspective paranoia.

I still hung out with my dealer Ian but he had begun to act strangely, his eyes so black and intense hinted at certain demons he was no longer able to contain. One night, he confided in me that he had sexually abused his younger sister Kerry as a child and had not been long out of prison for serving the sentence he'd received just a couple of years before when it had all come out.

Kerry, now sixteen, was dabbling with the gear (heroin) and was getting more and more aggressive towards him every time he was at his mum's. This also explained her attitude towards me – on the couple of occasions I'd been to his mum's, I'd been greeted with hostility from his mum and Kerry had looked like she wanted to punch me.

He kept saying he was sorry but I was disgusted. *Get away from me you dirty perve.* I took a taxi back to Pembroke and refused to see him again. As well as feeling revulsion, I'd been gobsmacked at his revelations. I didn't think paedophiles lived among us, people like me. I thought they belonged to the world of dirty old men that looked like weirdos or perverted care staff. Ian was my dealer for fuck's sake, one of my own. I saw him a few weeks later, dirty, haggard and skitzed out of his face. He tried to approach me but I threatened to knock him out. I didn't see him again after that.

My body had a couple of weeks much needed break from the speed, eventually recovering from the huge appetite and exhaustion that had overwhelmed it. Star made sure we had plenty of weed to smoke, an effective alternative to depressive, tiring amphetamine withdrawal and we would spend hours giggling like little kids.

I met Robbi during one of our missions into third block. He intrigued me with his designer stubble, weird dress sense, his popularity in the blocks and his love of rave dancing which he did constantly. He came up behind me one night while we were in his friend's flat and began touching my thigh, slipping his hand through the rips in my jeans. Slowly, erotically we kissed, that night ending up in his bed. He was different from the first block boys. At nineteen, and with his sexual expertise, I saw him as a man.

The next day my belly turned to jelly every time I thought of him and I spent hours worrying I would be fucked and fucked off but Robbi brought those fears to a halt when he came whistling outside my window that evening and sneaked me back into his flat for the night.

Star and I had been looking for a town house to share together in Birkenhead but after I met Robbi I didn't want to leave Pembroke. Bored of my excuses, Star moved into a beautifully furnished flat in Birkenhead. It wasn't long before I found a new supply and I was speeding daily again, sometimes having to snort a line just to lift my head off the pillow.

I made friends with a girl called Jane, an eighteen year old from third block who was addicted to slimming tablets. She was stylish despite her weight and kind of snobbish. At first, she'd nicknamed me 'spotty Marie from first block' behind my back. One day I got her to try speed in place of the slimming tablets she swallowed in vast quantities. She dropped her snobby front with me and we became close speed buddies.

Spring was coming and every Friday, Robbi, Jane and I, along with loads of others from second and third block went to The Drome in Birkenhead. On Drome nights I swapped my usual trackie bottoms for jeans

and tight tops but despite my tiny figure I felt fat and
bulky although I must have weighed all of ninety
pounds. I had a terrible self-image and I couldn't
dance no matter what I'd taken or how good the sets
were with DJ Trix and MC Cyanide whose mixes I
loved. Instead I'd just stand in the corner, rushing
deliciously from the speed and weak ecstasy we took.
In the toilets the conversations were all the same,
(*What's yer name? What yer had?*) All credit and
respect would go to the one who had taken the most.
Jane, Robbi and I threw in for an ounce of speed
every couple of days which we would cut up and lay
on to second and third block residents, writing their
names and amounts owed in my notebook. There
were always strong role reversals in my life; since
getting with Robbi I was now their dealer, the one
they needed and begged to lay them on one more, all
my previous shyness gone. I gave them about half of
what they paid for, greedy with my addiction and
forever scheming so as not to run out.
I did let myself come down sometimes, knowing a
little rest would refresh me, lower my tolerance
slightly and therefore make the speed hit me harder
when I snorted it again. On giro days, Jane and I
would pig out in Sayers on pasties and donuts, eating
until we were stuffed, our bodies claiming back what
we'd deprived them of before going off to score.

My Uncle Dom got back in touch with me. He lived
in nearby Rock Ferry and knew someone who was
friends with Robbi who had put two and two together
and realised I was his niece. When I smacked yet
another staff member and subsequently given my
marching orders, Uncle Dom came in his estate car to

collect me and my bin bags.

I didn't give a damn about being thrown out this time. Jane had just taken on a lovely modern flat in Dacre Hill and needed a flatmate to claim the other half of the housing benefit with her. It was the perfect arrangement. No nosey staff ruining my buzz, constant access to Robbi who kind of drifted up to the flat with us. Life was one long crazy party. LSD, speed and weed in abundance.

Chapter 24
Permanent Trip

Spring 1994
Sixteen years old, living with a friend and a like-minded, drug loving boyfriend, life was exciting. Robbi and I grew close, bonding in a way that only speed knows how. He was a mellow guy, a lover not a fighter and I loved getting off my head with him. He reckoned he had battled heroin addiction before coming to Pembroke with the help of his dad who had locked him in a room with an ounce of weed which had apparently killed his cold turkey symptoms. Knowing precious little about heroin at that time in my life, I believed him and looked at him in awe. Our conversations were deep, we connected.

Jane and I had this trip bond, where we instinctively knew each other's state of mind. Our trips always merged and we saw the same things. We talked about the beginning and end of the world, discovered universal secrets. I loved the hallucinatory world in which I now spent so much of my time; the music, the magical lands on our rave flyers, the drugged up fantasy which was my reality.

We continued visiting Pembroke Court, tripping in the filthy flats of fucked up friends, pushing our cut shit onto the inexperienced users who knew no better. I looked down on inexperienced users, as if I had something to be proud of. Every time we went to Pembroke Court we collected more of Robbi's stuff; speakers, amps, decks, tools and wires. Permanently out of our faces, the music played through Robbi's home-made sound systems enhanced our buzz.

He was forever wiring up new speakers, angling them

at all corners of our bedroom so that everywhere vibrated when the music was on. He had a good collection of trance too which I liked more than happy hard-core. It had a soulful melody and amazing beat which pulsated through me, complimenting whatever drug I was on. More importantly, every time he brought more of his stuff, I felt more secure in our relationship which had started off as me having more feelings than him. It was as if he was depositing pieces of himself with me.

One of Robbi´s friends from Pembroke Court sort of migrated to the flat with us and it wasn't long before he and Jane were bed-mates although they tried to keep it a secret from the rest of the world. We always had money between the four of us; in addition to our four giros, we claimed crisis loans for lost or stolen giros until the social refused to give any more. I was also entitled to a five hundred pound leaving care grant from social services for furniture and every week I went down, claiming I was buying some item of furniture. I would falsify receipts and take them back in the next week so I could claim more.
As for the flat, Jane and I each got three donated items from the St Vincent De Paul charity and furnished the living room with the ugliest flowery tangerine and brown couch that could have ever been made, next to a garish mustard yellow two seater sofa. I got some nice mirrored wardrobes from them though.
My already bad dress sense deteriorated further. I practically lived in pair of grey tracksuit bottoms and a denim shirt with a grey hood and sleeves. I wore my trustee black eyeliner but nothing to cover my spots

or blemishes, and a hairband round the front of my head over my ears with my long frizzy hair flying wildly but as far from sexy as you could get.

The more drugs I took, the clumsier I became - it was a standing joke that I always banged into things and knocked things over which is how my Auntie Tricia and Uncle Dom came to suspect I was using. I lived around the corner from them now and they always welcomed me into their house with a hot cup of tea or coffee and a plate of biscuits or cakes with cream, scones with jam. I went there on comedowns, my body craving the nourishment and sugar, my heart yearning for kindness from a real family member. They always told me they disagreed with what had happened to me and that my parents were the ones who were in the wrong. *You never took me in though, did you?* Several incidents of spilt coffees later and Auntie Tricia turned up at the flat to confront me with her concerns. My clumsiness was a big giveaway sign, she told me, as were my drawn cheeks and bags under my eyes and general appearance. 'I just want to help you Maria.' I denied everything.

We did have comedown days where we would just smoke weed and let ourselves sleep, indulging our bodies with much needed food. Beef flavoured noodles with melted cheese became our staple diet but on giro days we pigged out on chippy food and loads of chocolate. On these days, Jane listened to my stories of being in care and I even confided the truth of my 'rape' to her. She held me when I cried and acknowledged the fact that she knew those tears had been held in for years. After a couple of stimulant free days, we would score again and go wild.

Drugged daily on one substance or another along with my already obsessive, damaged thought processes, something was going to snap. It happened when we dropped a super strawberry, a potent version of the mellow strawberry we were used to. Robbi was doing knives and put some speed inside his squidgy gold seal weed, cannabis you could roll out like play-dough. I inhaled the smoke through a glass bottle. I took another, unaware that I'd just blown the proverbial fuse.

The couch has grown to twice its size, the giant flowers leer at me and I have an overwhelming feeling of having wet myself. I can't get up. I am rooted. What if they see the wet patch? I can't speak or move. The flowers are coming alive; glaring, staring flower eyes.

I had an overwhelming urge to empty my bladder and bowels and ran to the toilet. There were no windows in the tiny beige bathroom and the extractor fan was getting louder. I pushed but nothing came out. I got stuck on the toilet.

Voices in the fan, childhood memories, my sister, my brother, my parents, chanting rhymes. 'one, two, buckle my shoe, three, four, knock at the door... nineteen, twenty, MY PLATE'S EMPTY.' It was a rhyme that had haunted me one time while delirious from fever as it got louder and louder in my head, smashing my brain between its angry metallic recitals.

My parents are talking about me. Angry, accusing. I'm sorry Mummy. Don't get mad, Daddy. A fight my sister and I had once replays itself on the walls. I'm not sorry Teresa, you started it.

In the toilet of my childhood I heard my family sitting

down for dinner, in the flat's toilet I could hear Jane, Doug and Robbi coughing and spluttering after more speed encrusted hot knives. *Past, present, jumping back and forth; I am unable to leave either place.* Jane knocked on the door and I told her I was on a bad one. She reassured me Robbi would know what to do but the thought of him freaked me out further. "No, I don't wanna see him. Just ask him what to do." She came back with the information that fresh orange juice would bring me down and suggested we go for a walk to the shop to buy some, just me and her. I gladly agreed, desperate to escape the weird childhood images and claustrophobic flat.

Outside, The Alice in Wonderland effect had taken over. Jane was my life line; everything else was a threat, alien, out of sync, like giants had kicked the universe around and left me wobbling within. I gulped down the fresh orange juice and actually felt it change my perception, taking me to a new level, safe at first but quickly becoming frightening within minutes of arriving there.

I couldn't handle it outside anymore, sure I had wet myself again and back at the flat, I ensconced myself in the bathroom for another round of squeezing my bowels which actually did need to open now due to the amount of fresh orange I had drunk. Every sensation was hugely magnified. My rectum felt like it was being stretched so far that it was ripping and I tried to squeeze myself shut again, hold it in to stop it breaking me.

The voices kept coming back. I couldn't face my flat mates and crept to my room which was thankfully next door to the bathroom. Within minutes, my mind was readjusting all the familiar safe things in my room, twisting them into something horrible, mocking me and picking out my stupid pieces of life. *Mirrors everywhere, flashing beams at each other, talking about me. My reflection is witch like, ugly, scary. The mirrors are laughing at me, at how I preen in front of them when speeding, thinking I look good. Their evil laser beams terrify me.* I jumped up and turned them round, trying to get the horrible image of myself out of my head. Other hallucinations attacked me and I was rocking by the time Jane came in, my head in my hands.

Robbi was concerned so I agreed to see him. He prescribed more speed and remembering the last bad trip and how the speed had helped me get past it, I took two big lines of pink speed, one up each nostril. Big mistake, the trip was sent rocketing again, more orange juice, more toilet trips, more voices, childhood scenes driving me insane. I stayed like that for sixteen hours, a lunacy induced by my own self destruction.

I didn't recover from that trip; although the hallucinations subsided they didn't quite leave me. My subconscious was tortured by the stubborn dregs of LSD and I honestly thought the only way to get over it was to override it with a good trip.

Robbi also encouraged this whole-heartedly so a few days later I dropped half with him. Thank God it was only a half! I hallucinated having another evil speed knife and this trip also went bad. Even after coming down, I was hallucinating constantly. I saw faces and eyes everywhere, pot no longer relaxed me, simply induced more flashbacks. I couldn't even take speed as it sent me spiralling. It was like an old friend had turned on me. Everything had that trippy tinge around it and the speed I was so tired and lethargic I could barely get out of bed.

The party was over. After a couple of weeks of total abstinence, the strongest of the flashbacks began wearing off but all my perceptions remained distorted and strange. Robbi´s friend and Jane split. She and I had a massive argument and she gave Robbi and me our marching orders but we'd been looking for our own place anyway, I desperately needed a change in environment.

It was easy to find private rented accommodation that accepted social security in those days and we found a flat above a shop in New Ferry Precinct. I managed to secure an instant deposit for it from the social services as it was my first official flat since leaving care.

It was exciting to sign the tenancy with Robbi's name also on it. This was a big step in our relationship. I thought I was in love but in truth I was very possessive and needed to be loved and to feel secure. Robbi bought me a ring for my seventeenth birthday and put it on my engagement finger making me feel securer than ever.

Soon after we moved in, Robbi persuaded me I would be okay on just half an acid and a little speed. *Old habits die hard.* That night, my perception of Robbi changed irrevocably after he shaved off his overgrown beard that had once been sexy designer stubble. It had become a fully-fledged beard without either of us really noticing and I must have got used to him like that. My mind flipped inside out in horror. He wasn't Robbi anymore. The carpet removal made his eyes too big for his drug ravaged skinny face and in my drugged up mind, he looked like an alien, the devil, my worst nightmare.

To top it off, he had also fitted himself into pair of my jeans. *What the fuck?* I couldn't look at him. I wanted to run from this hellish vision. I wished my head wasn't so fuzzy on the acid.

"Alright petal?" He came over to kiss me and I froze. "Robbi, I'm tripping." *Fuck off weirdo.*

After a few days of regrowth, he began to look more like my Robbi again and I put the nightmare version out of my head but every time he shaved from then on, I couldn't stand being near him.

That was the last acid tab I took. Shadows now appeared everywhere. I was always twitchy and constantly felt malevolent presences behind me. I couldn't even go to the toilet alone once it had grown dark outside. The flat was haunted - by my own mind's mad projections. I couldn't touch speed anymore as it only enhanced the relentless paranoia and weed brought on heavy-duty flashbacks where I would go so white that I'd hide in the toilet, convinced I was about to lose control of my bowels or bladder. That awful feeling of having wet myself stayed with me, even when I'd been completely abstinent for months. Without drugs I reverted into a shell and lost the ability to even look people in the eye when speaking.

People were strange and I could often detect sinister figures beside everyone I knew, hear them talking to each other, telling me what the person was really thinking about me, which often wasn't nice. No one was to be trusted, except Robbi and Jane who I had recently made friends with again. Outside, the huge clouds looked as if some ominous presence had taken over the sky. I saw storms coming to destroy Birkenhead, the end of the world, visions of horror that petrified me. I made Robbi accompany me every time I went out. For that matter, Robbi wasn't allowed out of my sight, ever!

I began obsessing over our budget, rationing our cigarettes and tobacco to last us the two weeks as we now only had our combined giro of one hundred and forty a fortnight to live on. I controlled Robbi, every move he made, how high he had the music as it made me trip out if it was too loud, when he got a bath, where he went and who he could see. If he disagreed I would lose my temper, screaming abuse at him, accusing him that it was his speed knives that had pushed me to this state in the first place. *Nothing to do with me, God, no.*

I decided I was going to bed every night at a decent time (ten pm) - I think I was trying to turn into my mother - and that Robbi come with me as I was scared to be alone. I told him when to bathe and refused to let him shave. When he *disobeyed* and dared to shave, I would flip, recoil from him in bed and not let him touch me for a week. I wouldn't let him go on a course of lifeguard training that his probation worker booked for him, scared he would meet someone else. I banned him from taking trips and speed and only *allowed* him to buy a fiver's weed once a fortnight on payday. I resented him for being a giro pot head. Poor Robbi, those fortnightly Thursday evenings were his only escape from me.

Despite being totally abstinent, the psychosis symptoms would not leave. Robbi, also wanting some kind of drug, came with me to the doctor who prescribed us something called Meleril, which I later found out was an anti-psychotic drug used to combat the symptoms of schizophrenia. It didn't banish the apparitions; instead, it made us so drowsy that our boots felt like they'd been filled with cement every time we walked anywhere. The lethargy was like nothing I had ever known. After a couple of weeks, we stopped it and I got myself referred to Clatterbridge hospital to see a psychiatrist. He diagnosed I was simply insecure through being in care. *But what about the shadows? The paranoia? The incessant bloody mood swings? The ghosts?* I came away more determined than ever to control the only things I could, our budget and Robbi.

In some ways this was good, I made sure we attended our various probation and supervision appointments and my rigid budget dictated we bought enough food and paid our court fines and bills. Not good for Robbi though, I controlled everything he did. What I really wanted was for him to take the upper hand, to put me in my place, to show some passion and make me secure. I wanted someone to fight for me. Robbi's placidity was something I had loved about him at first but it made me despise him eventually. He would tell me he loved me but there was nothing really there. Jane always joked what I really wanted was to be a gangster's moll. The shadows gradually faded away, back into the recesses of my own mind but I was still a shell-shocked version of the girl I had been the year before.

Chapter 25
Welcome Sweet Relapse

Scared of complete insanity, I remained totally drug free and miserable. We lived our mundane giro supported lives in an area oppressed by negativity. I was old before my time, dressed like a dowdy middle aged woman and spent my days reading Helen Forrester memoirs. My evenings were spent smoking cigarettes and drinking hot sweet No Frills tea. *Tetley? You must be joking! Not on my budget.* Others from Pembroke also moved to New Ferry Park. It seemed everyone had fucked up on speed and were all living lives of self-forced abstinence.

Although controlling with Robbi, I could barely string a sentence together with anyone else. I bumped into my old friend Stephanie from my care days but couldn't even make eye contact while mumbling and stuttering. I shifted uncomfortably, blushed and said nothing when she incredulously asked what was wrong with me.

Although my paranoia and irrational fears began to leave me, I was bored, restless, agitated. Confined within a relationship with a man I no longer even fancied, we fought constantly. I would scream abuse and become completely out of control, yell at him to get out then throw myself in front of the door if he tried to leave. I belittled him in every way I could until he finally lost his temper, giving me some kind of reaction at last, yelling back and punching the window or wall. Then, I would cry and beg forgiveness, terrified of being abandoned, telling him I loved him, making him tell me he loved me and promise he would never leave me. My period, or the week running up to them, made me even crazier. At the same time as needing him I detested him, hatred mingled with a confused attachment.

Insecurity, my own lack of inner peace and self-confidence made me push him to his limits; punish him without even knowing why. I grew more possessive over him because the more shit I threw at him the more I thought he would leave me and despite not even wanting sex with him by that time, I couldn't imagine life without him.

As if life in Giro City wasn't bad enough, one evening we came home to find we'd been burgled. They'd taken our TV, our games console, all our games and rave tape packs. Not much by some people's standards but it was everything we owned. The social services refused to help me anymore and without insurance we weren't able to replace the stuff. Devastated wasn't the word. I looked at the gold rings I still wore on my finger, courtesy of my ex-boyfriend Kenny's burglary and felt a pang of remorse for having worn them with pride for the last two years. *Karma, I can't say it was a pleasure meeting you.* I wanted revenge. Sam's name was given to us, some local lad about Robbi's age, not hard at all. If we didn't do something then people would think we were an easy target. Robbi made so many excuses that in the end I totally lost all respect for him. *Was there any left at this point?* I began to fantasise about other lads I knew, thinking about them while in bed alone and on the rare nights when Robbi and I had sex, I would substitute his face for theirs, all the while becoming convinced that Robbi must be up to something, or would be given half the chance. I tightened his reins even more. Projection wasn't a word that formed part of my vocabulary at that time. I was an abusive control freak but saw myself as a victim of the world.

April - June 1995

My grandad died and I attended his funeral and then cried all the way home in the car with my Uncle Paul, not so much for my Grandad although I think that gave me the excuse to cry for my lost childhood and Uncle. That night, speed greeted me like a long-lost friend. I snorted it, savouring its chemical taste as it went down the back of my throat and within minutes I was animated and full of vitality. *Goodbye dreary drug free life. You were shit and I am never coming back.*

I started hanging out with Ann, a loud gobby girl of sixteen who thought she was hard because she'd just come out of care. Despite having previously disliked her, we bonded after a few lines of pink speed and she began coming round to hang out at mine and Robbi's. Speed rushed its way back into my life charming me with light, confidence and vitality anew.

I needed to end it with Robbi. I hated sex with him and had even been to the doctor's wondering if there was something wrong with me as I simply couldn't get wet. Sex was dry and uncomfortable. The doctor told me the cause was mental not physical, something which I didn't understand until I ended up in New Ferry Park one night shagging a male friend I knew from Pembroke. No problems whatsoever with lubrication. It was fast and furious and over within seconds but reawakened a lust in me that I hadn't felt for months.

Ironic really considering it had been me who been so suspicious of Robbi. My being unfaithful gave me the push I needed to end it. He begged me not to leave him but I told him we had grown apart giving him the old cliché 'I love you like a friend not a boyfriend.' Sadly, he agreed we would go our separate ways at the end of the tenancy which had been called to an abrupt stop by the shopkeeper underneath, due to our increasingly frequent rows that scared off the customers. However, he hung around me like a desperate stalker, hoping I would change my mind.
But I love you, Marie.
Fuck off and have a shave, I don't care anymore.
One night, I was on a comedown, half asleep when he came into the back living room where I was sleeping. I was horny - comedowns always did that to me – I would have fucked the milkman had he lain next to me at that moment. I opened myself to him, wet with amphetamine lust. I forgot about it the next day and as I was pushing some speed across a mirror he came in and put his arms round me.
"What yer doing?" I jumped away from him. Confusion slid across his face.
"For fucks sake Robbi, last night was a one off, a comedown fuck. It didn't mean anything.'
"Marie, petal, please don't do this to me." Once upon a time my heart had lifted when he called me petal.
"You need to move on." I put the speed up my nose, dismissing him.
That day, Ann and I, now best speed buddies, found a flat to share in Egerton Park and went on a speed fuelled mission to the social to get our two weeks rent in advance sorted out. When we came back there were paracetamol tablets scattered everywhere. Then

we found the note.

'Sorry, can't do this anymore, R x.'

Despite being irritated, I thrived on the drama as I
rang the ambulance to meet us at his mate's flat,
knowing where he would have gone. I didn't even
think of the pain and mental torture I had put him
through despite having suffered exactly the same
myself a couple of years earlier.

When Ann and I went to visit him, he was smiling
and dancing round in his hospital gown, apparently
fine after having had his stomach pumped. Parading
his drip round like a trophy he obviously thought I
wouldn't leave him now. I moved out the following
week, taking all the furniture with me (I had inherited
some from my late Grandad and the rest had been
acquired by me from social services) and leaving him
amongst a mass of wires, tools and speakers, his
esteem in shreds.

Egerton Park Winter 1995

I was writing in frenzy, speeding, rushing, manic. I
wrote of Maria, the baby innocent, the little girl, her
strong, religiously brain-washed beliefs, her
spirituality, her loving nature, her despicable
weakness, which caused her to be bullied and hurt.
I wrote of Marie, the fallen angel, rejected, forced to
fight, rebel and drug up since Maria had become too
hurt and angry to remain. My life traumas hit the
paper in angry black bullets, smudged in the places
where I gave way to tears. I wrote about them both in
the third person, pushing them away in order to
analyse them. Ann had actually been my inspiration
to write in the first place. Forever taking on the
identity of those I was closest to, I had written a poem

after reading some of hers and now I just couldn't stop.

After my brief period of chemical induced vitality, I had returned to being the timid, eager to please version of myself. Ann overwhelmed me along with my returned addiction. I put up with all her tantrums, of which there were many. I let her have her way on everything for which she repaid me by isolating me from her room and making sure that all the lads 'her' friends sat in there with her. I was grateful the nights she let me in her room and tried hard to be likeable, running to make cups of tea, offering to roll the spliffs, complimenting Ann and all but licking her arse for her. *What had happened to me?* She criticised my wild hair, lack of grooming, my horrendous weight loss - I was about five and a half stone/thirty-five kilos at that time - and whatever else came to her bitchy little mind. She even nicknamed me Mary because some guy I had slept with told everyone I had a hairy Mary although I didn't know this at the time. Thank God for my sister. Teresa – now suffering from a severe case of anorexia - visited regularly now and was my only real friend in the world.

Desperate to escape my own lonely company, I began to spend most evenings sitting downstairs with my neighbour and his friends just to avoid being alone in my bedroom, the lonely girl with no friends. Victor was nice to talk to once you got past his weirdness and strange looks. Tall and skinny with staring blue eyes, black hair, deathly complexion and stooping, jointed walk he was like something out of a dark elemental world.

I stopped taking speed for a few weeks but then I had no energy and couldn't stop eating. I developed a taste for jam on toast with sugary cups of tea and ate loads of it. My skin broke out in the worst case of acne I had ever known. *Come back little teenage spots, all is forgiven.* So sudden! I literally woke up one morning and my face had bright red angry inflamed lumps all over it which hurt physically apart from making me look like a freak and the topical lotion the doctor prescribed did nothing except cause dry patches around the outside of the acne cysts. Victor told me I looked awful and went on to point out that my face was bloated, I was getting a double chin and that I had looked better while I'd still been on the speed. *Well thank you for that!*

Ann moved out at the end of November, into a flat with her boyfriend. To my surprise, (and Ann´s disgust) Ann's friends still came to visit me most evenings. One of them, who I was sleeping with sporadically when the fancy took him, bought this huge dog, a staff cross named Patra that was as tall as me when she stood on her back paws. Somehow, he blagged me into buying her from him. That dog became my best friend.

In the beginning of December, I got my first job as a waitress at The Wimpy, a fast food restaurant. It was cash in hand on top of my dole and I began partaking in a little pleasure once again from my estranged lover. Just one tiny line, just a little lift, only to ensure I did my job quickly and efficiently, just for a little confidence boost to help me make small talk with the customers.

By the time Christmas arrived, I was taking more speed than I ever had before. Every morning I swallowed a big bomb and snorted a few lines, topping up the bombs all day in work, sometimes sniffing a line or two in the staff toilet. I would get home wired, full of pent up energy, walk Patra, clean my flat and then spend the lonely night time freezing cold in my flat that had no heating, nothing to look forward to except work the next day, empty in my white powder desert.

The speed made me over efficient in work at times and once when I was sent to clean the toilets I had to be brought downstairs two hours later, higher than usual on detergent fumes, on a pure mission to get every bit of grime out of the grouting between the tiles. Even then, no one seemed to suspect I was constantly on something.

I started going out on night missions with Patra mostly ending up at my local dealer, Minty's. I liked hanging out in his, he always sorted me extra speed on top of what I bought every day with my daily earnings. If I was wired he would tell me to roll a spliff from his never ending stash and also let me crash there when my body finally exhausted itself, waking me for work in the morning with a coffee and a bomb.

His crazy side kick, Grinch, was always there, wired up, looking out of the third floor flat window onto the busy New Chester Road, watching for government spies. "I know they're watchin' me. Get on to that one, black sierra, F redge, full of bizzies, every night it passes here. Look! Can yer fuckin' believe it? There's the silver one now, unmarked police car. You can see the camera in the aerial. I know the sounds of their engines now, they speak to me." Minty and I would piss ourselves laughing. Poor Grinch he was simply further down the slippery slope than us but it was one and the same.

I ended the year by almost overdosing on Ecstasy and speed at Club Kinetic, a rave club in Stoke, suffering a very near death experience that still didn't serve to teach me anything.

Chapter 26
Doctor Will

January - 1996

I met Will one night while in Minty's. The persona I
first encountered was a comedian who'd had Minty,
me and everyone else in stitches laughing at Grinch
who he was able to take off perfectly. As he'd got up
to leave he had looked almost shy as he asked me if I
would like to go with him to his flat. Minty was
packing up for the night and I hadn't wanted to go
home and be alone so I went back with him to his flat.
He was very courteous and polite, fully into his
second chosen role of the night, that of the polite
English gentleman, as he asked me about my use and
listened, umming and aaing concernedly

"Have you ever injected?"

I shook my head.

"I tried it a couple of weeks back."

"What's it like?"

"You get this rush...it's like, hard to explain. You get
it in your throat." He went over to a cupboard and
pulled out some needles that were still in their
packets.

"Do you want to try?"

Fascinated and having been curious for a while about
injecting speed, I nodded. He got out two spoons,
placed a little powder speed on each and added some
water. He held a lighter under my spoon, burning it
until the speed had dissolved, then, after drew the
concoction into the barrel through a filter, he flicked
the barrel until there were no air bubbles in them
before attaching the spikes.

He got out a little red cord and tightened it round my arm into a tourniquet. The gentleman became a doctor, at home in the medical type environment he had created, from little touches such as the disinfectant smell of the Sterets with which he wiped crook of my arm to the painless yet much feared pin prick accompanied by instructions to tense then relax my arm.

He explained to me that only once the needle was correctly inside a vein it was possible to draw blood into the barrel. I watched the dark trickle of my blood mingle with the pure clarity of the drug before it disappeared into my arm.

"Do you feel it in your throat?"

I shook my head.

"It's 'cos I only put a bit on. I was worried how you'd react. We'll try more next time."

Will accompanied me home, all excellent manners and gentle ways, buying me chocolate and drinks on the way. He was interested in all the shit I chatted to him and even helped me fix my hair with the little plaits I had started putting in the front of it. He gave me another injection for work before kissing my cheek goodbye; such decorum.

That morning I contacted the local syringe exchange as advised by Will who had drilled home the importance of being clean, and the two exchange workers came out to my flat that night armed with yellow NHS bins and hundreds of clean works and Sterets. I was now a registered drug addict.

Feb 1996

Pleasure rushed through my veins and up my throat, taking my breath away, rendering me ecstatic. My breath was infused with the warmth of the hit, so powerful I forgot about the important things of life such as breathing. Euphoria flooded my brain and I felt myself going under. My pulse raced uncontrollably as I gave myself over to this orgasmic intensity.

The rush was unbelievable. It felt as if it would kill me as it took my breath away, choking me and it was a death I wouldn't have minded dying, the exquisite pleasure was so immense.

"Breathe the rush Marie, breathe," Will advised gently yet urgently.

I did as he said, trusting him implicitly, drawing oxygen into my lungs, inhaling deeply and deliberately. He removed the needle and put some tissue on the pin prick. Perversely I found it a huge turn on, the needle he'd put into my arm piercing me in more ways than one. The clear liquid fascinated me as it blended with my blood, the colours fusing together with perfection.

Will seemed mesmerised by the sight too and had taken a few seconds flushing the beautiful contents of the syringe before putting pressure on the plunger to deliver me to heaven. He hit me up perfectly, his needle binding me to him. I felt loved as he looked after me, ensuring I was breathing and dealing with my used needle.

He took my place on the stool in Minty's tiny bathroom. Minty had sorted us some paste, a purified form of speed, uncut and far more potent than the stuff sold on the streets. It wasn't powder; it was solid and sticky. Will was Minty's best mate and got all sorts of freebies and I was his protégée, the first person he'd ever injected which made me feel special.

He was so clean, good looking; nothing like you would expect an intravenous drug user to be. His skin glowed with health. He was well dressed and, at thirty four, was sixteen years my senior. He tightened the tourniquet around his solid tanned bicep and picked up the prepared syringe, tapping out the air bubbles. His pleasure arrived the moment that the needle touched his flesh and he caressed his vein with the sharp flint of steel, prolonging the moment.

I was hypnotised by the whole process. I was racing, getting higher on the rainbows shooting through my mind that actually increased after the hit in contrast to regular speed. Paste was something else. I hadn't experienced anything like it in the couple of weeks I'd been hitting up since meeting Will who now played about with his needle for what seemed like ages, drawing the blood from his arm, pushing it in a little and drawing it out again. The act of injection was his pleasure and he was trying to enhance the initial hit as much as he could.

"Will you're sick mate," laughed Minty, "just get it in for fuck's sake and stop messing round. You and yer fuckin' needle fixation."

I carried on gazing at Will adoringly. He was the epitome of speed; talkative, funny, witty in his varied role plays, confident, intense and dangerous.

After Minty had his hit and we were all chatting bundles of shit, animated and bonded from our shared pleasure ride, Will grabbed me by the hand and pulled me out of the bathroom.

"We're going back to yours," he said urgently, "I'm gonna fuck my slave, hard. You'd like that, wouldn't you?"

I felt shy. Will had always been my older concerned

friend who I trusted to inject me.

"Well?"

"Okay,"

"Okay what?" Cross at my hesitance, he hissed the word master at me.

The sudden perception of his dominating side gave me a thrill, "Yes, Master."

I was rewarded with a sudden kiss on my lips. The second we got out of Minty's borrowed Sierra he dragged me into my building.

"Hurry up you little bitch, get upstairs."

I knew this was part of his role play and it excited me when he lightly slapped my face on the way upstairs to my flat. He threw me back on the bed, kissing me hard while wrenching my trackie bottoms down from my hips. He ragged my top up, then his own, rubbing his bare chest against my naked breasts. He bit my nipples and plunged a finger into my moistness before shoving his hard cock inside me.

I loved being totally overpowered by him and being fucked so hard that I had to stuff the pillow in my mouth to keep me from crying out. He was turned on by my passiveness, responding to it by fucking me ever more aggressively. I was dripping wet. Pleasure rippled through me as I pushed my pelvis upwards to meet his thrusts and I pulled him deeper and deeper inside me.

Sex on a paste hit was amazing.

"Tell me you love me, Marie, you little bitch," he growled.

I told him I loved him over and over until he told me to shut up. Hurt stung the bubble of my buzz as I awaited my next instruction. I was disappointed as none were forth coming. He pulled his jeans back up and put his coat on.

"See you soon, behave yourself. No more hitting up 'til you see me again. Who's your master?"

"You are,"

"No one else touches my wench, okay?"

Despite being disappointed that he was leaving - we both had hours of life left in us - yet thrilled to be called 'his' wench, I grinned my agreement. I heard him outside singing "Maria, Maria, I love you Maria," his use of my parents' name for me making me feel truly loved. I loved him too. I wanted to be just like him.

I had been injecting for about a month when I walked into The Lodge for my first ever appointment with a drug counsellor. My concerned syringe exchange workers had booked me into to see the youth drug worker, standard procedure for under twenty-ones. The only thing that had made me actually keep the appointment was the fact that I thought I may well be able to get a free supply of speed amps from the centre. I had no intention of stopping what I was doing despite the horrible comedowns and tell-tale bruising and punctures all over my arms.

"Marie?"

A man with light brown curly hair stood looking expectantly at me. I nodded slightly and followed him through the door guarded fiercely by the receptionist to a small room with a desk and two chairs. He introduced himself as Terry.

"So, Marie, I see you were referred by Joan and Anne."

Joan and Anne were my syringe exchange workers who came out regularly, armed with huge bright

yellow NHS needle bins, Sterets and literally
hundreds of clean 2.5ml barrels and small spikes.
Although, both in their forties they would whistle and
throw stones at my window to get my attention and
bang on the door as if they were my mates, something
which amused me. They were down to earth as well
as caring and non-judgemental.

Terry began going through some kind of standard
assessment of which I couldn't answer half the
questions.

"How often do you inject? How often do you take
speed, coke, ecstasy, LSD? How often do you smoke
marijuana? Have you tried heroin? How long have
you been taking drugs for? What was the first thing
you took? Do you normally use alone or with
friends?"

The questions were endless.

"I dunno. Every day."

"How many times a day do you inject?"

"Depends."

I didn't want to tell him that I was given loads of
freebies in return for the clean works I supplied from
my flat in case they stopped giving them to me. Most
of my junkie mates didn't want to register with The
Lodge themselves nor did they want the exchange
workers going near their own homes. I couldn't care
less myself; this way I obtained free drugs and didn't
leave myself open to catching diseases such as
Hepatitis B, C or HIV.

"I need to know the amount of speed you inject
regularly in order to determine what help you can be
given."

"Like I said, it depends. If I've just scored, I inject
four, maybe five times daily. Sometimes I'm just

given it. But it's proper strong. Stronger than what most people get. It's paste, pure and solid."

"Hmmm, speed isn't usually very pure at all by the time it gets to street level. And it tends to be powder."

"Well, I know the dealer." I had only ever had paste once.

"Do you inject yourself Marie?"

"Now I do, yeah."

"How did you start injecting? Did someone help you?"

I nodded, unwilling to mention Will's name.

"Can I see your arms?"

I rolled my sleeves up. My skinny white arms were puckered with tiny red marks and also displayed some impressive bruising where I had missed my veins and wasted the hit.

"Your veins are tiny hun, you won't be injecting for long. Has Anne talked to you about rotating your sites?"

"Yeah, she said the same but that if I look after myself then my veins are less likely to collapse."

"Has she spoken to you about using your groin?"

"Eew gross and there's no rush when you do it that way."

"Marie, what's happened to you in your life to make you want to live this way?"

I stared at him blankly. What the hell had my life got to do with it? I just lived for my hit. Because I liked it.

"Nothing."

"Someone, somewhere must have hurt you badly. Eighteen year old girls do not do this to themselves without some reason."

For reasons I could not even begin to comprehend, I

burst into tears. I angrily pulled my arm under my nose and rubbed fiercely at my eyes with my other fist.

"It's okay to cry you know."

Terry waited patiently, until I had got my ridiculous sobbing under control.

"Who hurt you?" he asked gently.

"No one, I mean, my mum I suppose when she kicked me out but I can't remember anything big."

"Marie, lots people have suppressed memory syndrome. Don't worry, it'll come to you. I want you to write a diary. First of all I want to know every time you have a hit or take anything else. Also, it might be an idea to write down any feelings you are having or anything you remember that seems significant."

I nodded, wondering when he was going to talk about alternative drugs for me. When it seemed like he never would I ventured, "Terry, can't you prescribe me anything? Like smack heads get methadone, isn't there anything to give me to get me off the speed?"

He smiled ruefully, "I shouldn't say this, but it would be easier if you *were* on heroin. There are various medicines to replace heroin but speed is different. Also, the damage that speed does to your mind and body is irreversible whereas once a heroin addict's withdrawal is over, his body can return to normal."

I was shocked.

"Really? How is that possible?"

He shrugged, "Heroin itself does no lasting damage to the body or the mind. It's the lifestyle and addiction that affects the user detrimentally. Speed is a harsh chemical; a manmade drug that literally destroys the body. I want to help you Marie, while you're still young and before you do too much damage."

"But what about speed amps?" I persisted. "Surely they could stabilise me and then you could reduce me?" I needed him to give me something, something that would stop the relentless depression, lethargy and exhaustion that took me over when without any supply.

"There's only one man on the Wirral prescribed amps, and he is a special case. Hopefully you will never be at his level."

He told me this man hit coke and speed to his neck and was regularly in and out of the local psychiatric ward. He ended the appointment telling me that he would expect me back the same time the following week, and to bring me with a written diary of my drug and needle use. He also referred me to Response, another organisation for young people in distress that gave food parcels, condoms and clean needles.

I gave Victor his first hit, enjoying the feeling of power, repeating Will's advice about being clean, never sharing anything, not even spoons and always using Sterets. That winter was freezing and the world seemed constantly dark when Will wasn't around and despite his warning, I continued hitting up without him. Crap powder though it was, Victor always had speed and something was better than nothing to hit up. I loved the smell of the sterile packets containing clean works and Sterets that my exchange workers brought me in great quantities. I loved the whole process. I would spend hours out of my face pumping my arms up, tensing them until I could see my veins, washing them obsessively and putting cold bandages on to reduce the marks.

I developed some type of obsessive compulsive

disorder and I began using Dettol in my baths as it reminded me of obsessively clean Will who used Dettol for just about anything. I would get on my hands and knees, scrubbing the kitchen floor with Dettol and bleach, cleaning the same place over and over until my hands were raw.

I had a constant stream of friends throughout this period but the friendships rarely lasted longer than a few weeks. When I'd first started injecting, Claire, a sister of one of the lads I had met through Ann, moved in with me. She also came to work at the Wimpy with me and we would get high together at home although Claire never injected and only used recreationally. As she was well respected in Rock Ferry, certain people like Ann couldn't get away with their derogatory behaviour towards me. Her brother, Paul, was a big man around town too and all the lads looked up to him.

People came flocking round to the flat in Egerton Park every night, dropping acid and smoking weed. I never took acid but I didn't bother to hide the fact that I was injecting from them, although I never did it in front of any of them except for Claire and her best mate Tracy, a girl who really looked up to me, something I really didn't understand. Apparently, she thought I was pretty? *Really? Give me some of what you're on.* She liked my style. I wore little plaits at the front of my hair, sealing the ends with beeswax and putting silver and purple beads on them with tight fitting beanie hats, thinking that I looked ambient and hippy like in a cheeky, attractive way; individual. Claire had shown me the benefits of tinted moisturiser, mascara and how to plump up my lips by dry brushing them with a toothbrush; she had also encouraged me to buy leggings and tight little tops to make the most of my slim figure. Although she sometimes took speed with me, it was just a phase with her. She was a lot more stable and encouraged me to attend my drug counselling appointments. Much to my disgust, she would let Terry in every time he came chasing me because I had failed to turn up. Terry continued encouraging me to explore my past through writing, informing me some of his other cases had remembered repressed memories of being sexually abused. In one case, his client had remembered all her sisters had been abused, except for her, and that had made her feel guilty and also, undesirable. It had affected her as deeply as if she herself had been abused.

He tried all possibilities with me but I remained stuck, desperately wanting to remember the thing I must have blanked out in order to find the key to escape the world into which it had submersed me. He often took me to see his 'success stories' recovered heroin addicts, hoping that would encourage me to turn my life around but I would go home from the appointments and hit ever more speed. The truth was he had no idea how to deal with my speed needle addiction but it wasn't for want of trying. Terry did his best.

As my drug use took its toll I became more irritable. I would snap at Claire and Tracy giving them short moody answers, agitated to the point of blowing a circuit after spending nights repeatedly injecting, yet getting nowhere near the rush I craved on the cheap cut to death powder speed. I felt agitated and irritated inside and out, as my body protested against the abuse to which I repeatedly subjected it. I needed paste. I had only to hit a tiny bit of that and I was up in rainbow land for hours, talking my head off to anyone who would listen, writing crazily, filling books with my cloudy insights.

While at Claire's grandparents' house one Sunday I tried to talk her into robbing money from her Granddad's purse, growing ever more annoyed when she kept hesitating until she put her foot down and said, "Marie, you need to give it up. I can't rob my grandparents. I wouldn't ask you to rob yours."
The next night we sat up planning how to rob the till in work. I swear, we must have gone over the same stupid plan for six hours or more, every time I thought we had it sussed, Claire would double check something and end up going through it all again.
It was a fiasco. We couldn't get it together enough to go through with it. We had both become twitchy, nervous and agitated, making our mission impossible. The managers seemed to know we were up to something and not once did they leave us alone by the till. We gave it up and I was sacked a couple of days later.
Eventually, Claire moved out in to distance herself from me, my moods and my chaotic lifestyle but she stayed in touch and often invited me to her flat, attempting to replace my habit with weed. With her, I enjoyed some mellow stoned escapes from the crazy life I lived but always returned, hopelessly addicted to the hit.
I had no morals by then and initiated a few more to the joys of the needle, getting off on the power trip and pretending I was a female Will. The night Tracy

came to me; she'd been upset about an argument with her ex, the father of her two year old son, and asked me to help her inject herself. Part of me was reluctant but I prepared the works anyway, talking her through it, advising her on the correct way to draw up the melted drug though a clean filter to avoid a dirty hit, something that left its victim with a pounding headache and literally made you feel like you were going to die. I had suffered them a couple of times. Hell wouldn't compare.

I attempted to spike the surface of her arm where a vein was just visible but no blood would go into the syringe.

"Your veins aren't strong enough," I told her, "I can't do it."

"Just try, Marie, please."

Again and again I tried until I was crying, telling her I couldn't do it. I made her promise not to say anything. I actually felt ashamed of myself. The sight of her cherry splattered, paper white skin made me feel sick and I desperately wanted to forget the whole thing. Screw the power thing, I was no Will and I swore to myself I would never attempt anything like this again unless helping other struggling junkie friends with their hits; that was etiquette, intravenous law.

Someone came to warn me Claire had found out what had happened and that she wasn't happy. Despite my seemingly hardened ways, I was still terrified at the thought of physical violence from other girls and was shaking when I opened the door to her. Claire, however, wasn't a bully and told me straight off she wasn't going to hit me but then continued by telling me that she was disgusted with what I'd done as well as disappointed and hurt. A good hiding would have

hurt less than her unhappy eyes glistening with tears as she begged me to get some help before telling me she couldn't have any part of my life anymore. She also advised me to get away from Will and my other junkie mates, telling me they were turning me.
I knew she was right but couldn't break away from them.

Chapter 27
Junkie Life

March/April 1996

Over the next few weeks, The Lodge became a sanctuary for me. I was always greeted like a long lost friend by Anne, Joan and the other workers. They never treated me like a lesser person like so many did and were never too busy to sit down with me and ask how my life was going. On occasions when I had taken way too much speed and was suffering temporary drug induced psychosis in which I would see red laser lights directed at me and be convinced that someone was going to kill me, they would take me in and let me talk my madness out of my system. Other times, I would spend hours in their treatment rooms, crying uncontrollably for hours. Terry prescribed me Prozac but I tried to inject them, convinced that anything that entered my bloodstream though the eye of a needle would make me feel good. Prozac powder wasn't made to be injected and would bubble up on the spoon making it almost impossible to draw up into the syringe but I would draw up as much as I could and force it into my ever willing veins.

I had actually taken Terry's advice regards the writing although I never did manage to give him an exact summary of my drug use, I found myself writing more and more, in a strange format that was a mixture of poetry and a fantasy story, always in the third person about a little girl with long dark hair and a white dress but she was so hazy. I would write and write until I found answers and relief in my words. I kept getting the feeling I was about to grasp at something, some knowledge, some new memory, something I'd repressed like Terry had suggested but never quite got there.

When I wasn't at The Lodge, I was forever looking for my next high. The best times were when Will gave me paste, the worst where when I had to resort to hanging around Victor's who still couldn't hit himself up properly and therefore had to sort me his cut powder, which he sold for Minty, in exchange for my help and clean sterile needles. He usually had the ingredients in for sweet cups of teas too, which I craved when coming down and I used to clean his notoriously filthy kitchen in exchange for hits, drinks and food.

Sometimes, I had no choice but to come down, let my exhausted starving body sleep and when I did this it was like the sleep of the dead. My poor dog Patra would be stuck with me while I could be practically comatose for two days and nights and I would wake to piles of dog shit and pee all over the flat. One time someone managed to break into my flat and rob fifty acid tabs I had hidden under my bed without me waking. Patra was soft with everyone and would have probably begged for some affection as the culprit robbed her mistress. This didn't bode well with Victor to whom they had belonged but he soon forgave me as he had no one else to administer his injections.

I lived for the times when Will and Minty came because their visits always brought with them free paste hits and nights of lust-filled pleasure. I felt important when they sought me out in front of all the Rock Ferry crew who used to look down on me. It was me who was singled out and due to the fact they were infamous in the area I felt like the gangster's moll I had always wanted to be. When they turned up I would just leave whoever was in my flat and go with them.

Sex with Will had a dark edge which tapped into something within I hadn't previously encountered. When I was at his he would take such good care of me. After making me suck his cock, pulling down my knickers and fucking me and playing out his various roles he would make me bathe, order me to eat Weetabix and give me the biggest handful of vitamin tablets you could imagine.

"It's important to look after yourself when you're into doobs," the doctor would advise, doob being his code name for needles.

He had long since abandoned the gentleman persona. When I was there, other girls would call in to get speed. When they'd gone, he would tell me what he liked about sex with them, which ones liked it rough from behind, who sucked cock the best and I had no choice but to swallow it. I had no claim on him but lived for the nights when he was all mine. I hung doggedly onto my perception that we had a bond no one else could break as I was the only girl he had ever hit up.

He would disappear from my life for days then turn up randomly. I regularly spent the night keeping vigils by the window, yearning for him. I honestly thought I was in love with him. The windy nights tricked my over stimulated mind into believing a car was pulling up or there was a stone at my window. Every noise had me running to the window. These vigils became more frequent and intense as I became more obsessive.

"Who's been treating my patient?" he enquired in the professional manner he always adopted for our hypodermic sessions as he rolled up my sleeve one Saturday night.

"No one."

"Really? I think you are lying. Maria, Maria. This isn't good. You have a perfectly good doctor right here."

The way he said my name filled me with both excitement and foreboding. No one but my parents called me Maria but this fact helped further convince me that he cared deeply for me. Little head game on his part. When you are on the amount of stimulants that I was, anything could click. The most random coincidences become meaningful and trick you into believing the most ludicrous things.

"Doctor Will is gonna show you how it's done."

After flushing my blood for a while he slowly pushed the plunger. He watched me as he released it, smiling as I whimpered in reaction the huge swelling appearing in my arm where he was deliberately missing the vein. Apart from being painful, a missed hit didn't bring on any kind of rush. My throat thirsted for the sensation his paste hits usually brought.

"Will..."

"Shh, you have to learn. You should have listened to me," he affirmed calmly, not letting me pull away until every last drop was released.

Will was soon preoccupied in pleasuring himself by playing with the needle in his own vein. When his ritual was over he broke an E in half, placing it on my tongue.

"Thank you, Master," he prompted, looking at me

warningly.

"Thank you, Master," I repeated automatically, nervous as to how this was going to go.

He softened, leaning over to kiss me gently. I responded immediately. I was as addicted to him as I was to the needles. He pushed my head down to his groin, exposing his cock for me to suck and I could smell female scent on him. He told me about another girl, Kirstie.

"She is so fit, Marie, blonde, perfect. Can you smell her, taste her? Tastes good, doesn't she?"

The sickness in the pit of my stomach at his cruel, taunting words prevented me from making a sound.

"Thinks she can do as she likes though," he went on. "Got a boyfriend, the cheeky bitch, won't finish him either. That's why I'm here."

He eased my legs open after removing my leggings.

"And then there's you. Won't do as you're told either. Hitting up behind my back. Who's your Doctor?"

"You are. I'm sorry. I just need it all the time now."

He entered me and laughed, rocking me gently to his rhythm.

"Maria, Maria, queen of the doob. You're the first you know. The first girl I ever introduced to the doob. That makes you special."

I leaned back to encourage him further inside me, my heart flooded with warmth once more. I knew deep down I was special to him and all the Kirsties of the world would never change that.

"I wanna fuck you up the arse. Marie, let me fuck you up the arse."

"No."

He bent his head down to my ear, nuzzling me and kissing me, sending delicious thrills running down the side of my neck.

"Please, it's what I like best. It will make up for disobeying me too."

"No Will, I'm scared. I don't want to."

"I'll be gentle."

He pulled out of my wetness, leaving an unfulfilled sense of longing within me. He turned me over effortlessly and placed the tip of his cock at the opening of my anus.

"Ready?" he whispered, stroking me, caressing me, kissing my ears, showing me more physical affection than he ever had.

"Don't hurt me."

It felt uncomfortable as he slowly twisted himself like to the first inch of my anus but then he thrust himself suddenly as far in as he could, making me scream out in agony. Rip. Tear. Split. Agonising pain rocketed through my entire body. My cries weren't my own; I sounded more like a wild animal as I yelled and screamed out into the night. He laughed in response and put his hand over my mouth as he thrust harder into me.

The horrendous throbbing overwhelmed my entire system until it felt familiar as if I had always known it and that familiarity gave birth to a terrifying thought. Realisation dawned and sudden vile images flashed through my mind. Just as I thought I was about to pass out, he shuddered and came.

I was too weak to speak.

It wasn't only what he'd done to me that temporarily stole my voice from me, it was the realisation, the absolute certainty that this had been done to me before. Suddenly it was clear what Terry had been talking about. I must have been raped anally as a child and completely forgotten it. Although I couldn't actually remember any details of that hideous thing done to the little girl I once was, I knew beyond a doubt that it must have been my Uncle Paul as he was the one who was closest to me as a child. It all made sense; my stimulated and damaged thoughts convinced me over and over again that this was the truth. All that was left for me to do now was to expose my paedo priest uncle for what he really was and then all the bad would fall away from me.

(N.B. –As a child I was never sexually abused by anyone in any way. They were all false memories due to the drugs, the fact I had been looking for an answer and the abuse I really had just suffered at the hands of Will). My Uncle Paul had never been anything but good to me).

Will slunk out of my flat minutes after he had cum and for once I was happy to let him go. My thoughts turned into screwed up words which I spat out on paper, further convincing me into a repressed childhood nightmare memory.

My ordeal of shame wasn't over. The next day, Victor laughed at me in front of not only Minty but all of his friends too, saying I was one dirty skank, that I had sounded like a stuck pig while taking it up the arse from Will and that everyone had heard me.

I was mortified and slammed out of Victor's dirty hovel before they saw me cry. My back passage was in so much discomfort that I could barely walk, I had bled significantly and even just the thought of going for a poo made my cross my legs and breathe in sharply although all of this physical stuff disappeared into the abyss of my newly found knowledge derived from the medium of forced anal sex.

I heard a soft knock at the door. Minty was there, grinning at me, his moustache giving him a definite look of the deceased Freddie Mercury.

"Don't mind Victor, he's a dick. Probably wanted it up the arse himself. Don't cry, hun."

He hugged me and then suddenly he was unzipping his fly, grinning manically at me as he promised me a hit of paste, caught hold of my hair and pushed my head down until I could feel his hardness, warm against my face. Knowing I had no choice and telling myself at least I could get a hit out of it I took him into my mouth. Thank God he didn't smell at least. Being a speed freak, he took meticulous care of himself; we all laughed behind his back about his obsessive eyebrow plucking.

He moved my head up and down so that it was more like a glorified wank, ignoring my tears. He stood looking at me after he came, leaving his disgusting floppy little willy in my mouth and I asked him pathetically for my paste hit.

"Not got none on me love. But here's a fiver, get yerself something nice."

He threw the note on the bed laughing and leaving me alone in my humiliation.

"That's Kirstie, Will's girlfriend," Victor threw me a sly look as he pointed out the pretty, classy looking blonde getting out of the taxi outside Minty's as we pulled up in Victor's battered old mini. She smiled at us as we got out of the car. So she was Will's official girlfriend now?

Will and Minty had both turned up a couple of days after they had hurt me, apologising for what they had done, giving me some weed and advising me, as if they were my best friends, to smoke that and take a break from the speed for a few days. They acted like a couple of older brothers who had played a harmless prank on their little sister. Will had promised he'd never do that to me again and seemed genuinely ashamed. Of course I'd forgiven him; a faithful bitch always forgives her master.

We all went to Garland's in Liverpool that night. After several hits of paste, I had looked fantastic, in my own perception anyway, in cut off denim shorts over black tights and a tight fitting pink top. Kirstie befriended me in the club, offering me some of her own paste.

"Isn't it amazing?" I enthused while swallowing the little bomb - even I wouldn't hit up in a club toilet - "the buzz is proper clean and pure, the hit's fuckin' out of this world and it takes you into another reality." She giggled, swallowed a tiny bomb and told me she'd never hit up and spent the rest of the night dancing with me rather than Will who was really into his buzz that night, doing dance offs with us all.

After the club shut we all went back to Minty's to continue the stimulant party.

"We're like a family," Sophisticated Kirstie was almost childlike in her observation, much to my amusement as she had also entered into the paste zone now despite laughing at my earlier enthusiasm.

On a mission to fuck with my head, Will brought Kirstie to mine about half an hour after I had left Minty's for home.

"That bitch needs putting in her place," he stated, glancing first at me, then Patra who was laid out on the bed in front of me as if she was protecting me from the pair of them who were perched at the top of the bed. *Which bitch?*

"Shall we torture her?" Kirstie drawled, her eyes sparkling and her lips twitching.

"Later. I wanna see you two fuck first."

I felt uncomfortable as they both looked at me expectantly. I cleared my throat nervously, "I'm not a lesbian."

My words were almost inaudible. The combination of the ecstasy along with the amount of speed I had hit and sniffed that night had somehow silenced me and despite the fact I should have been talking for England, my thoughts were locked inside.

"Or you can watch me fuck Kirstie? Unless you're jealous," he laughed.

I couldn't reply, my eyes were darting everywhere, my dry lips pursing and pouting, my face contorting as the stimulants took me to the brink. He continued taunting me, telling me that Kirstie was way fitter than me, leaving me without any sense of self-worth at all. I was literally squirming. Kirstie was this sexy hot girl, real girlfriend material, Will's actual girlfriend and I felt so ugly and naïve and stupid next to her.

"Aww, Will, leave her, she's so innocent," Kirstie smiled at me sympathetically, her voice seeming to carry warmth and genuine affection for me and I forgave her previous words about torturing my dog. After hours of Will's cruel mental abuse, he and Kirstie left, both of them kissing my cheek on their way out. What kind of fucked up shit was that?

To my surprise, a couple of days later, Kirstie turned up, holding out a bar of chocolate and a packet of ciggies telling me she only worked up the road in a nursery and was on her lunch break. She had felt bad about leaving me so skitzed that night. She looked so young and friendly dressed a casual navy blue sports jumper and tracksuit bottoms that it was hard to believe she was that same seductress that she'd appeared to be while with Will.

She began coming round most lunch times. Just turned nineteen, she was five months older than me. Fun, vivacious and generous, she lived at home with her mum and brother. She'd also been an A level drama student albeit only for a couple of months and seemed in control of her drug taking, that's to say she didn't inject and looked really healthy whereas my use showed all over my face in acne and on my arms in tracks. Best of all, she never judged me for being a needle user and took me under her wing. It was a friendship born from strange circumstances but one that was completely genuine on both sides.

At my parent's house – May 1996

"Uncle Paul doesn't want this to carry on but if you continue with it he will have no choice other than taking you to court for slander."

My dad stated this in cold tones that did not hide his anger with me for what he assumed to be a vicious accusation made up of vindictive lies. I had phoned my mum the week before to tell her of my recently awakened memories. However, while that night had so convinced me of the vile acts that had befallen me as a child, to my surprise no solid memories had actually surfaced. I really couldn't remember any occasion of my uncle ever being anything other than loving towards me.

The truth was I too had severe doubts but didn't quite know how to say so. I was desperate to find a reason for my fuck up of a life, locate the key for my drug use, to solve the puzzle Terry had set me. Lots of his clients had uncovered frozen memories of sexual abuse and then got clean easily. I had honed in on that one possibility instead of looking into various other forms of help he had offered me.

"I believe that you believe it," Teresa, now just seventeen, told me emphatically when I asked her what she thought.

Her words were my light bulb moment. What had actually happened with Will was the reality I couldn't deal with and it had rotated on its head inside my tortured wired up mind. Even though I resented the fact that my dad could be so cold, for all he knew it might be true, I finally conceded in a small voice, "I don't think it really happened either."

Nothing further was said that day. Before I left, my mum packed me a bag of food telling me that no matter what, I was still her daughter and although she wouldn't give me money as she knew where it would go, she wouldn't see me starve. *Oh so magnanimous, Mum.* I didn't see until many years later, the enormity of that simple act considering the horrible allegations I'd made.

Teresa was the bridge that kept me in contact with my family at that time. Without her, I believe all contact would have severed completely. She visited me regularly and bought tiny little pieces of weed from me at twice the normal price knowing I needed the money. She brought me food every time she visited, shared her ciggies and often took me round to our parent's house as if to remind them that they had another daughter too.

Chapter 28
Poets

I continued speed writing, disguising my feelings in metaphors. Sometimes, when I was really 'skitzed' as we called the psychotic state of paranoia caused by too many hits and not enough sleep, I would write out my panic, and question God only knows who about my state of mind. This would calm me and within a few hours I would find myself picking up my pen and paper again and answering my previous questions. The writing came through automatically. I can only describe it as a force, something within me. When I read it back I found good advice, wisdom and insights. *Where did they come from?* The energy behind my writing came out as words such as light, insight, ending the night, always in rhymes; it would give me the answers that I had searched for just hours earlier. When I was skitzed, the questions would form, when the drugs were leaving my system, the answers would arrive and I found myself turning to this particular therapy more and more. *All this misery, seemingly in vain, (vein) unspeakable torment, perpetual pain, psychotic thoughts turning her brain, rushing feelings, making her insane*

I even showed these poems to my mum, in an attempt to confide in her my injecting drug use. I wanted to see if she could guess the truth that I was injecting. *But do yer know what I mean, Mum, what I'm trying to tell you?* Puzzled, she replied that she could see a very tortured soul and a rough talent for writing.

I began to write more about the child I had once been, piecing together the poetic tragedy of the innocent making her first communion in a little white dress at the age of four. I told Terry that I could only write like this when I was high, again putting forward my case for injectable speed amps. *But I need them Terry, I'm on paste, not just speed, my problem needs meds, my problems are worse than the rest.* I knew I almost had him convinced to prescribe me the amps but he kept with his excuses was that I was so young and that apparently for me there was a chance of recovery although I couldn't see it myself. Without speed, I was unable to function mentally or physically for sheer exhaustion.

My junkie lifestyle saw me deteriorate in every way. The men who hung around our flats would flip out sometimes, a result of too much speed and use me as their punch bag. I had none of my care kid fight left and my body was so weak and underweight that I couldn't have defended myself had I tried. Will was also becoming an abusive nightmare.

He turned up at my flat while I had a male friend there and punished me violently, bursting in after having been tipped off by Victor that I had this guy in my flat. His energy lit up the place, eyes blazing around the room, taking in every detail, chippy wrappers, rizlas, weed, scorching every offending item in their wake.

"Nice and cosy here hey Marie?" He seemed so polite until he kicked Patra off the bed, calling me minging dirty junkie scum.

"Dogs DO NOT sleep on beds. It's a fucking disgrace in here, Marie. Marie the Minger," he laughed at his own wit.

He ignored the lad in question apart from reminding him he had a girlfriend already and telling him I was a minger, continuing to humiliate me verbally and

physically, kicking me, throwing the table over and
sweeping all my things off the dresser onto the floor.
Then, after another kick to my shin, he went to leave
and politely said goodbye, like nothing had happened.
"Where's your MANNERS?" He bounced back into
my face when I didn't reply, too busy choking my
fear and humiliation back down. "When someone
says goodbye, you say goodbye properly. Did your
mother never teach you anything?"

He employed his headmaster's tone of voice. "And
now you will say goodbye when I say goodbye.
Understand me?"

"Answer me!" He exploded when I didn't speak. He
spat in my face and kicked me again. *Move over
headmaster, the maniac is back.*

Finally I managed, "Goodbye, Will."

"Goodbye, Maria. I am just trying to teach you some
manners. It's for your own good."

It hit me that again he had called me Maria, while
'telling me off' just like my parents. It made me think
that maybe he was right, that I had no manners, that I
deserved his crap, that if I had listened to my parents
when I was a child then I wouldn't be here in this
mess. That maybe I was lucky to have him; that he
could teach me the lessons I had refused to learn as a
child. My thinking turned on its head as I convinced
myself once again, that he was in my life for good
reason.

Kirstie and I grew closer and I looked forward to her
lunch time visits. At night, we would walk endlessly
round the streets; our fast pace and furtive movements
drawing attention from drivers who would slow down
and stare. *Government spies.* We witnessed suspicious

things such as random BT vans parking outside my house while they pretended to work in one of the houses. *Undercover police.* A bit extreme, all we did was break into cars and rob tapes and small change for chocolate. We would shout at the cars, 'we're fuckin' onto you' wondering why the drivers always stared so much at us. Sometimes we would crack up laughing at each other's huge dark eyes, freaked out and terrified, hysterical to the point we would sometimes wet ourselves. I would walk her home to her mum's when dawn was breaking and she would sneak out biscuits and chocolate cereals for me to take home.

Kirstie introduced me to various new people. Barry was an older man in his forties. He often invited us round to his and invited us to help ourselves to chocolate biscuits, tea and cigarettes. His place was a comforting haven where I could escape to when the madness of my flat became too much. Barry always made lewd comments but we would laugh at him and call him a porn star, ripping him for his moustache that could have been straight off a porn movie. He was harmless though and we spent many evenings chilling there.

Kirstie was light hearted and fun loving by nature and got me to see the funny side of myself. She would laugh at my facial contortions such as my speed induced mannerisms, my most notorious being my top lip pursing and sticking out when I was skitzing. She would mimic me and call me moody, not in the least intimidated by my moods. Kirstie reminded me how to laugh.

Kim was twenty-two; tall and slim with short cropped blonde hair she had a polished, classy look. Not a trace of the junkie she had just become appeared on her face. Kirstie thought a lot of her and always said we should meet as we had a lot in common with the needles, Will and his apparent control over us and our weird poetry writing.

Apparently Kim was jealous of me as I had been the first girl Will had introduced to the needle, something which I understood as I would have felt the same if the situation had been reversed. She turned up at mine randomly one day demanding to see Will. When I told her I hadn't seen him, she came in and offered me a hit of her speed.

Kim and I bonded over that first hit *Speed - bringing enemies closer* and I started going to down to her flat which was in a huge tower block in Birkenhead. Kirstie sort of faded into the background for a while. We spent days just hitting up and hitting up, relentlessly pumping our aching veins to the limit. She had house bricks of speed in her fridge, supplied by her dad, a known dealer, for her to sell. I went to Response, which was just around the corner, daily to exchange and obtain clean works, such a responsible little drug user.

Kim and I would write poem after poem, comparing the prose and the many possible subliminal messages contained within. We could guess each other's inner most feelings and fears; crack the code. Delighted she could work out my twisted words and thought processes, I gave her everything, something which I later realised was the way she was able to manipulate me.

The first time I slept with Will again since meeting Kirstie and Kim was in Kim's flat, in her bed, while she was in hospital suffering a suspected miscarriage of Will's baby. I'd been with her at the family planning clinic when her test had showed positive a week earlier. Kim had continued hitting up even though I knew she wanted that baby, felt it was a connection between her and Will.

She never admitted her own desperation where he was concerned, always tried to make out she was playing him as well as he played her but I saw the anguish in her face, however well masked, when he was with Kirstie, could read in her poems the pain and confusion which reflected mine exactly. If Kim didn't want me to understand her she should never have let me read her prose, I understood messed up prose better than Enid Blyton stories.

I set about cleaning her kitchen once she had left for the hospital and then Will buzzed up. I prayed he wasn't in an abusive mood, the last time I'd seen him hadn't been nice.

"Where is she then?" he asked after kissing me on the cheek, the gentleman was back.

I told him what was happening.

"I knew she'd miscarry, all those doobs. But come on Marie, d' you even think she's really pregnant?"

"Well yeah. I was with her when she did the test."

"You can fake them you know." *Can you?*

Will perched himself on a work top, watching me clean for a while.

"Come and clean Kim's room with me," he ordered.

I hesitated, recognising the intensity in his eyes.

"Come on Marie, when was the last time we had together?"

Kirstie, Kim, me, the power of three, Will's mini harem? It was all so fucked up.

"I want you so much, Marie, you little bitch. You've

been driving me insane with your snotty looks and bad manners, sucking up to Kirstie and Kim and forgetting about your Master."

I wanted him too, not physically but emotionally I craved him; his affection and dirty sex was much more preferable to his verbal taunts and violent outbursts but the problem was I loved Kim like a big sister and knew she would hate me for this. She also funded my habit.

"Will, we shouldn't, "I protested feebly.

He had coaxed me into the bedroom by now and was pulling his jeans off.

"Shh," he put his fingers to my lips.

"Will, no. Kim, the baby. And Kirstie too."

"So loyal," he laughed, "they aren't be so loyal to you."

He pulled me down on to the bed and close to him as he determinedly eased my top off. I didn't put up much resistance because deep down he was fulfilling desires I had run from for weeks. He pulled his own jumper over his head and thrust my face to his chest urging me to suck his nipples.

"I want you, you little slut, "he breathed as he pulled my knickers down over my hips. "Open your legs. Don't make me force you."

He was so affectionate, so loving in the way he stroked my hair and ran his hands up my back. I was weakening despite the guilt that was eating me up as I thought of Kim. I wasn't as concerned for Kirstie as I knew she just wouldn't have been bothered.

He laughed as he eased himself into a position that granted him access. The tip of his cock slid around my treacherous clitoris, which, despite my guilty conscience and outward refusal of him was wet and pulsating almost painfully. I tried weakly to push him off and whispered "no, please don't," knowing it was no use, that he would take me now, no matter what. I breathed in sharply as I felt him move inside me, automatically parting my legs and arching my back up to him as my unfaithful body welcomed him home. He moved slowly, in and out, prolonging my pleasure for once.

"So young," he breathed, "so small," he stopped and looked at me, "so soft," another pause, "so lovely," he pulled me close to him then and fucked me quickly but softly, his pace getting more rapid as he worked his way to his own release.

"Only thirteen," I thought I heard him say as his thrusts got more frantic.

"Tell me how old you are," he whispered into my ear as he forced himself to slow down.

I was puzzled. "Eighteen."

"No, thirteen. Tell me you're thirteen."

I nodded, lost in his sexual affection. As he came, my mind was racing. Did he know my horrible experience of losing my innocence at thirteen? Had he connected that much to me? Was that what the so young, small, soft and lovely was about? Him realising my vulnerability, wanting to take away that pain by re-enacting a forced incident of sex, yet with so much affection and pleasure, gentleness and love. Had he intended to heal me of the first time?

I was so twisted up within my amphetamine riddled mind that I had no idea I had probably just fulfilled a sick fantasy of his that had nothing to do with me or my past and everything to do with him and his unhealthy interest in young innocent girls. For me, I could only think of his soft words, his gentle touch, his apparent need of me so strong he couldn't take no for an answer.

"Will, please don't tell Kim, she'll hate me for this," I pleaded.

He laughed, "She won't find out, well not from me anyway." His eyes said otherwise as they swivelled round her bedroom.

After he'd gone, my conscience screamed at me. How could I have done that knowing she was probably losing his baby? My mind had said no but my body had screamed yes. Part of me wanted to own up to her, the other knew I'd never say a word. I spent hours writing my guilt out into evil fairy-tale style poetry and metaphoric twisted prose

Kim returned the next day, cold, withdrawn and in denial of any pain caused by the loss of her unborn. I was eaten up with guilt about what I had done and also of the feelings I harboured for Will, feelings I knew would incur her jealousy, anger and sense of betrayal if only she knew. After that incident, I continued to spend most of my time with Kim. Our lives were spent injecting and writing. Another hit, another poem. Rush, write, analyse. Whacked out poems and prose. Speed rush, throat burn, pleasure and paranoia. Why are my veins disappearing?

Kim was obsessed with the head games she believed that people played. Her poems often contained the words manipulation, intimidation, corruption. It seemed everyone was playing a game, especially Will. My own Will-influenced poems were incoherent ramblings desperate to understand him, and in doing so, maybe myself. Influenced by my religious upbringing, my poetry was filled with analogies of

God and Satan, the fight of the dark against the light, the good and bad, the pure and the wicked, the tyrant and his victim.

I was convinced Kim suspected what had taken place with Will and me that night. She started playing Alanis Morrissette's 'Do you forgive me love?' endlessly and urged me to listen to the words which said things like, 'do you forgive me love, when I laid in your bed?' watching my face closely for a reaction. She made comments about always finding my hairs everywhere, saying I should let her cut my hair which was wild, frizzy and out of control. I wondered if she'd actually found my hair in her bed, or something damning, maybe that's what the gleam in Will's eyes had been about when he had said she wouldn't find out from him. She often said her motto was to keep friends close, enemies closer and I wondered if she meant me. My mind was ever alert, racing and paranoid.

My desperation for needles was really showing; insults wherever I went, junkie bitch, ugly slut, skitzo, dirty speed freak. I also found that while when alone with me, Kim was the best friend ever but in front of others she would distance herself from me and become all superior and bossy, treating me like an embarrassing child. I tried harder to be a good friend to Kim, to make up to her without her knowing what I had done. I cleaned her flat regularly, went to the shops for her, listened to her and found empathy with everything she said.

My mind became filled with my new knowledge about head workers and head games I began viewing everyone as if they had an agenda, a secret mission to destroy me, to take me down, make me crack. I would go for days too scared to drink tap water in case the government had put something in it. By now I could eat while speeding, such was my tolerance but my paranoid thoughts wound me up so tight that I jerked constantly and couldn't eat for nerves and for fear of being poisoned. Kim was annoyed when I told her these irrational fears, which made me even more paranoid. *What is she annoyed about? Is she guilty of something? Annoyed cos I got on to her plan?* That particular psychosis left me once I had a much needed three day sleep of the dead.

Victor was missing - no one had seen him for two days. Kim´s supply was out and we went on a mission, rooting his flat, in all the drawers, cupboards and behind the couches. We lifted the carpets, all the while both of us seeing mirages in the desert, our desire for speed manifested so strongly that we kept seeing it everywhere. I often did this when I had been up for too long, bending down regularly on the stairs of our flats every time I saw a bit of white paper or discarded chewing gum. Rooting was typical amongst speed freaks, addictive, manic, obsessive searching for nothing.

I was jumpy; imagining every bang outside in the wind was him returning. Eventually my guilt got the better of me, or maybe it was my paranoia and I persuaded Kim to give it up. Will came round that night and laughingly asked us if we'd seen Victor. He knew of our rooting and of Victor's disappearance. Had he been watching? I knew he spied on me at times as he always hinted at things I'd done. I remembered him telling me that he had sent people in to The Wimpy to track me and see how I'd reacted to my first hit.

When we told Will we hadn't seen Victor for a couple of days he smiled mysteriously then got out his speed and shared it with us, more stimulants sending my paranoia into overdrive. The next day Victor came back. His eyes flashed angrily as he told us Will had kept him prisoner in his flat and made him clean the floors with a toothbrush.

Later that day when Kim had gone, Victor came up to my flat and banged loudly on the door.

He was off his head, his eyes scarily huge as he told me he had a gun and that he was going to throw every last bit of shit out of my flat and then blow my head off. I was terrified and managed to shut the door in his face. I really believed he would shoot me as he looked well skitzed and in that zone one could do anything. I hadn't slept for days and felt like I was in the middle of a horror movie.

"He won't do anything," Teresa reassured me when she visited that day. "He's all talk."

Why couldn't she feel my fear? This was real. That night I slept restlessly. Harsh comedown, wired, hungry, craving ciggies and drugs, I felt wretched although the ferocity of my comedown had taken the paranoia off Victor's threats and I didn't feel so scared. There was a soft knocking on my door about four am.

"Marie," I heard Will call softly.

He got into bed with me and pretty soon I was sucking his dick, comforted by having him in my bed. I slept easily as he held me tenderly, a baby in his arms.

Chapter 29
Paranoia Amplified

June 1996

I moved to a nicer part of Rock Ferry. My parents actually let me have some of my withheld inheritance money from my grandad for the deposit. Kim fell out with me because she had wanted me to move to Birkenhead with her but my speed enlightened brain had seen another side to her and knew it would be like living with Ann all over again. Kirstie, who I had made friends with again after she had fucked Will in my kitchen and broken the sink, and I would spend hours looking out of the window at the church opposite, convinced *they* had planted cameras. BT, Manweb Electricity, North West Water; no one was who they appeared to be.

Kim declared an invisible war on me. She was now hanging round with a crew of sixteen year old joyriders sorting them with speed to ensure their loyalty. She wrote me poems, cursing me in hidden codes, her deep hatred camouflaged behind well-chosen prose. My regular injections kept me well on to her.

I started pretending I wasn't in when she came then I would spend the night furtively listening for her return. When I did let her in there was always some plan, some agenda to her visits and the lads with her would rob stuff out of the shared kitchen and dining area, which belonged to the three men who lived downstairs and run around really loudly disturbing the other tenants who complained to the landlord.

I would start to hate her but as soon as she wrote me a coded poem and presented it to me like it was part of the mystery of her enigma, or made me a new tape filled with Tori Amos, Kate Bush or Alanis Morrissette that seemed to carry hidden messages for me, I was ready to forgive her, believing that at last she had decided to return to being my wise and caring friend.

Kim became my psychosis.

I felt her presence everywhere, the cat creeping up on the mouse. Every night, while out and about, wherever I was, I would see her face laughing at me. I felt often I was in the portal between our world and hell and literally ran from trees and bushes, sure they could reach out their devil arm branches and transport me to hell. She was the devil's wife, a white witch turned bad, dark queen of the underworld. I was losing my mind, my grip on reality but I couldn't stop injecting.

After she got her younger sister to punch me in the face one night on some teenage trumped up accusation about a dirty look, I never let her in my bedsit again.

Kirstie and I became closer and closer, confiding our innermost secrets to one another. With Kirstie, I could be open and honest and her with me. I even admitted to her how scared I used to be of girls my own age and how I was terrified of fighting. This was something no one admitted in Rock Ferry and Kirstie just loved me even more for it, telling me it was okay not to be a fighter.

She introduced me to Fleetwood Mac and I fell in love with the song Rhiannon, captivated by the welsh witch who was strong, wild and beautiful, didn't suffer fools and was illusive to men. I played it repeatedly, much to Kirstie´s amusement, Stevie Nicks´ lyrics touching me profoundly.

Kirstie even invited me to Alton Towers with her dad and step mum. We took loads of photos of us posing in the grounds, Kirstie, ever sexy, with a red rose between her teeth, me forever in a denim dress and black boots, frizzy hair everywhere. Later, I thought of this day whenever I listened to the Trainspotting CD's 'Perfect Day.' That was a lovely escape from the madness.

Back in Rock Ferry our speed habits got worse and we made lots of equally paranoid friends who all told us of their various theories about the undercover spies that stalked us. Microphones in the pipes, hidden cameras in the lights, microscopic robots that only became visible to human eyes when the veil was lifted by our mind enhancing drug. We would listen by the pipes, stare at the lights and tell the cameras we were onto them. Then there were my other conspiracy theories, the religious ones totally backed up by this crazy witch girl whose body would contort shockingly as she took on her various tarot personalities and tell me I wasn´t who I pretended to be. Her face and voice would take on the person she was with while she told them she was a high priestess. She ended up in Clatterbridge psych ward very soon after we met and she accused this fat old guy of raping her while she was out of her face on speed.

Fat Tim, an extremely overweight bearded man in his fifties with white hair who was as addicted to speed as we were and who spent his days rooting the tips for whatever valuable items he could find, would have been very capable of it too. He was the type your mother warns you against as a child; speed and hot cooked meals while on a comedown were his offered sweets and I had seen the way he fed the crazy witch girl speed knowing it made her manic and then proceeded to play little head games with her.

Sept 1996

More trouble with Kim came my way when Adam, a recent boyfriend of hers, turned up at mine after having bored of Kim and her stupid games. A dark-haired man of twenty three, with large hypnotic blue eyes, magnified more by his pale complexion. I liked him instantly for the charming, funny guy he was. The first night he hung out with us, he talked incessantly for hours, convincing us all that he had twenty grand and two kilos of coke stashed in some flat in Liverpool that he would bring the next day; we never saw any of it.

That night he first came we all went out on a midnight walk. The moon was full, bright in the sky and it had cast a magical glow on my world. I saw glimpses of a future where Adam and I were together, running in fields, free from the oppression of the drugs and Rock Ferry. It's like I knew that I would marry him years later.

I spent the next day with him just hanging out with him and it was great until Kirstie turned up and Adam switched all his attention on to her. When she left to go home for her tea, he walked her down the stairs and when he came back up, he bragged of how he'd kissed her. I hid my feelings, obviously he would like Kirstie better than me, everyone did, but I'd thought we may have had something.

Later, when I was rushing off a massive hit, Kim

turned up; her fury made manifest in the winds howling that night as she banged the doors and threw stones at my window. I was irrationally fearful of what she would do, knowing she'd come because Adam had dumped her and that she would blame me as her spies had probably told her that I was the one who had been with him all day. Another wired up paranoid night.

When I went outside the next day, I panicked every time a car went past in case it was her. I imagined seeing her everywhere I went or her lying in wait for me when I returned home. I don't know exactly what it was I was so scared of but my fear of her had blown up to unrealistic drug induced psychotic proportions and she had become the epitome of evil. She even got one of her little joyriders to spike Patra with an E which I took as a personal threat with a sinister message for me instead of seeing it for exactly what it was, a not so harmless prank. Although she was, in reality, doing her best to cause trouble, my fearful reactions and obsessive thoughts about her mind games were well out of proportion to what she was doing. *Undiagnosed Borderline meet drug-induced psychosis at its highest level.*

After Adam had switched sides she was like the proverbial woman scorned and began breaking into neighbours' cars, damaging the property and getting her lads to hang around outside intimidating the men who also lived in the building I lived in. Eventually the landlord, fed up with all the complaints, gave me a week's notice to get out of the premises. *Mission accomplished Kim.*

October 1996

I ended up homeless for three and a half weeks. I stayed here there and everywhere, sleeping on the couch of whoever would have me until Will invited me to stay at his flat for a few days on the condition I brought my telly and video. My stuff was all in some girl's shed and we wasted no time collecting it. I was elated at the thought of living in Will's; his violence towards me had subsided completely in the last few weeks and he had been really sweet to me one night when I had been ill with a fever. Will had his own agenda though and the first night that I was there, he tried to sell me to Little Billy, the local drug dealer's son, in an exchange for a hit of coke. I refused to let Little Billy anywhere near me and ran back to Will's who threatened me with a slap if I didn't shut up about it. I lasted in his for about a week before he threw me out, keeping my telly and video which he later sold. I still loved him and hung on desperately for him to come and make me his once again.

Chapter 30
A Little Family Support

Winter 1996

My sister and I found a house to share. Our parents, amazingly enough granted her a six week trial of independence and sanctioned out a little more of my withheld inheritance from my granddad for my half of the deposit.

At first it was exciting moving into a flat with my sister. The landlord seemed a pleasant man - before we moved in that was. On finding there was no heating whatsoever we waited for two weeks for him to provide us with one portable gas fire for the front room which soon became our bedroom, front room and dining room due to the freezing conditions in the rest of the flat. It was colder inside than outside that winter.

To get a bath was an all-day affair as someone had to make sure the emersion heater stayed lit for an hour before we ran the water, no easy feat when there was a hole in the wall right by the flame through which we could see into the street. The landlord didn't care and as our housing benefit was late coming through he threatened us with eviction so in the end we just put up and shut up.

Teresa, who now attended Sixth Form College and was studying psychology had begun dabbling with speed by this time too but her extreme skinniness was caused by her anorexia. We spoke at length while under the influence, of our childhoods and the possible reasons for my prolific drug use and her eating disorder. It was a common ground between us and helped us understand each other.

However, I was so vile to her at times that she only lasted living with me for three weeks. Apart from using all her stuff regularly as if it was my right, I made her buy what we needed to survive when I'd run out of my giro money. She had a little part time job at a chippy in Wallasey and often handed me part of her wages despite me having no rights to them whatsoever. Bath bombs, Body Shop soaps, fruity shampoos and lip balms, I took my pick, delighting in her luxuries. I saw the elegant tartan trousers and A-line above the knee dresses she favoured as nice extensions to my wardrobe.

I had no respect for the fact they were her belongings but at the time I didn't see that. I think part of it was that I saw all her possessions as things that resembled the huge difference in our lives. She had never been in care or disowned or left on the streets by our parents, she had everything I didn't so I saw it as my right to use what I wanted. I was jealous but didn't realise it.

For her part, she was so relieved to be away from Mum and Dad and their religious regime, which had worsened by far since the days I had lived there that she rarely complained to me about my awful behaviour. The only times she ever got annoyed were when Patra got in the fridge and ate her chocolate Nutella, licking the jar clean out.

My paranoia, coupled with Will's head games where he would flirt with Teresa all the while checking for my reactions had me convinced that something was going on with them. I felt I had two personalities sometimes. When Teresa wasn't there, I would hear her voice speaking, then Will's, like they were downstairs. I would pace the flat like a caged animal yelling, "I can fuckin' hear yers," while stamping my feet on the floor. The voices would stop but then they would start their plotting again. I never could make out exactly what they were saying but I heard my name mentioned many times by both of them, followed by Will's cruel laughter.

I was convinced they were having an affair in the downstairs flat and spent a lot of time during the day while Teresa was out with my ear to the floor, even going downstairs to knock on the door. The neighbour, eighteen year old Frankie, must have thought I was nuts when he answered the door to me with my wild hair and huge dilated eyes, asking him knowingly if he'd seen Will or my sister. The fact he looked a little freaked out further convinced me he was in on it. When Teresa came home though, I would forget my suspicions and see her as my lovely sister, only to have the bad thoughts return the moment she was out of sight.

One night I came back from Will's and knocked on the front door for twenty minutes; no answer although I knew Teresa was in due to the mortis key being in the lock. After finally splitting one of the panels open with a hammer I borrowed from Frankie and opening the door from the inside, I ran upstairs. Enraged, I ran over to her and began pounding her in the head with my fists. She woke up screaming and terrified.

"How could you not hear?" I screamed in her face absolutely out of control, "How could you not have? I had to hammer the door in. I know you're up to something with Will you little slag. This is proof."

How I figured it was proof when I had just left Will's and there was no way he could have been there, I do not know but at the time this fact was irrefutable in my speed soaked brain. I was full of remorse the next day and kept apologising but she froze me out and went home to our parents for a couple of days. I had no remorse, simply jealousy that she had that luxury whereas I was never allowed to stay over. I was sure she would tell our parents what had happened and that they would all be talking about me, the shame of the family, the devil's child, the schizo.

A few days later Teresa and I fell out again, both of us on raging comedowns without smokes, food or even the ingredients needed for a cup of tea. This time she fought back and we absolutely trashed the flat during the scrap which went on for hours. The rage was like it had been when we'd been children, transported back in time, ineffectual fists flying, desperate hair pulling and biting.

Finally exhausted, we had managed to make a roll up between us from the remnants of an ashtray and I was screaming at her to find a match to light it, when someone knocked on the door. Mortified we looked at each other, praying no one had heard the wild animals we had resembled moments earlier. Adam, now Kirstie's official boyfriend, was amused as he said he'd heard someone calling for the police as there was a terrible fight going on. United again now in our desperation for him not to know it was us we looked at him wide eyed, pretending we had no idea what he was talking about.

Sick of my mood swings, assaults and constant talk about the numerous taxis which were stalking me and doing undercover surveillance on the flat, Teresa moved out shortly afterwards and got herself a bedsit near Wallasey Promenade.

Life got more miserable after she left. The flat was so cold I had forgotten what warmth was. I had to sleep fully dressed under piles of quilts and rarely had money to buy a new gas bottle. I read dozens of Sweet Valley High University books which Teresa had left in her hurry to get away from me, books which were aimed at younger teenagers but I read them avidly. The secret groups and sinister happenings in the underground of the university reflected the conspiracy theories ever-present in my mind. Everything I read seemed to have been designed solely for me to read at that time in my life, be it Paul Milton's Paradise Lost, or Sweet Valley High. I read meaning into everything.

I alternated reading with sleeping during long days of forced abstinence. Then Giro Day would come and I would enthusiastically bathe and clean up, oblivious to the cold with chemical warmth lighting me up. Will started visiting again, seeking me out to cash his giro with him and sorting me whenever he had anything. He told me he felt responsible for getting me to end my needle use and put us both on a needle detox; swallowing copious amounts of speed bombs instead, our replacement; methadone to a heroin addict trying to get clean. For a few weeks, we were constantly together, not sleeping together but enjoying each other's company. With speed addled minds we would stare at the North Star convinced it was a satellite, planted there to watch us all.

Will opened up to me a lot during this time, telling me about his own past, enabling me to understand his moods, his violence and his hang ups about cleanliness. His dad had regularly battered his mum and would send the kids out shoplifting for food as he drank all the housekeeping money. If they got caught they would also be in for a beating. He told me that he was always the dirty kid in the class, bullied for being a tramp and I felt his pain so acutely it convinced me I was in love with him all over again. Sometimes he would appear to be like a little boy, lost, scared and confused, at other times he would seem powerful, evil and I could see two separate personalities fighting for domination of his mind as his face contorted visibly. It was wise to get out of his way when he was like that as his mind's eye could flip me in an instant to being the cause of all his anguish, resulting in another terrifying violent episode. I adored him shamelessly; convinced I could help him, I excused everything he did, blaming his past for his present behaviour.

Kim turned up out of the blue telling me she missed me. She casually commented on the rumours I was seeing Will officially, surprising me with her compassionate smile and saying she didn't mind as she now had a boyfriend in the North End. I didn't trust her at first but after a few poems and an invite to Macdonald's, we were hitting speed several times a day, bonding anew through our shared self-abuse. *Hit, rush, poem, blood spill, burst vein, bruises and tracks, guilt;* insanity taking over my written words, the nightmare was more intense this time round.

Adam had been getting his giros sent to my house and one day it came when he and Kirstie owed me a tenner which I urgently needed to get dog food, ciggies and milk. After two days of trying to get in touch, I signed the giro over to myself and cashed it, taking the tenner that was mine and putting the rest to one side and not touching it.

The next day, Adam turned up, Will in tow, demanding his money and accusing me of having robbed it. I threw the money at him, all there minus my tenner, and furiously shouted that I had been trying to call him and Kirstie for days and I had cashed it just to get the money they owed me as Patra was starving. Suddenly, Will, tongue between teeth, slapped me round the head several times. He then picked up the hexagon glass top of my coffee table given to me by Fat Tim, a present from his tip rooting, and threw it at me, followed by the metal base. I ducked, protecting my head with my arms. "Will," I cried out as he picked up a hammer, incidentally the one I had used to smash in the door panel before attacking my sister, albeit not with the hammer. *Come back Dad with your controlled childhood chastisements.* Bruises splattered my arms and legs for days afterwards. Nothing broken, still alive, face intact: Breathe the Will rush, Marie.

Mentally and physically battered; depression caused by lack of stimulants wore me out - Kim had accompanied Will to his after the hammer episode and not come back. I yearned for some affection, a mother's warmth, sweet tea like my dad used to make me. I had never felt so alone. I couldn't stay there in that house, round those people anymore. The dark night of the soul lasted for days.

For the first time in months I thought of my Uncle Paul, of how close we'd been and how much I missed him. I wished I hadn't accused him of that awful twisted abuse and decided to get in touch and try to explain to him that I was sorry and explain that it was the drugs which had convinced me that the horrors inside my mind were real. My Uncle Dom arranged for my Uncle Paul to go there so we could talk; a safe place given my horrific allegations.

I woke the morning of the scheduled visit with some sense of purpose, more positive than I had been in years. I hadn't seen Will or Kim for a week and I'd had time to clear my head a little and free myself from the hold of manipulators and their spiked offerings containing the opposite of peace.

I apologised to my Uncle Paul and he forgave me instantly but told me it would take a while to repair the trust and he wasn't comfortable being alone with me for the time being. He told me how hurt he'd been and reminded me painfully of how close we'd been before I'd turned; 'went funny' was how he put it. He also told me gently that people would be more likely to help me if I showed willing in helping myself, but that the world would turn its back on me if I made no effort.

His words switched a light on in my brain and I told him excitedly that he made sense, feeling once again like the innocent child who had avidly listened to his every word. It hurt that he wouldn't be able to trust me but I knew I had caused that and was determined that one day he would trust me again and love me again he once had. He told me he had always loved me, very dearly, but that I'd pushed him away. We agreed to begin rebuilding our relationship.

The next day I enlisted my dad's help to come and see a flat in Wallasey with me, time to get out of Rock ferry. I moved there just before Christmas full of good intentions.

Despite spending all of Christmas drug free, by New Year's Eve I had relapsed, back in New Ferry with Kim in her new flat. She had made me an offer I couldn't refuse when she told me concernedly that she would take me in hand once and for all, help me become sophisticated, educate me on the ways of the world. I hadn't heard of the term guru but that is what I yearned for and what she wanted to be. Her education of me started and finished with her shagging every lad who showed an interest in me, this was for my own good she explained, and buying a Tori Amos tape and telling me to really listen to the lyrics. I homed in on Crucify Myself, how very fitting.

For those couple of months, I hit up so much I almost lost my veins. I constantly had track marks and acne fired up my skin with clusters of angry pustules and big painful red lumps. I would try and deal with this by using Dettol on my face, even bathing in the stuff as I felt dirty and unclean. I bathed as often as I could but never used make up or styled my hair and eventually I let Kim cut it into a short and very ugly bob.

She also talked me into giving Patra up after agreeing with Will my dog was "holding me back. *My surrogate parents*. Poor, hungry, skinny Patra, although I would buy her food before I fed myself, her food never came before the drugs I needed. I loved her but was a terrible dog owner and even I could see she deserved better. I let her go to a young hippy guy who had a farm in Wales. Saying goodbye to that big faithful dog was so hard for me but at last she escaped starvation, neglect and the madness of my mood swings and lifestyle which included no freedom to run anywhere when I was comatose from my many comedowns. I had loved her but not enough to be able to care for her properly.

We got worse than we'd ever been; careless, unclean, often running out of needles and having to resort to getting them back out of the big yellow sharps bin and boiling them before using again. They would get blunt and we would have to stab our flesh several times to successfully hit a vein. The bin stank of stale blood and made me balk but the need was so great that we couldn't wait until we got to the chemist to do an exchange and Kim didn't want workers from The Lodge calling round and bringing her house on top. The self-disgust would disappear as soon as the heat hit my throat and I had another Dettol bath.

Will took to calling me Marie the Minger in addition to other pleasantries, Toxic Waste, Scummy Bitch, Spotty Minger, Custard Cream Face "You were born to be abused Marie, born to be abused." Sometimes he would make me repeat the fact I was born to be abused. *Yes, Will, I was born to be bused.*

He would turn up in the middle of the night, sometimes kicking me awake from where I slept on a mattress on Kim's bedroom floor, spitting at me, insulting me, booting me hard, knowing I had no way of defending myself against him. He would call me a tramp for sleeping on someone's floor making Kim smirk with condescension as she looked down at me. I hated her so much for that given that she was supposed to be my teacher and therefore a protector of sorts.

One night, unable to deal with anymore, I reversed the charges to my mum and dad and they agreed to pay for a taxi for me to get home to them. However, convinced I had more to learn from Kim I went back the next day.

My self-abuse was relentless, my only break being a weekend in which my Uncle Paul had planned a day trip to Stafford for me with him and my parents, reminding me how it felt to be part of my family again, the same little girl who had sat on Uncle Paul's knee on the train so many years earlier after going to some random place for the day. We had a lovely day. I was treated to a new sixteenth century poetry book, some new candles and a massive meal at a sweet, little restaurant near Stafford railway station.
My drug addictions didn't seem real as I laughed and joked with my family, none of us irate with each other for once. Uncle Paul's presence, like it always had been, was healing and positive. I felt hope, like I could return to a nicer time, a purer world.
I could have returned to my own Wallasey flat but still chose to go back to Kim's that night. Between us we had nothing, no money, cigarettes, nothing. We scavenged around the streets at dawn for ciggie butts, scrounging money until we had enough for a packet of cigarette papers. We drank bitter, disgusting black coffee and smoked paper thin roll ups made from trampled dirty ciggie butts. The contrast between the day spent with my family and this hurt me physically. How had I come to this? A raging drug addict, a dirty scavenging tramp, when I was once so talented and full of promise: how had I ended up like this?

Chapter 31
Born Again Catholic

Spring/Summer 1996
After the Stafford trip, I began visiting Wallasey and
my parents more often and during a lunch trip that
they treated me to at a local Chinese restaurant; I
noticed a job offer in the window and asked one of
the waitresses about it. San, the owner and boss came
out of the kitchen to see me.
"You start Saturday." he told me gruffly in broken,
accented English.
That first night I turned up at work on the Saturday at
five-thirty as instructed in order to have some dinner
before we opened at six pm. I arrived there in my
denim dress underneath an extremely out of shape
mini jumper with hugely stretched long sleeves. San
was horrified when he saw my attire and had his
much more softly spoken wife Leigh take me upstairs
and give me a white shirt and apron to wear over my
dress. I was told to buy a black skirt and white blouse
for the following week.
God knows how he didn't sack me as I spent the night
dropping things, confusing the orders and upsetting
the regular customers with my lack of knowledge of
their orders. I was so paranoid and jumpy and
couldn't even look the friendly kitchen staff Anna and
Bern in the eye when they tried to make conversation
with me.
"You seem very nervous love," Anna had a voice
clear as a bell with a defined local accent. She was
round and motherly but had a fierce side too which
thankfully only appeared when she shouted back at
the temperamental San every time he shouted at her

or anybody else which was often. She was the only person who would dare.

At the end of the night after I had to be told to stop hoovering after having gone into one on the carpet and seeing imaginary bits of fluff everywhere. I had earned eighteen pounds for six hours work plus tips which turned out to be around fourteen pounds for each waitress making thirty-two to take home in total. I felt rich.

I settled in more at the restaurant, gradually coming out of myself and although I still used drugs, I got to work every Saturday come hell or high water, getting dropped off back at my Wallasey flat where I would stay until the Sunday and then return to Kim's. I loved that job, free food all night plus copious amounts of creamy coffee and coca cola and the luxury of integrating with 'normal' people.

A couple of weeks before Easter, I moved back to my Wallasey flat. Kim was getting pissed off with my constant presence and I was sick of living my life by her rules and of being manipulated by her. I packed up my clothes, got the bus to my parents' and asked my mum if I could stay there for the night. I just couldn't handle being alone.

"You will never learn to live alone in your own home if you can't stay there. I am saying no for your own good." My mum was adamant and my teary protests of feeling unwell didn't move her. I stormed off, shouting abuse at her.

God knows what possessed me to go St Alban's church but that is where I ended up. Father Nick recognised the crying, angry, older version of me. He was calming, welcoming as he invited me in to sit down and had his housekeeper bring me some tea and cake. I poured it all out to him, everything that had happened since going into care even telling him about the terrible accusation I had made about my Uncle. As I cried, he reassured me over and over that it was all okay, that God would take it away from me now, and that I was forgiven, no penance, nothing.

I felt whole, cleansed and revitalised. The room seemed to take on a rosy hue. The only thing I could liken it to was God the Holy Spirit. Father Nick absolved me from all my sins, like in proper confession, and told me I was welcome to come back any time to talk to him. I went back to my flat, a spring in my step, all fear of being alone gone.

From then on, I began to rediscover my religion and also a relationship with my mum who I'd gone back to see the following day, proudly telling her I had now been absolved and forgiven for all. She suggested I talk to Father Joe, the priest from her church in Liverpool who had come to the hospital with her when I'd first gone into care and taken an overdose.

The rainbow colours arrived again as I spoke with him and I truly believed I was in contact with God once more. I began attending church again, starting with every service during Holy week; Holy Thursday, Good Friday, Holy Saturday and Easter Sunday. I renounced the devil with the rest of the congregation at the Thursday service and reverently kissed the cross at the Good Friday service. I believed I was renewing my soul, making myself pure again and felt great comfort from being in church.

Every Sunday, I went to church with my mum and brother, meeting them on the Liverpool bus. My dad still went to the local church; he did the collections and was the treasurer of the St. Vincent de Paul charity, a role he took very seriously but since the day my mum had fallen out with Father Nick years before when he'd refused to endorse her theory that I was possessed by the devil she had attended the Liverpool church on a daily basis.

I felt I was glowing inside while attending Sunday Mass; felt the communion host create a real communion between my soul and the Holy Spirit but this never lasted for long. I think part of the happiness I experienced was also that I with my mum again and felt loved as she guided me back into the thralls of the family religion.

After church, I would sleep the afternoon away. My body, still exhausted from extreme stimulant withdrawal, craved excessive amounts of food and sleep. On those Sunday afternoons after church, I suffered terrible bouts of sleep paralysis and felt convinced it was the devil or an evil spirit that attacked me. On speaking to my mum, the fountain of all knowledge on all things religious, she agreed the devil was trying hard not to let me go. The fact I was on my way back, my soul cleared by confession and nourished by communion apparently made him more determined than ever to bring me back to the dark. I prayed to God for protection before I slept from then on.

I started taking prescribed antibiotics for my acne and my skin began to clear as the days went by. I was totally drug free and my body filled out. I began to develop breasts for the first time in my life since I was thirteen when they had attempted to grow then disappeared. My hair had grown a bit from Kim's awful cut and I managed to tame it with wax into a long layered bob.

I bought fashionable clothes, having more money now with my earnings from the restaurant. My look became short skirts with tights and ankle boots although I always wore tracksuit tops as a coat. I had put weight on everywhere to the point of feeling bloated but I couldn't stop eating. I had made friends with the girl who lived upstairs from me and she fed me all the time. In addition to her generous portions, I lived on multiple packs of custard creams and hot sugary tea, replacing years of lost blood sugars. I craved sweetness and my body was holding onto the fat, saving it up for the next rainy day that would surely befall it.

I enjoyed the comfort and novelty of having food in the cupboards. I slept late every day and still felt tired all the time but told myself it would wear off, it was just withdrawal.

I felt attractive and this was affirmed when I decided to go up to Kim's to collect some of my things which were still there. Kirstie, who happened to be there when I got there exclaimed delightedly, "look at Marie's boobies! Where did they come from?"

Kim glared at her, then at me and my new found assets. She looked haggard and I think it was the first time I had ever looked better than her.

Since I had last seen Kirstie, who hadn't spoken to me since the giro incident, she and Adam had been arrested for the armed robbery of a post office. The robbery had made local news, due to the involvement of the armed response unit in hot pursuit of Adam and Kirstie in a robbed car. Adam was in Walton on remand, awaiting sentencing. Kirstie had been arrested with hundreds of electric cards still on her person and had been charged with conspiracy to commit robbery but had managed to obtain bail as it was her first offence. She'd also moved into a flat in Wallasey above her dad's nursery on King Street which was just down the road from my mum's and we arranged to meet up.

Will, who was also at Kim's, was impressed, probably by the newly arrived boobs and the fact that I was a whole new page to be turned now that he hadn't seen me for weeks, never mind the fact my skin had by now cleared dramatically. He left when I did, asking where I was going and I accepted the small bomb he offered me in the taxi to my flat, just for old times' sake. I was up like a rocket, my body enthusiastic in her welcome of the lover she had been apart from. Will was charming and considerate, easily seducing me once again despite my newly rediscovered religion. When he left in the morning I was glowing with happiness but then the guilt set in. After snorting the two lines he had left me, I felt the need to justify my sin on paper, mad amphetamine influenced poetry where I swore an oath that I would only ever sleep with Will for the rest of my life and therefore it couldn't be immoral or wrong as that was as good as being married. Indoctrinated catholic guilt plus amphetamine – a powerful mix.

I swore he'd be the one to whom I would devote my mind, body and soul, (after God of course), and that I would pray for him every day. Therefore, I reasoned in my scruffy writing, I would be bringing another soul back to God too. All this was written in rhyme and led me onto writing biblical metaphors. I wrote sermons and lectures, long rambling poems where I attempted to understand the mysteries of God, life, the universe and of my own tortured soul. I went to confession as soon as I could to clear my sin properly from my over active conscience.

Kirstie, Teresa and I were soon hanging out together, this time roaming the streets of Wallasey, bright in comparison to my recent perceptions of Rock Ferry and New Ferry. For a while we stayed off the speed, instead buying weed regularly, a great replacement drug, harmless and fuzzy. I continued my regular church attendance and Teresa and Kirstie were amused by my devoutness. Teresa, for her part, kept up the pretence of going to church every Sunday with my dad but didn't take any of it seriously whereas I was a rapt born again catholic.

I also went to Will's regularly, always taking some weed with me as he was also abstaining from speed, and we would smoke together into the early hours, then I would stay over in his bed while he took the couch. We were different people without amphetamines and got on well. I spent hours praying, for him, for me, for our love that I still believed was lying dormant. I fervently repeated decades of the rosary while on the bus to his New Ferry flat and often went to church to light a candle for him.

One night, I was sleeping over and woke up to Will on a mission, looking for cameras in his vents. He'd obviously been hitting up. I felt like he had betrayed me as he had sneaked out to go and score. Angrily, I told him none too nicely that he was skitzed, there was nothing in the vents and that he was stupid for hitting up again. Needless to say, he flipped, absolutely battering me, *slap, kick, punch, rewind, repeat* before bashing my leg with a steel fire extinguisher (the bruises from this left my leg discoloured for about two years afterwards). He then threw me out dressed in only a dressing gown and pair of knickers, no money, keys or anything. I got a taxi to my mum's who rang my landlord to get me a spare set of keys. His rejection hurt more than my battered leg.

Teresa came to see me later, bringing me some chicken and sweet corn soup and crackers. We spent the night smoking weed and munching until we slept. The next day we spent stoned, venturing out only to the bakers on Poulton Road to get pasties and cakes. Despite what had happened I felt much better. We did this every Monday night from then on throughout the summer.

Along with Kirstie, we spent the sunny afternoons smoking weed in Central Park and going to various beer gardens to enjoy ciders and black. We used sunbeds regularly; ate loads, bought clothes, acted like regular teenagers, went clubbing and smoked ourselves silly. It was Teresa's last summer at home as she was due to go to university in the September. We all had little jobs on the side to support our dole money, Teresa in a local chippy, Kirstie in a pub near Birkenhead Park Station and me in the Chinese. I got on well with all the staff and enjoyed my shifts there and by then was working four shifts a week. My relationship with both parents was far better now. They liked Kirstie, we often went round to have cups of tea with my mum.

From prison, Adam had banned Kirstie banned from hanging round with me, the bad influence. *Who me?* At Kirstie's request, I ended up writing him a letter assuring him I was a good friend to Kirstie and off the needles now, in truth not quite but I believed I was doing well, better than I had been anyway. He relented and let us be friends. He was so controlling. He made Kirstie write him a ten page letter every day. She also took him heroin although he had never used it on the outside.

Gear was out of your system within three days whereas weed took twenty-eight days to completely clear, ensuring you tested positive on random urine tests. He told Kirstie that everyone in prison took smack but never got a habit. She did all his washing while he was still on remand, visited every two days, wrote the ten pages every day which I would help her with, sent him postal orders, money, stamps and writing paper.

And then she succumbed to temptation and her own curiosity and got out of her head one night on the smack she had bought for him, just to see what the fuss was about she told me. I knew it was never going to be just that and hoped and prayed she wouldn't carry on.

It wasn't long before we started taking speed again, believing ourselves to be past the addiction and able to use it recreationally. I never wanted to get to the state I had been in but when I went to Rock Ferry one Sunday to buy a one off eighth of speed, the pull of the needle reigned me in and I had a hit with the dealer, just to be polite...

The rush was orgasmic and I went to church that evening absolutely out of my face, savouring the experience, loving the communion bread and wine, marvelling at the sermons and my apparently faultless memory which remembered the words to the creeds and all the responses in mass off by heart. I started doing this most Sundays, just one hit a week was okay I told myself.

After mass, I would be inspired to write my own sermons. I believed it was God speaking to me, through me and as I said the rosary, I wondered why it was said that speed was so bad when it brought me closer to God. I thought of myself as a type of dark angel, fallen from heaven in order to bring people back to the light; good justification for my continued recreational needle use.

Chapter 32
Heroin

Summer/Autumn 1997

Lisa, her brother Ryan and their heroin habits moved in above me with Lisa's youngest son, a little toddler called Jonny. Her other little boy lived with his Nan in Sheffield and her husband was currently in prison. She and Ryan had been born to addicted parents and although Ryan had fallen into it as a teenager, Lisa had spent her life begging her mum, dad and brothers to stop, that was until she had her second baby and developed a nasty postnatal depression. Her mother told her it would help and help it did; helped her forget the depression along with her values and her previous freedom from addiction. She was now prescribed methadone, smoked gear on top daily, crack rocks on payday and shoplifted to support her habits. Lisa was lovely despite all this and was always really sweet to me. Ryan sometimes half-heartedly flirted with me but I wasn't interested at first.

By the end of that summer, Teresa had departed for university and Kirstie was regularly taking lines off Adam's prison grams. My new upstairs neighbours fascinated her. She was always making excuse for us to go and see them. In my opinion, smack was a dirty drug that wasted its victims leaving them like zombies and I hated seeing my beautiful friend Kirstie, grouched out and drawling with that typical smack voice after tooting the dirty brown powder.

On my twentieth birthday, I ended up sleeping with Ryan. The day before, I'd nipped up to Lisa's and he'd just got out of the shower, put The Doors on and begun singing, clothed only in his towel, his wet curly brown hair making him look like Jim Morrison. Lust hit me. I hadn´t seen Will since the last beating and when I slept with Ryan on my birthday night I felt sure I had begun a new relationship.

The next day, he avoided me and I felt the rejection intensely. I obsessed painfully, embarrassingly, doing ridiculous things like sitting on the wall outside waiting for him to come home, telling his friends I wanted a word and constantly hanging round Lisa's. Desperate to fill the empty ache, as well as to get him to notice me, I resorted to hitting up regularly again. I could be the 'queen of his doob,' - *yes I actually thought this*.

I injected myself in front of him; sure he would become interested again now he knew I was like him. Heroin was his mistress and speed was my master. I begged him to tell me why he had changed and he simply said we had to be adult about it. He then told Kirstie it was just sex, nothing more, information I dragged it out of her by going on and on about it. I chased, he ran; I was crazy with speed infused, amplified feelings of abandonment.

Kirstie was tooting gear frequently by then, cold turkeys would hit her hard. The night she came to mine, nose running, pupils huge, shivering and ill, begging Ryan to sort her some of his watered down methadone was the night I ran back to Will's, knowing instinctively he would want me back now. *Dear Satan, I am coming home.* Will was like an older concerned brother welcoming me into his flat as I told him about Ryan.

The gentleman was back, the one who had kissed my cheek goodbye after introducing me to my first needle. This time he pulled out some foil from a

drawer and looked at me for my reaction as he got his
little bag of brown from out of his pocket. The doctor
and his patient, same roles, different stage.

"I haven't got a habit you know, but I got so skitzed
on the speed that I had to do something to sort my
head out. Have a little line, It'll make you feel better,
help you lose the obsessive thoughts and forget why
you're skitzed."

It made perfect sense to me. My old master was
obviously the one to introduce me to heroin. Despite
having begged Kirstie several times to stop the gear,
right now I just wanted to feel better and escape my
obsessive empty sickness. I couldn´t take it anymore.
Will placed a small amount of gear onto the foil
explaining that he hadn't quite got the hang of tooting
and always wasted it if he put loads on. I watched him
suck the smoke up through his foil tube. He then held
it for me as I tentatively sucked the smoke. Oblivion
medication. Almost immediately my thoughts stopped
racing, my demons slipped away into the unknown
and my emotions were fuzzy in cotton wool bliss.
We smoked a few lines and later I floated back home
on a bus and cancelled my shift at work. Nice little
chill out. I soon got twitchy and agitated however as
the amphetamines fought the heroin. I went next door
to this smack head, crack head couple I knew, Ian and
Raquel. Ian was relatively good looking but Raquel's
looks were totally destroyed by methadone, rocks,
tranquilisers, downers, sleepers and God knows
whatever else. She had once shown me a photo of
herself before the drugs and she'd been stunning. She
told me she'd started with the gear because it was the
only thing that blocked her nightmares from
childhood sexual abuse. By the time I knew her she

was one of the most prolific users I had ever come across.

After much wheedling on my part Raquel got out her gear and once again my world was enveloped in cotton wool.

Until that afternoon when my landlord turned up and gave me a week's notice, accusing me of being a smack head. *Wow that showed quick! How did he know?*

After looking for flats all week, hitting God knows how much speed as no one would give me gear, I turned up at my parents, desperate and skitzed out. "Look what I've been doing to myself!" I cried, ragging up my sleeves to show my mum the bruises and needle marks. "I need help."

My parents took it in their stride. I think at that time they had accepted I would probably never change. I had abandoned my newfound religion and they didn't offer any help.

I felt so wretched that evening that when Kirstie and this other girl Alana, a weekend only user who had worked in the chippie with my sister, came round to Lisa's later I told them I wanted to throw in with them for their gear. Ryan came in with us too although he looked disapproving at the fact I was involved.

The gentle fluffy feeling that the smack had given me a few days ago hadn't been a fair appraisal of its potency. I knew first time users could be sick and thought I'd been lucky. This time, it overwhelmed me. I gouched out and vomited all night. The next day I was still sick and just about got through my shift at work.

After that, I reverted again to speed. The last thing I needed was extra thinking time but the needle rush was so enticing and I needed something. The day of my eviction I was off my head, speeding so fast but not getting anything done. In the end, Kirstie and Alana had to help me bag everything up. Lisa had invited me to stay upstairs with her until I got a new place. My thoughts were racing, my veins pounding and I was so jittery and nervous that I couldn't sit still while I waited for her to get back. The world was fast and noisy.

Lisa came back and wiped away my comedown with my first hit of coke. Oh my God! The most intense rush I had ever felt knocked me to my knees. Euphoric hit, so much pleasure my whole body felt like it was about to explode in ecstasy. After a few minutes, the rushes left and I began to feel restless and twitchy once more. Angry and agitated, I began pacing. Each passing second, my voice became more staccato, my words clipped and panicky.

Lisa told me some gear would bring me down nicely and she was right. As soon as I smoked a few lines I felt better. Calm, relaxed, wonderful. No sickness this time, just nicely drifting. Fuzzy, fluffy baby in a blanket, snug and drowsy in my new drug's arms.

The next day was the day Princess Diana died and left England reeling in her loss. It was also the day Ryan got arrested for a burglary and was subsequently sent to Walton on remand by the court two days later. A week later, I received a letter from him. I responded immediately.

Now that Ryan was locked up and not taking drugs, at least not like he had been on the outside, he apologised to me for the callous way in which he'd treated me, telling me I was pretty and sweet and it was because he didn't like himself very much that whenever someone else liked him that he felt they must have something wrong with them. I accepted and welcomed his explanation.

I began writing and receiving letters a couple of times a week, visiting him twice weekly while he was on remand and even doing his laundry. *So desperate to be loved, so desperate to be like Kirstie with a prison boyfriend.* Adam really did love Kirstie though and they had enjoyed a very intense relationship on the outside - my one night stand did not really compare.

I got a little studio flat two floors above Raquel and Ian's. My new abode was a hovel inside and out, only accessible by a fire escape. By now I had replaced speed completely with smack and weed, although I only smoked a couple of brown lines every couple of days. Once, I took gear into Ryan and almost got caught but managed to hide the bags in between my cheeks and gums narrowly escaping prison myself. No more gear for Ryan from that day on.

Kirstie was on methadone now, forty-five ml daily after I'd made her come up to The Lodge with me to see Terry who sorted her script in the record time of two days. Her habit just grew and grew as she kept smoking on top of her script. I thought I was okay; like Alana, my use was small and recreational, *how the drugs delude us all.*

Alana was so aggressive with her pale red hair and cold blue eyes that I was quite scared of her. She was really possessive and once got so jealous about Kirstie and me that had to make plans in secret to hang out together without her. One time she had a huge go at us for "fucking her off for each other" as she put it. She even threw a coat hanger at me in my own flat, yelled at us for ages then making Kirstie and me lie down cuddle her all night long. This was because we had gone to see a friend without her. I cursed the day my sister had introduced Alana to us before escaping off to university in Derby leaving us all stuck with her. She reminded me of Begsby out of Trainspotting.

She always sought me out and wanted to be around me and I often blanked the door but then she'd go into the flat on the floor between Raquel and me and bang on the ceiling with a mop until I had no choice but to answer the door, pretending I had been sleeping.

She also made sure she caught me by picking me up from work every Saturday night. She told me I was only allowed to smoke with her but smoking with her was stressful as she went mad every time I missed a tiny bit of smoke. The lines she put on the foil were miniscule and most people would have missed the smoke but she was such a bossy bitch with me. "CONCENTRATE! DON'T WASTE IT." She would shove me and I would desperately try not to miss; scared she would actually hit me.

After we smoked some, she was slightly more pleasant and we would walk around the moonlit streets, drawling and gouching on street benches, thinking we were it.

I got Will to try his first coke hit and I took pleasure seeing him keel over and urging him to breathe. The pattern had come full circle, a temporary but full role reversal. I stayed over there with him after we smoked some of his gear to come back down. The next day, I was trying to book a visit to Ryan and after an hour of being on hold and having the call disconnected before being able to book the visit - typical for the prison visit booking system - I threw the phone down in anger. Will lost it. Tongue between clenched teeth he landed on me with his fists, screaming at me to respect him and his property. He dragged me into the bedroom, *bang, bang, bang, slap, slap, punch, kick*; he grabbed my throat strangling me. I went limp and felt myself blacking out just as he released my throat from his grip. "Get in the bathroom and clean yourself up," he yelled, face inches from mine.

Petrified, I dived into the bathroom and locked the door. Noticing the bath still full of water I quickly unplugged it, my trembling hands struggling to find the plug. I knew he would drown me if he came in the bathroom and saw the bath tub full and the flimsy lock wouldn't keep him out if he had a mind to come in. I prayed the water would go down quickly as I knew Will hadn't finished with me yet.

After I'd washed my face and dragged a brush through my hair in an effort to look more presentable, knowing anything would set him off again, I opened the bathroom door apprehensively. Just as I had predicted, the storm wasn't over, his light blue eyes were flashing agitatedly.

"Where are you going, Marie?" he asked me slowly, dangerously as I tried to leave quietly.

"Home," I answered, trying hard not to sound too cocky or too scared.

Nothing would have stopped that second beating though and he laid into me wildly. He realised his weak punches were doing nothing and began once again to strangle me. His hands got tighter and tighter around my neck and he screamed, "yer gonna die Marie, say bye-bye to yer life. I'm gonna kill you, yer stupid bitch. Say bye. Say bye to your life. SAY IT!" he yelled frenziedly.

I tried obey him. Everything was receding as I struggled for breath. I felt my life slipping away. His voice was muffled as it screamed "I wouldn't even get time for a scummy little bitch like you, I could just bury you and no one would care enough to look."

Please God, don't let me die like this.

Suddenly he let go and threw me out of the door, at least I was dressed this time.

After going to my mum's but receiving no pity only "I told you so" from both parents I went back to my flat and gained some sympathy and a couple of lines from Raquel and Ian. I slept with a hammer under my pillow for the few days that followed.

The next day, Kirstie, Alana and I got arrested for robbing a handbag out of someone's car. The bag contained an eighth of speed which Kirstie and I bombed immediately. The police arrested us literally within minutes of the theft, knowing automatically that the junkies who lived up the fire escape who were responsible. Being locked up is bad enough, being locked up speeding is unbearable! Flashbacks from the Will incident kept playing out on my cell walls and I kept jumping up in a panic, almost hallucinating him in my cell.

Worse still, despite taking the full blame for the theft so we could get out quickly, I was also arrested on an old warrant, stemming back to some stolen car offence from when I was fifteen. I was kept in overnight and taken to court in Staffordshire the next day in a sweat van. The police told me I was going straight to Risley but by some unusual stroke of luck I was simply sentenced to the loss of my license and told to make my own way home from Staffordshire as part of my punishment. *Where did they get those magistrates from?* Banning a license I didn't even have and leave a convicted joyrider stranded ninety miles from home…lucky I couldn't drive. My parents came through for me that time and actually faxed the money for my ticket home through to Cannock police.

A few days later when I was sitting in Raquel's, Will turned up. I jumped when I saw him but he told me to chill. Apparently he'd bumped into Lisa and Raquel at The Lodge and they'd all scored together.
"Come and have a hit of coke with us,' he invited. However scared I was of him, the allure of the rush was too strong to refuse. He asked me to stay with him in Lisa's front room that night and though I didn't want to, I was too scared to say no. The last thing I wanted was to sleep with him again and I felt guilty about Ryan who I was supposed to be being faithful to. I was passive, unresponsive and when he tried to kiss me I turned away, revolted by the smell of the bad tooth he'd always complained about but which I'd never smelt until that night.
I had never learnt how to open my mouth and shout no to sex. I felt self-loathing and disgust and prayed he would hurry up and cum so it could be over. Of all the things I ever went through with Will; that last night is the one that still features most in my

nightmares. It was the last time I had any involvement with him.

November 1997
Over the next few weeks I took smack more frequently but didn't see myself as having a problem. I didn't go full cold turkey without it, didn't need it daily, just felt a little tired, achy and slightly strung out without it. Kirstie had a huge habit now; I tooted small amounts to self-medicate. Kirstie, despite her methadone script, tooted whatever she could, whenever she could until her eyes rolled back in her head and her face hit the floor.

Sometimes I would stay home and look after Lisa´s little Jonny while they went out shoplifting and would get a few little lines for my trouble, other times I went out shoplifting with Kirstie. *Asda, making heroin dreams come true.* Nescafe, bacon, cheese, chocolate, all easy to steal and even easier to sell half price in the pubs.

I met Kerry, the younger abused sister of my old dealer, Ian. She was friends with Lisa and started coming round to see her and this time we got on really well. Even with her long straggly blonde hair, dark roots and bright blue eyes enhanced by the tiny tell-tale pupils, she was really pretty and had a big smile. She seemed a different girl from the snotty hard faced one I had briefly met years before.

She turned up one night crying her eyes out, all her stuff in bin bags.

"Me mum's bin bagged me cos I got into a fight with her about our Ian." She faltered and I felt this need to talk to her.

"He told me, ages ago, what he did to you, you know.

Said he had touched you and stuff for years but that no one believed you even when he got found guilty in court. I stopped hanging round with him after he told me that."

"He told you?"

I nodded.

"Oh my God! He's never admitted it at home, even when he was locked up for it, he never admitted it. Me mum didn't speak to me for ages 'cos of it and still acts like nothing happened. She says if it did happen then I encouraged it." Her voice broke off again and I hugged her.

"It's okay, I bet she knows deep down it's true but can't admit it to herself."

Kerry nodded and told me that the fact he'd told me made her feel better as at least it was some type of acknowledgement. From then on she came round most days. She was forever trying to get off the gear and would go for three days at a time without it, suffering severe withdrawals, determined to beat them but always ended up giving into her addiction. Her boyfriend was in Walton with Ryan and we sometimes did our visits together.

Lisa got locked up a short time later and I ended up taking two year old Jonny to Lisa's mum in Sheffield with money that I managed to get from one of my old social workers gave me for the journey.

Although an addict for over thirty years, (now stable on a daily methadone script), Shirley was a deep thinking poetic woman. Her flat was cosy and I was so glad little Jonny now had a haven, a refuge and the possibility of a normal life. I was becoming one of their family, the dutiful daughter-in-law, taking care of Ryan and now doing the right thing by Lisa's little boy. Before leaving the next day for home, Shirley gave me some methadone as I was feeling really feverish and achy and told me I was welcome anytime, something I took her up on a few times over the next few months when I needed a break.

I developed a taste for brandy and often popped into the pub before my visits to Walton. I loved the warmth it gave me and it really enhanced the gear. Ryan complained a couple of times that I looked pinned and warned me I was getting a habit.
"You look bad Marie," he told me, "pale and yer eyes are always wasted. What are you doing?
"I only dabble, "I told him, "and who are you to talk? Your habit was way out of control when you were out. You can't say anything to me."
"Sorry for being worried," Ryan said sarcastically.
I got home and got wrecked with Kerry. When Alana arrived later on we were gouching all over the place, barely able to speak or lift our heads from the floor. Moggies, DF's, vallies, complimented with a nice half of brown and a bottle of rum I had stolen out of the open window of a car on the way home. I felt lovely. Alana went mental. She still had a thing about controlling my smack intake. When Kerry and I tried to convince her we hadn't taken anything, she stormed out and we couldn't stop laughing.
I didn't have a habit. I no longer suffered paranoia, no longer hit up. I had said goodbye to all stimulants; speed, coke, crack, no thank you. Vallies, moggies, methadone, gear, brandy, rum, weed, yes please; *I didn't have a habit.*

Borderline

Part 4

Redemption

Chapter 33
Sick

Jan - May 1998

I had been feeling ill for weeks, after Christmas it had got progressively worse and I regularly awoke feeling sick and still exhausted, as if I hadn't slept. I was suffering a lot of diarrhoea too, especially on the nights I worked at the restaurant. I would be up and down all night expelling the contents of my constantly loose bowels. I couldn't stomach alcohol at all, every brandy I took came back up after ten minutes and when I smoked I felt sick. My joints hurt and I ached all over.

Alana and Kirstie laughed when I told them I thought I must have a habit, Alana even called me a wannabe smack head although she did concede that I looked terrible. I decided to go back to see my old counsellor, Terry, at The Lodge to try and get a methadone script, convinced I must be in some kind of withdrawal.

I had to go to The Lodge three times in all over a two week period to finally get a script. Those journeys were sheer hell. I had no energy, and felt so ill I don't know how I managed to get there and back without collapsing. The pains in my stomach made me double over at times. I never had enough bus fare to get all the way there and had to walk from Birkenhead bus station up to The Lodge. It was a bitter winter and the cold ripped through my bones as I dragged myself up the hill.

The only thing that kept me going was the thought of the blessed methadone, which I believed would end my sickness. Luckily for me, Terry always managed to get me the bus fare for my return journey and I would stagger off the bus, thankful my ordeal was over and I could get home and into bed. The only thing that indicated to me that I wasn't suffering from a smack withdrawal was the fact I could sleep endlessly.

I managed to get myself a small meth script and for a few days I did feel better. I actually liked methadone more than gear; I gouched nicely off my morning dose and enjoyed the warm feeling it gave me. However, it didn't mask my symptoms for long.

Alana came round one afternoon with some leaflets she had picked up from the doctor's about hepatitis and HIV. As we read through them I realised that I had all the hepatitis symptoms, even going off tobacco and alcohol were listed.

"No way have I got hep. I've never shared a needle in my life. And I haven't hit up for ages, three months at least."

"You've been ill for ages though," Alana seemed concerned and I was a little surprised at her caring attitude. "That dirty bitch Raquel probably switched the needles or something, the dirty, scummy fuck."

Raquel had active hepatitis C and Alana hated her because she fancied Ian and couldn't understand why he preferred to stay with Raquel than be with her. They weren't having an affair or anything but Alana had fixated badly on him. She had battered Raquel outside ours too, just for being Ian's partner.

I didn't believe Raquel was capable of that and pushed it out of my mind but I woke up one day feeling so achy and sick that I decided to go to Rock Ferry to get some extra methadone from Kirstie's dealer. I made it as far as Woodside before my stomach rebelled vehemently and I spewed all over the bus floor. I heaved several times more before my stomach settled down again. I had broken out in a cold sweat and the right hand side of my stomach was killing me.

I got off the bus which was stationary due to a driver changeover and got a taxi to my parent's house where my mum took one look at me and told my dad to call a taxi. She took me straight to the doctor and held me in her arms as I cried in the waiting room. The doctor, although sympathetic and suitably concerned, said all I could do was drink plenty of fluids, take painkillers and rest. They never prescribed medicine for viruses. He also told me he wanted to run some tests.

My mum came with me to Mill Lane the following week and held my hand as they took my blood - ironically, I was terrified of having blood tests. A week later, the doctor explained that a problem had been detected in my liver function and explained gently to me that they would need to do more specialised tests for specific liver problems. I knew at that moment that I'd somehow contracted hepatitis but I still willed for it not to be true.

The following week I could deny it no longer. "Hepatitis B," the doctor's kind face didn't look happy to impart this news and passed me a tissue as I broke out crying.

My dismal future flashed before my eyes. I was going to die a junkie death, turn yellow like Raquel often did and have everyone think I was dirty. I would never be able to have kids, or another partner without infecting him and my life would be full of illness.

"What am I gonna do? I've got this for life now

haven't I?

"I don't know," he replied regretfully. "I believe hepatitis B is milder than C but I need to get some more information myself on it. You have a script don't you? And a worker at The Lodge? I suggest you go and see them. They'll have lots of information at the drop in place, the exchange. Make an appointment to come back and see me in two weeks but come again if you feel ill in the meantime. We are going to have to keep an eye on your liver function."

I went to Raquel and Ian's who were really sympathetic but very surprised I had been diagnosed with hepatitis B and not C as that is what they all had. They told me that some guy who had used to come round the year before had switched the barrels one time to pretend to me he was giving me a clean barrel so I would sort him some speed. It had been washed out but still, it had been used. This guy was also HIV positive and they advised me to go and get tests for that too. After crying in their flat for an hour and getting a little smoke from them, I went to my parents' who were surprisingly compassionate and supportive. My dad made me cups of sugary tea and my mum shared her cigarettes with me all night. They even let me stay overnight in my old bedroom. Teresa called from university and I sobbed out loud on the phone to her.

I started crying again when I arrived at The Lodge the next day and saw Terry's familiar, cheery face. He took me in to see one of the nurses, Linda, who was an expert on all types of blood borne diseases. She was a young Scottish woman who immediately put me at ease, as did all the Lodge staff, and told me that hepatitis B had a recovery rate of between seventy and ninety per cent. Hepatitis C was the one that lingered, usually turning its victims into life-long carriers like Raquel and Ian. She asked me lots of questions about the illness I had suffered and said it sounded like I had acute hepatitis B but that the worst was over.

"The illness is in the potentially fatal stage but your body has fought it off. You are unlikely to get that ill again even if you do go on to become a carrier. You're still very young and if you give your liver a fighting chance you are likely to clear it altogether."

She went on to explain to me lots of things about the two different strains and told me that hepatitis B was sexually transmitted whereas hepatitis C was blood-borne, which made me wonder where it had come from, obviously not that used barrel.

She stressed that I had a much better chance of clearing it if I stopped drinking and taking the hard drugs I was becoming very accustomed too. She told me the stigma attached to illnesses even such as HIV was nowhere near as bad now and also that there were excellent treatments to prevent it from ever turning into full blown AIDS should the worst come to the worst. She agreed with me that I needed the test but that it may be best to wait a while until I'd had the chance to digest the hepatitis diagnosis and had started my recovery and methadone reduction.

I left there that day with a sense of hope and a strong determination to heal myself from this illness. The last thing I wanted was to become a carrier for life and I also believe that if I made a strong effort to stop drugs and drink that God would not punish me with a HIV diagnosis on top. I was bargaining with Him from the moment I left The Lodge.

Kirstie was lovely when I told her my news, squeezing my hand affectionately, telling me with that one gesture that she didn't attach a dirty stigma to my illness. Our friendship was drifting though. Together we had been arrested three times in that last month for shoplifting offences and the police had warned us that if we were arrested again before appearing in court, we would both go straight to HMP Risley. For once in my life I had taken heed of the warning but Kirstie was a prisoner to her own addictions and within a couple of days of our last joint arrest had managed to get arrested again and sent to Risley.

I visited her there and we wrote but I was losing her. We both got given probation in court but the moment she´d been released from custody she´d gone straight off to score. She'd decided she wanted to try hitting coke, just to see what the fuss was about. To that day, Kirstie had not used a needle but nothing I could say would deter her and it was then we really began to walk our separate paths.

It was time to get clean.

As the weeks went by, the hepatitis started to leave me. My joints ached less and I felt stronger. I began reducing my methadone dose and stopped using other drugs altogether apart from tobacco and a spliff or two at night, which Lynda said was definitely the lesser of all the other evils I could have been subjecting myself to. The first few days I had felt really rough, strung out and hadn't been able to sleep at all but sheer willpower made me stick to my methadone dose. Sometimes, I suffered huge cravings for a little smoke, just to be able to sleep and feel a bit less achy. I was surprised at my self-control when it came to saying no to sly little toots downstairs with Raquel but this illness had shaken me and I was more determined to recover totally than what I had been about anything before.

Desperate for my parents' approval and God's leniency with the HIV results, I started attending the local church again and I also joined the choir. I felt comforted being in the warm church every Friday evening for choir practice and every Sunday morning singing at the front with all the other choir members who welcomed me lovingly into their fold. Being in church was the only other thing I knew apart from my life of crime, social service care and drugs; polar opposites, always at the extreme. I was searching for something but at the time I had no idea what. I was either religious or an addict, no happy medium.

April 1998
I went back to college, Carlett Park in Eastham, where my brother, Liam, now almost seventeen, was re-doing his G.C.S.E.s. I had spoken to my parents at length about wanting to move away to Sheffield, mainly for when Ryan got out, but also for a new start and for college and we all agreed it would be a good idea for me to get used to studying again before enrolling for full time courses in September.
Liam spoke to his tutor about the possibility of me doing my English Literature G.C.S.E. as I still loved to write my poetry and had always enjoyed creative writing while at school. After scoring very highly in the aptitude tests, he agreed that I could start, despite

it being so late in the year as long as I put in a lot of work at home. I readily agreed started college twice a week.

Ryan´s mum, Shirley, who I still went to see every few weeks, was extremely proud that I had taken the first steps of my educational journey. One of the books I had to read and review was Wuthering Heights, which we'd discuss for hours on end while Alex, one of Ryan's brothers, took the piss out of us although when the fancy took him he could get just as deep and meaningful himself.

Shirley and Alex were like my extended family and I had confided in them as well as Ryan about my hepatitis B. Ryan had been fine about it and said he'd had the vaccinations so even if I was a carrier it wouldn't affect him. Strangely enough he'd received the second vaccination in August, literally a couple of weeks before he'd slept with me, making me wonder if that vaccine was in fact live and had somehow infected me. It was either that or Will but I was not getting in touch with Will to check that one out.

I decided I'd had just about enough of Alana who still turned up at my work every Saturday night and wasn't happy at my refusal to smoke her proffered little brown grains. She turned up at my flat most week nights too. I knew she left her chippy at 11:15 pm so every night around that time I would turn all my lights out and literally hide under the duvet. I couldn't just tell her to fuck off like most people would have. For a few nights, the banging went on for twenty minutes or more but she eventually took the hint and left me alone.

I became a lot closer to my parents, especially my mum. Now I was back at church and living a good little catholic life, my mum really was supportive in the only way she knew how towards all my efforts to clear myself of hepatitis. She taught me simple little prayers and told me of their power, *Oh Sacred Heart of Jesus, I place my trust in thee.* This one saved souls from purgatory allowing them to enter heaven; in return for these prayers the souls would then plead with God on behalf of the one who had helped save them. I repeated these prayers over and over like a mantra, hundreds of times a day. *Oh Sacred Heart of Jesus, I place my trust in thee. Deliver me from the curse of HIV, let me clear the hepatitis B.*

Chapter 34
Love Hurts

May - July 1998

One night walking to work, I heard my name being called from out of a window of an old house on Liscard Road. To my surprise it was Jane, who I hadn't seen since I was seventeen. It turned out that she'd also ended up injecting speed for a couple of years but was mostly drug free now. Incidentally, she too had a HIV scare hanging over her, having ended up living with Grinch, the speed freak from Minty's, who had recently overdosed on heroin and died. The autopsy had discovered he had been Hep C and HIV positive. Jane had been given the all clear on the emergency tests but was still waiting for her follow ups as it can six months to show up in the blood. She had got together with a lad called Pete who lived downstairs from her, a lazy fucker who never moved if he could help it, even having a pee cost him to move his idle ass from his bed. He was an ex-heroin user but still heavily scripted on over a hundred ml of daily methadone. Jane confided that she'd been taking some at his request so she could test positive for opiates and qualify for a script to bump up Pete's dose further. Pete never mixed with anyone, terrified of getting back into the gear again preferring his self-inflicted methadone house arrest.

My hepatitis symptoms had cleared and it was only occasionally that I still felt the ache in my joints or nauseated when I smoked cigarettes, in general I felt much better. I still had the HIV test hanging over me, not to mention all the other possible diseases I might have contracted but I was praying every night that I would be clear. *Dear God, I go to church and I am even a choir girl now.*

Jane talked me into finally going for my HIV test and Lynda took my blood telling me they would also check for other illnesses such as syphilis, and whether or not I had managed to clear the hepatitis completely. *Oh Sacred heart of Jesus...I'll be a good girl now.*

I was completely methadone free after Terry convinced me that the daily two ml I was hanging on to was more psychological than anything else. Two sleepless nights filled with waking nightmares and restless leg syndrome was all it had cost me and I was both opiate and stimulant free. I just smoked a spliff to relax me at night, which was nothing in comparison to what I'd been doing before and taking the Dihydrocodeine that my mum offered me for period pains was also excusable, surely? I mean, they were my *mum's* tablets and came on prescription so they weren't detrimental to my recovery.

It was in the May of 1998 that I officially met Saul, Raquel's brother. I knew he was married as I had seen him before, at Christmas, while he, his wife Louise, and their kids had been staying with Raquel, their kids beautiful but neglected, just like Raquel's children. Now, he was staying at Raquel's again but his wife and kids were nowhere to be seen. He was also a raging addict just like Raquel.

Saul had charm and lots of it. Although his good looks were ravaged by his addictions he still had a certain appeal to him and after a few days of knowing him I looked forward to the compliments he gave me every time I went to Raquel's. *You're proper fit*

though, your eyes, oh my God, gorgeous. Sexy girl,
here she is. I hadn´t had compliments about my looks
from a guy hardly ever and his constant flattery made
me feel good.

"You're married though," I protested when he tried to
kiss me one night in my flat.

"I'm not, we split up. Look," he showed me his bare
wedding finger. "She's in the hostel with the kids and
I'm here with our Raquel, you know that."

"You go over there every day though."

"Yeah, to see the kids. I'm not with her. Don't you
think if I was, she'd be over here too?"

I wanted to believe him because he made me laugh
and I was growing more attracted to him the more I
saw of him although I fought myself on it; apart from
anything else he was hopelessly addicted and I'd
worked hard getting myself clean.

Nevertheless, it didn't take me long to fall; his charm,
wit, humour, his persistence, his relentless pursuit of
me. *I've been praying for someone like you Marie, a*
sexy fit girl like you. God brought you to me. You can
save me too, like you saved yourself. You can get me
off the gear and give me a good life. He would turn
up sniffling, eyes watering, pupils dilated, shivering,
and sometimes doubled over with stomach cramps in
full blown cold turkey to prove to me he was getting
off the gear. Despite his withdrawal pains he would
laugh a lot more than when he had taken gear and his
humour was infectious.

"God I want you so much," he would growl at me
then laugh, "I get proper horny when I'm turkeying."

I went back to The Lodge to collect my results. The
anxiety I felt as I walked in to Lynda's room was

amplified when she didn't tell me the results immediately on entering. I sat down, my hands trembling and my heart pounding as she turned to me. "Do you want the good news or the good news?" She smiled beatifically.

"Wh, what?" I stuttered, barely daring to believe there was only good news.

"Marie, your HIV results were negative chick, and also conclusive as you have not used a needle or slept with anyone for more than six months. Your Hepatitis B results confirm that you have completely cleared the virus from your system. You are neither a carrier nor infectious to anyone. Well done you!"

"Oh my God! Oh my God, thank you!"

"There are antibodies in your blood now, which will always remain there but they are the same antibodies that someone would have after having the vaccination and will protect you from ever contracting it again…not that you are going to put yourself at any risk! Now you are going to practice safe sex," she twinkled at me. "Being drug free suits you by the way, your eyes are sparkling and you look amazing." After my all-clear novelty had worn off, my good intentions about not putting myself at risk also faded slightly. The third of June was Jane's twenty-third birthday and also the first night I slept with Saul. I had been round at Jane's all afternoon; the couple of vodkas, a single Valium and a Dihydrocodeine were just one offs. By the time I had smoked a couple of joints I was high and reckless. My relapse was inevitable really as I hadn't dealt with any of the things that had led up to me becoming addicted in the first place, simply escaped to an adult version of my catholic childhood.

I got back home to find a note from Saul telling me to knock on Raquel's when I got back but he must have heard me clanking up the metal fire escape because when I turned round he was grinning at me.

"Alright Mee?" I loved his pet name for me.

This time when he tried to kiss me I didn't push him away and was surprised by how gentle his kisses were. They soon became stronger and he pulled my hair back lightly, drawing me closer. We spent all night together, passionate in our love making because it was far more than just fucking, the best I had ever had. No condoms, I wonder who else would put themselves at risk so soon after such a huge sexual health scare?

Over the next few weeks, Saul spent every night in my flat with me. He went to Liverpool in the daytime to see his kids and sometimes brought one or another of them back with him to stay over, thus further convincing me of his separated marital status. His kids were really sweet to me and Raquel and Ian were really happy that we were together.

"Part of the family Maz," Raquel would beam toothlessly at me.

I went with Saul to the hospital to collect his own HIV and hep results and we hugged when he got the all clear too. He was always complimenting me, giving me confidence. When I wore short skirts, he would tell me how sexy I was and show me off all the time to Raquel and his mates. *She's well fit my Mee.* He kissed and cuddled me constantly, took me to meet his mum and told me daily he loved me, that I was the best thing that ever happened to him, holding my eyes as he made me fall harder for him.

If he wasn't with me I would feel a sick panic that he

wouldn't come back, that something would happen to him. When I heard him at my door or saw him walking over the road, my heart would leap and all my anxieties would disappear. I wanted to be with him all the time, I adored him. I would count the hours at work until I could get out and take a takeaway home to him and spend the night together listening to Fleetwood Mac and Queen.
We couldn't get enough of each other.
I hated it when he hit up though, when he tightened the belt around his arm so much that I feared his circulation would cut off while he desperately tried to find a vein. *Needle stabs, blood splatters, rotten cherries.* When I'd been injecting I had almost always been clean about it and able to find a vein, even those horrible few weeks in Kim's hadn't seen me in his depth of depravity. Part of me felt disgusted when I saw him like this, a dirty, desperate smack rat, but as soon as the belt was off and the ugly process complete, he would tell me he was sorry, that he couldn't help himself. He liked a drink too and there was something about his whisky tinged breath that pulled me in deeper. I craved it like I craved Saul and everything about him minus his needle fixations.
Ryan got onto the fact I was no longer his devoted little prison girlfriend when I turned up on a visit with an unsuccessfully concealed love bite. Saul had marked his territory, jealous that I still went to see Ryan. Despite the concealer, he noticed it straight away and walked off the visit after I admitted I'd been seeing Saul. He wrote to me a letter a few days later thanking me for all I had done for him.
It hurt more breaking off my friendship with Shirley who I'd grown to love. She had no hard feelings

towards me though and told me my time with her had enhanced her life as it had mine and that I had done a great service for her family with her little grandson as well as with Ryan.

I started having a little swig of Saul's methadone in the mornings before he left to help me deal with the emptiness I always felt when he was gone. A few small lines with Raquel during the day also helped fluff me up and prevent my horrible sick nerves of neediness from affecting me so much. I was convinced he still had something with Louise but he denied it, reassuring me he was just there for his kids during the day while she worked.

My mum told me he was a bad influence, calling him a silver tongued charmer and warning that his charm disguised something darker. I think she also saw the change in me caused by the opiates I had sworn to stay away from.

Despite using again, my college plans were still in full flow although now we had decided upon Stafford College instead of Sheffield and one Saturday morning in July I went down there with my parents for an open day. After speaking to various tutors at the college, I enrolled for Performing Arts, English Literature and Music, where I would begin my clarinet once again. I felt I had achieved something big by enrolling for these courses, hoping they would bring out the talent that I had buried deep and that I could have a whole new life in Stafford.

I liked the idea of being a full time student and of doing something with my life. I assured myself I would be okay stopping the small amounts of gear and meth I had been doing and Saul had already decided he would move to Stafford with me, although this I kept back from my parents.

I arrived home that night, optimistic and positive, to find an empty flat. *Where are you, Saul? You promised to be here.* Full of dread, I ran down to Raquel's. A sheepish looking Raquel opened the door frantically mouthing 'Louise' at me.

"Alright Marie?" Louise appeared behind Raquel.

"Alright."

She was pleasant and smiling but her hard eyes and grim mouth didn't make me want to mess with her. She was really skinny and bony but she had the North End ingrained in her and I knew who would come off worse in a fight.

"Saul got arrested," she informed me, "your keys are in custody with him. I tried to get them for you but they said you gotta get them yerself. So I'll walk the police-station with you. Me and the kids will stay with you the night to wait for him if that's okay? Saul says yer always let them stay over. Dead nice of yer to help him and me kids out the way yer 'ave been."

I knew at this moment, even without Raquel's attempts to further warn me by putting her finger to her lips and shaking her head wildly, that Louise was definitely still very much with Saul and I nodded, trying to compose myself. Inside I was gutted but my survival instinct took over and I walked with Louise to Manor Road Police and signed for my keys. Tamsin, her twelve year old daughter linked arms with me all the way there and back while I chain-smoked the ten cigarettes Louise had generously bought me. Tamsin was excited that now I could be mates with her mum as well as her dad. *God this is horrible!* Their little boy, Leo, climbed onto my knee for a story back at my flat like he always did when he stayed over.

Louise commented that her kids really liked me and she was happy that Saul had a friend like me, now that she knew there was nothing going on. She also let me know that the reason Saul was staying at Raquel's was because he had been kicked out of the hostel and that their only chance of being rehoused was if she stayed in the hostel, hence why she was there and he wasn't. *Oh!*

Tamsin had already told me that the hostel was horrible and that they had to share a room with another family that stunk and always gave them nits but as much as I felt sorry for them I was desperately attached to Saul and the battle between my heart and my catholic guilty conscience commenced.

He turned up in the early hours and after disguising shock at seeing his wife and kids there he got under the covers with Louise, a knife to my heart but what else could he do? I wanted to cry when they began shuffling around together and finally told them not to be at it in my house as I was still awake. They stopped; mercifully, as I really couldn't have listened to them have sex.

I hated him for putting me through this and when he turned to face me as the early dawn rays lit up the room, mouthing that he loved me, I turned my back. I wanted them out of my flat but within hours I was yearning for him, my heartache sickening me. I was so addicted to him.

"She'd fucking kill you Mee, I don't want that for my little Mee. She won't let go. We will be together properly but we need to wait til you go to Stafford."

He pushed me gently back on the bed that afternoon, begging me to wait til he could end it with her properly and kissed my tears away before going down on me, telling me he needed to feel close to me, to make me better. "I'm not a perve Mee, I just love you Mee, need to taste you."

His sexual addiction to me convinced me of his love. He drank me desperately as my tears fell, like my nectar was his life source.

For the next few weeks I was alternately miserable and elated, my moods depended on Saul. I felt rougher as the days went by and began using more and more methadone, especially when Saul had taken Valium.

"Why are you such a slut Marie? To want a married man like me. You're desperate," he would drawl, skagged up voice, pinned eyes.

We would argue, I would cry and then he would be so sweet again. I would swallow a couple of Valium myself, smoke on his rock pipe and toot on his gear. My feelings towards him were too intense; my life revolved around him. I went to church, to confession, begged the priests to tell me my love for him wasn't a sin. They never could. I listened to his excuses, tried to leave him, told him not to come anymore but my resolve weakened every time I answered the door to him. *Borderline love equals total obsession and attachment.* I stopped going to church knowing the church disapproved of my relationship.

Our time together became far more limited when Louise got allocated a flat in Toxteth. "We still have Stafford," he would promise me in the dead of night, holding me close while the rest of the world receded, making me believe there was only me and him.

Then came the afternoon from hell where Saul turned up absolutely out of his face, angry with me because I hadn't gone to his new flat the previous night while Louise was staying at her parents in the North End after work. I had felt really sick and tired and could not summon the energy to get there and I was also worried about being on Louise's territory. As soon as he saw me he began shouting abuse at me, as well as screaming at Raquel and kicking cars. His kids were hysterical but he was oblivious to their cries.

"Phone me mum, Marie," Tamsin begged me tearfully, "she's in work but she'll come. I want me mum."

Louise was working in the Wimpy in Birkenhead where I'd once worked but got a taxi and arrived within minutes of my call.

"Go for that little slag," a vallied up Saul yelled at her, fuming that I had called Louise. "You were right about me and her, yeah you were, fuckin´ do the slag, Lou."

I escaped up the fire escape into my little flat just in time to escape a good hiding. Saul got locked up in the end after totally flipping and jumping in front of a police car. I spent that night crying myself sick at my mum's.

The next day he rang me from the police-station while I was at work, pleading for forgiveness, swearing he couldn't remember telling Louise about us. "Please, Mee, don't bail on us now. It was the vallies, you know how they make me. I won't do them no more, I promise. I love you babe, I'm so sorry. I'm going straight to Walton on remand now til court but I'll get a transfer to Stafford."

I love you so much Saul, I need you too. Whatever it

takes babe, even killing myself slowly as I'm doing now.

Chapter 35
Pregnant

August 1998 – April 1999

I thought that with Saul off the scene, maybe my emotional sickness would settle down a bit -at least I knew where he was and it wasn't with Louise or off his head gouched out in an alley somewhere - but I was constantly nauseated. Raquel told me she thought I was pregnant after she noticed me balking while having a little toot in hers.

"Look at yer boobs Maz, they're pushing out of yer top. Haven't you noticed? And my first signs are always balking off a toot."

My breasts continued to swell more and the nausea turned into regular vomiting. Furthermore, I was hugely constipated, my hair was greasy and I was absolutely exhausted. I confided my fears to my mum three days after the non-arrival of my usually regular period. She surprised me by staying calm and reasonable.

"If you are, I will support you. I don't agree with the way it has been conceived but I will be its grandmother no matter what."

I went for a test at the women's clinic at The Lodge the following Tuesday. I had just turned twenty-one that weekend. Jane had found out she was pregnant a few weeks back and went there to collect the weekly meth script Liam had made her blag. The test was positive, the blue lines appeared immediately. In just eight more months I would be a mother. My decision was immediate. With or without Saul I was going to have my baby and be the best mum ever.

I loved my baby from the moment I saw the blue line in the test window, despite the fact it was yet a tiny ball of cells, slowly unfurling and expanding inside my womb. I felt strangely protective over it and also myself. I quit smoking that day. I also stopped the antibiotics I was taking for my acne, vowing I would not take street drugs of any kind and that I would get scripted and wean down until I became totally abstinent from methadone, once again. Terry fast-tracked me a new methadone script before signing me over Karen, the designated key worker for pregnant women.

My parents didn't know I was scripted and would have been worried to death over the effects of methadone on their unborn grandchild so I saw no need to worry them with it. I was absolutely determined that I would be off it as soon as safely possible and therefore my baby wouldn't be born suffering withdrawal. If I reduced my meth slowly by couple of ml every few days, I would be off it by the time I was around five months pregnant and my baby would be absolutely fine.

Saul acted as if he was over the moon about our baby when I told him the news on a visit a couple of days after I'd found out. I had already decided that if the baby was a girl I would call her Rhiannon after the Fleetwood Mac song we both loved. He told me he had an even better reason to get rid of Louise now and that he would be with me in Stafford when he got out.

The sickness became overwhelming, twenty-four hours a day, from the second I woke up in the morning until I went to sleep at night, and even that was punctuated every couple of hours with the urge to vomit. Morning sickness, if only! I was exhausted and losing weight rather than putting it on but I still felt utter elation at being pregnant.

I confided to my parents I didn't think I'd be able to handle going to Stafford. My mum looked relieved and agreed I would be best staying near family. I tried to get on with my studies for my English G.C.S.E. but the sickness got so bad that I couldn't concentrate on any writing. I spent every evening reading various novels by the Bronte sisters that I had to read for my college course and running to the toilet to be sick every few minutes.

I wrote to Saul to tell him that I was letting him go, that he should be with Louise and their kids as she needed him more than me, that she had three who would miss him whereas my baby would never miss what it had never known. I cried while writing it but I had my family now, who were supporting me more than I ever thought possible and I knew Saul was no good for me or this baby. My separation anxiety from him had begun to pass since his timely removal from my life.

As for my sickness, it got to the point where I was drinking water just to have something to bring up other than my own stomach acid. I quickly learnt tea was milder on the throat when regurgitated compared to juices which burnt like acid. Milk turned into soggy bread like lumps and I couldn't even handle the smell of coffee let alone drink it. The upside was that it did make it easier to give up smoking as even the smell of a cigarette made me balk.

By the time I was almost seven weeks pregnant, I was so sick I could barely stand. My dad took me to the hospital where they admitted me and put me on a drip, offering me anti-sickness medication which I gallantly refused, stating I didn't want to put the baby at risk. My supportive parents stayed with me until the nurses took me up to a ward.

I spoke to the nurse about my methadone after my parents had gone and she assured me they would have an emergency script for me the next day. It was dangerous to go cold turkey off anything while pregnant as the baby suffers it too and risks miscarrying. I hated the fact I had to take it at all and had already begun reducing.

I was taken down to the out patients antenatal department for a scan and saw my baby's heartbeat on screen for the first time. Seeing that tiny fluttering on the screen made the sickness worth-while and strengthened even more my resolve to become completely drug free. I recovered my health and my appetite and after three days they released me from hospital. However, that weekend I was admitted back into hospital again.

The same pattern was repeated for the next couple of weeks, with me getting better each time I was in hospital and ill again when I was out. The drip helped me for some reason although there was no medication in it, just saline to rehydrate me. They told me my condition was called hyperemesis.

One of the times I was waiting with my mum at my flat for the hospital taxi to come and take me to Arrowe Park Hospital, Saul turned up. He told me he'd been released on bail again and had come to spend the day with me.

"Didn't you get the letter?" I asked him, excited to see him despite myself.

"Mee, you and me are forever, I'm not letting you do this to us."

He held me tightly. We kissed, he didn't even care how bad my breath must have smelt from my constant vomiting, how badly my skin had flared up with the worst acne I'd ever suffered or that my hair had lost any semblance of the life it had once had. He loved me like no one ever had and I cried when I had to let him go to get in the taxi with my mum.

"I love your daughter, Mrs McClure."

"Leave her alone then." My mum was nobody's fool.

"I'll be round as soon as you're home again," Saul promised me, leaving my heart raw at the sight of him fading as the taxi drove away.

Part of me was so relieved Saul had decided not to let me go. It took away my guilt of wanting him so much. *God, I tried to end it.* He phoned the hospital to speak to me every day while I was in and came round when I got home, lovingly caressing my still flat belly and huge swollen boobs.

I cried when he left the next morning but he promised he would be back soon. It was tough knowing he was living with Louise but even with my success at staying abstinent from everything, even tobacco, I could not beat my addiction to Saul.

"If you'd moved to Stafford, we could have been together now. I would've looked after you."

My sickness diminished slightly after five separate stays in hospital although it didn't stop completely. I managed to get back to working on Saturday nights at the restaurant and San would make me beef with ginger and spring onion. Saul continued to turn up randomly, usually about once a week but I never knew when he would come. There were no mobile phones then and I didn't have a landline either. If I wasn't in he always came to Jane's looking for me. When Saul was determined, nothing could stop him. I loved it so much when he chased me; I would drop whatever I was doing and go home with him, over the moon at the thought of a whole night with him.

I joined a women's group run by Arch Initiatives that I went to with Jane every Monday afternoon. The group was especially for female users and ex-users, those maintaining a script or those still using street drugs. The support workers were lovely and provided a different activity every week such as arts and crafts and glass painting. Sometimes they would have a hairdresser come in and give us free haircuts and blow dries. There were always lots of tea and biscuits provided and everyone was always interested to hear every stage of mine and Jane's pregnancies.

My face had broken out so badly by the time I was twelve weeks pregnant I could barely see the once pale skin for the angry, inflamed cysts but Saul still told me I was beautiful. He fed my low ego and boosted me up. *I need Saul I need Saul,* my constant mantra. Despite being so lovesick and physically ill, I continued reducing my meth and was a successful non-smoker apart from the one spliff I smoked at night to regulate my moods and switch off my feelings. I felt so guilty for smoking it and tried hard to stop but without it I just could not switch off.

Jane and I spent most days together but I was only truly happy when Saul was with me. He used to phone me at an agreed time at the local payphone and sometimes he would get me to meet him over in Liverpool where we would walk round the art gallery,

St Paul's Market and down by the docks. We never had any money and he would ask the market stall holders for bread and ham for us to eat then we would bunk the train back to mine. The next evening, I would walk back with him to Birkenhead Park station along the dock road, desperate to prolong our time together, then walk home alone, freezing in the dark winter night, lost and empty, wondering when I would see him again.

Probably due to my immune system being weakened by all the sickness, I caught terrible colds throughout the winter that made my temperature rage and knocked the life out of me for days at a time. Some women blossom and bloom during pregnancy, I was not one of them. My mum took me in and nursed me back to health every time I was ill and cooked me warm nourishing meals.

My dad helped me find a new flat around the corner from them, which I moved into just before Christmas. I spent every day at my parents´ house, sharing every step of my pregnancy with my mum, each twinge, the first flutter, kick and turn of the baby. Once the baby started kicking she never stopped and I would proudly cradle my swelling belly. My mum was the first to see my twenty week scan pictures and the one in whom I confided every fear, hope and dream I had about my baby, which I was becoming more and more certain was a girl although I had asked them not to tell me at the scan.

My mum was secretly very pleased at the fact she was becoming a grandmother although her rigid catholic beliefs did make her say to me from time to time, "I don't agree with how the baby was conceived but I will love it anyway."

She knitted cardigans and booties and welcomed me and my bump back into the family. Jane and my mum were my best friends throughout my pregnancy, my rocks and I don't know what I would have done without either of them.

When I had turned twenty-one, the rest of the money inherited from my granddad became officially mine and I used it to furnish the new flat and turn it into a home for my baby and me. For the first time in my life I owned a washing machine and tumble dryer. I got a landline and sky TV put in, bought furniture for the baby's room, a Moses basket for her to sleep in and made the flat really cosy and comfortable.

New Year's Eve, the last day of 1998 was the day I swallowed my last dose of methadone. I was five months pregnant. I suffered a couple of sleepless nights, the dreaded restless legs and a few minor aches but that was it. I also stopped with the nightly spliffs. However, the depression, apathy and boredom really set in and if I hadn't been pregnant I would have relapsed.

I started going on these downers where I would spend hours crying to my mum, panicking, convincing myself I was going to be an awful mum. Terrified of failure, relapse, and of screwing my baby up, I would go round in circles about whether or not I should give her up for adoption knowing that was the last thing I wanted - arguing with oneself is a horrible symptom of Borderline and one that still affects me a lot now. My mum listened patiently every time and reassured me that my concerns were normal and that she had faith in me. *Yes! My mum had faith in me.*

I was officially discharged from The Lodge but was offered no after care support such as relapse prevention programs or Narcotics Anonymous. I didn't even know what NA was until reading about it in a Catherine Keyes novel a few years ago. Apart from the weekly women's group I had no official support in place. My continued abstinence was down to me and me alone. Everyone, including my probation officer, was confident that I had reformed and that was there was no danger of relapse. All my urine samples were clean and all I could talk about was my baby and the new life ahead of me.

I sill craved Saul with every inch of my being. I often braced freezing cold nights sitting on train stations for hours with him, both of us putting off his getting on the trains that came every fifteen minutes, preferring to cuddle up to each other. He ripped my heart out every time he left and only ever gave me pieces of it back.

After spending a bitterly cold February afternoon in Liverpool city centre, Saul took me back to his, assuring me Louise was at work and wouldn't be home. My shock at the bare floor boards, naked windows and filthy beds paled in comparison to Saul attempting his hit right in front of the three children. He even made Tamsin help him tighten the belt around his arm.

Saul sensed my disgust and told me "don't you be fuckin' judging me," reminding me I had been an injecting drug user too. Yes but not in front of children! I knew I needed to break it off with him and that he shouldn't be around my baby or indeed any child with his ferocious habit.

I didn't go back to him after that.

A couple of weeks later, Saul got locked up again and wrote me long love letters with red hearts coloured all over the envelopes filled with fervent promises that when he got out he really would be with me and drug free. He promised he had done a fast detox inside and that we would have a good life, me, him and our baby. I was desperate to believe him and his letters filled with promises and hopes of a future with a clean version of him filled my lonely days.

On the twenty-ninth of April, 1999 I gave birth to a gorgeous perfect baby girl after a short six hour labour, supported throughout by my mother. No signs of drug damage; my placenta was one of the healthiest my midwife had seen. I was transformed by the arrival of Rhiannon. I looked into my new born daughter's bright eyes, coloured by that beautiful temporary new born shade of blue, already alert and focusing on me. I saw so much hope and new life there and an all-encompassing love was born. I cradled her tenderly as we contemplated each other. *My baby girl, Rhiannon.*

Chapter 36
A New Life

April 1999 – August 2002

Rhiannon was a beautiful, gorgeous little baby but also a difficult one as she cried a lot and constantly demanded milk and cuddles. I adored her. Breast feeding bonded us like I never would have imagined and the fact it was me, my milk, my body that sustained her every need gave me a sense of self-worth I had never experienced before. I was so proud of being a mother, her mother, although I did struggle emotionally and with the fact that she barely let me sleep.

Jane was an amazing friend and her little boy was just eight weeks older than Rhiannon. For the first few weeks of her new life, when she was so demanding I couldn't even put her down to make a sandwich, Jane would come round and make me healthy meals, invite me to stay with her when she saw I was depressed and together we discovered life as young mums could be just as much fun and a lot more fulfilling than our previous drug taking lives had been.

Saul got out of prison a week after I gave birth but never came to me as promised. I spent days sitting by the phone, doing nothing but breast-feeding, nappy changing, cuddling my daughter and pining for her father, hating the fact that every time the phone rang it wasn´t him, sick with abandonment. He turned up ten days later to see his new born daughter who screamed the entire time he held her, her face screwed up in crimson anger. He informed me he had moved with Louise and the kids to Wallasey and wanted to carry on our affair. Apart from being terrified of what

Louise would do to me, I didn't really want Saul around my baby despite still having strong feelings for him.

It was time I learnt to fight back. I needed to be able to physically protect myself from the Wills and Louises of the world so that I could keep my daughter and myself safe. I began twice-weekly women's kick boxing classes in the local martial arts centre on Manor Road. The adrenalin high I got from this released so many natural endorphins that I knew I had found my alternative high.

At home, I practiced turning on the balls of my feet to do the roundhouse kicks until I mastered it. Every time I got tired, I would imagine Will kicking me, strangling me, spitting at me and this would spur me on. I also met some really nice 'normal' women who weren't into drugs and accepted and liked me for exactly who I was.

I severed all contact with Saul when Rhiannon was a couple of months old after he ignored me in the street one day, vallied up as usual. He'd only ever bothered to visit twice in all that time anyway but I cried for hours that day he ignored me. They the last tears I ever cried for him as I knew the best thing for Rhiannon and me was not to have him around.

When Rhiannon stopped breast feeding at four months I began smoking a spliff or two in the evenings to relieve the emptiness and depression that had never really left me despite the love I felt for my baby daughter. I was determined not to relapse on to anything else. I didn't crave speed or coke at all and although sometimes I wanted the cotton wool fuzz of a heroin toot, I loved Rhiannon too much to give in and made sure I only ever smoked my spliff when she was asleep at night.

So many times I tried to stop it but the truth is I could not function without it. After just days of not smoking it, I would be anxious and nervous, my thoughts racing, panicking and only a spliff could switch it off. If I wasn't anxious, I would get really empty and bored and the familiar old irrational rage would bubble under the surface.

Regardless of all this, I maintained a relatively stable life. I had started attending mum and baby groups, took Rhiannon on various playdates and to baby swimming classes. She was always really well dressed and I spent lots of time playing with her, cuddling her, reading to her and being the best mum I could be. I had regular visits with my health visitor, Paula who I liked very much. She always told me what a good mum I was and after hearing some of my horror stories regarding Will, arranged for me to have weekly counselling with a lovely woman at the local rape and sexual abuse crisis centre.

Despite never having been sexually abused as a child, other deep rooted childhood issues, which I had never confided to anyone, rose to the surface and poured out bitterly as I told my counsellor of everything I had suffered, leading up to my parents abandoning me into care. However, I didn't tell her of the way my own behaviour had changed so drastically at twelve years old, of the quick as lightning mood changes and the disorientated feelings I had suffered. I very much identified with myself as a victim of my past who was becoming a strong survivor of the present. I blamed my parents for everything that had befallen me at the same time as appreciating they had come back to me and loved me now.

I angrily confronted my mum and dad who in turn became angry with me as they denied the physical and mental abuse of which I accused them. I thought I was going insane, *more false memory syndrome?* Teresa was my rock throughout those months of counselling and assured me I wasn't going mad as she too remembered everything that I did. Those memories are what form the early chapters of this book.

Although my parents never acknowledged neither their culpability for the things I accused them of nor any responsibility at all for all the things I had ended up becoming, we still maintained for the most part a close relationship although at times I would explode on them and storm out of the house screaming abuse. It was our mutual love of Rhiannon which always brought us back together.

My counsellor was amazing and with her help I began discovering my inner strength. I felt a bit of a fraud for receiving counselling from the rape and sexual abuse centre as the sexual abuse I had suffered from Will was only a tiny fraction of my baggage and I never had managed to get it clear in my head whether or not my teenage ordeal had been officially rape. My counsellor assured me I had every right to be there and I spent numerous sessions with her talking and crying brokenly as I relived all the horrors of Will, the needle induced psychosis, the way I had LET my so called friends treat me.

Too easy to blame my past; I never saw that the problem was far more complex, something inside me, my brain chemistry. My life had been so traumatic and there were so many possible reasons to explain why I was the way I was that my undiagnosed mental health disorder had no chance of being exposed at that time in my life.

My counsellor encouraged me to go to a survivor's group where I began writing poems again. Writing was pure therapy. That, the counselling and the kickboxing were the foundations on which I started to rebuild my life. The weekly talking and daily writing helped me lead a relatively stable life even though I did still have those feelings of being weird, not quite right. It took years to discover the monster I was really fighting.

I had cut off from my entire past, all of my drug taking mates and was worried when I bumped into my old friend Kerry and her new boyfriend when Rhiannon was eight months old. However, she was going through a similar process of recovery that I had and was at that time two months pregnant and one month clean. I was so timid back then, not even able to look her or her boyfriend in the eye and she joked I was like a little church mouse.

It was around that time that I started a self-esteem and confidence building class at the local college. As I broke out of my shell, I became quite cocky and verbally aggressive. Kerry watched my transformation over the months, sometimes complaining at my attitude, sometimes laughing. Our relationship got stronger and stronger and her baby, Kellie, became Rhiannon's best friend too; they grew up more like sisters than friends.

Kerry and Jane both got jobs with me at the restaurant and the three of us spent a lot of time together, both in work and out. I became so much more confident as a waitress and loved working now I had lost that awful speed nervousness and crippling shyness. I discovered my sense of humour and had to be told to stop talking several times while on shift by San, the hot-tempered little Chinese boss. *Malay always you talk too much.*

When the Wallasey Martial Arts Centre shut down I continued kickboxing with a world title fighter, Karl Kilbride. I never trained seriously or more than twice a week but held high in my priorities my twice weekly classes. I got a best attendance certificate as it was a standing joke that I never ever missed class come rain, wind or snow. When Karl went off to Holland I started Applied Karate classes with Fred Fox, a legend to this day in Wallasey who sadly passed away in 2009. RIP Fred.

Fred's classes brought me an inner peace as well as the adrenalin release I craved. He made me believe in myself, told me I was strong, and never let me quit no matter how tired I was from fighting all the men in the class. He told me I could knock a man out with my elbows, something which meant the world to me given my past with abusive men. Those lovely guys in that class went really easy on me and truly helped me rebuild my shattered self-image where men were concerned.

Aggression replaced my lack of confidence and my anger became increasingly difficult to manage once more. I tried meditation classes, desperate to put out the angry sparks which so often lit up and exploded. Impossible. I could never switch off and felt angrier if anything because I felt like such a failure in class.

Everyone else in the class would have this serene look on their faces and then there would be me, twitching, grimacing, practically in pain in my effort to keep still.

I spent a year at the Wallasey College doing various twelve week intro courses. As well as the self-esteem building, I did assertiveness, Intro to Indian Head Massage and Intro to Counselling. I then enrolled for various diploma courses in massage and counselling. The counselling course was also instrumental in my increasing self-awareness and personal development and I began keeping a written journal. Writing remained one of my greatest self-help tools.

I loved being a college student, especially when I enrolled for massage and had to wear a white tunic with smart black trousers and shoes. I finally felt like I belonged somewhere and took huge pride in the fact I was working towards something.

Body massage wasn't what I originally wanted to do but in order to undertake the Indian Head Massage Diploma; I had to do basic body massage first. The tutor from the intro courses also introduced me to chakras, crystals and reiki. I was no longer religious or addicted, no more extremes, but these spiritual practices appealed to me. I began collecting crystals and got attuned to reiki by one of the customers from the restaurant, a psychic lady who also gave me weekly reflexology and thus inspired me to go on to learn that particular healing art also.

I read endlessly about angels, self-healing, positive affirmations - Louise Hay´s 'You Can Heal Your Own Life' became my bible. I found the Conversations with God Book 1 by Neale Donald Walsh a soothing balm for the scarred remnants of my guilty catholic within and The Celestine Prophecy opened parts of mind that had long been asleep. I read avidly about energy healing, chakra healing and various other spiritual practices. I thought maybe being attuned to reiki would bring me some magical, miracle cure; it did help somewhat but nothing could help my emotional states, be they overwhelming anger, depression or irrational anxiety and fear.

I had only been in one relationship since having Rhiannon, a guy who didn't want anything too serious. My natural obsessive tendencies had surfaced at the beginning and the days without him had felt empty and hopeless. I had got bored of him in the end and now, without drugs or a boyfriend in my life, despite my mood swings, I was definitely functioning a lot better than I ever had before. As well as college, work and kick boxing, I enjoyed blow dries, highlights, sun beds, nice clothes and a great toned figure although my acne still continued to plague me. I tried everything, even resorting to Accutane which still didn't clear it despite having a 97% success rate. *Acne, the bane of my life!*
One of the things I really didn't like about myself was my lack of firm identity. While on my college counselling course, I was Little Miss Wise for My Age, strong, empathic and full of promise. My co-students, all women several years older than me, respected my maturity and told me I was wise beyond my twenty-three years. However when I was around younger women, girls I had known as a troubled adolescent, I would revert to the wannabe tough street kid, swearing needlessly, reminding them I did kickboxing and totally the opposite of the strong

young woman I presented at college. With my parents I was moody and emotional, with Kerry and Jane or my sister, I was strong, confident, funny and happy; I still didn't know who I really was.

Despite my identity disturbance, I was a good mum. I doted on my baby girl and was totally in love with her. Rhiannon was a lovely, inquisitive child with a lot to say for herself. She was like a petite little pixie with her cat green eyes and fairy soft skin. She was fair haired and had cute little ways like sucking her fingers and carrying her beloved teddy everywhere. Everything she did made me love her even more. She was confident and happy and my parents adored her as much as I did. Her little voice was so posh too and she always enunciated all her words very carefully, something which made us all laugh, My parents helped me by taking care of her when I was working and Rhiannon's first few years were happy ones, only blighted a couple of times by my horrible temper.

Saul turned up again out of the blue when Rhiannon was eighteen months old, drunk and vallied up. *Wow so ugly! How had I ever fancied that?* After automatically going into my protective kickboxing stance when he became aggressive, he put up his fists to fight me, bouncing around ridiculously, not quite the boxer he once had been. I punched him twice in the face and kicked him out of the door and then got an injunction on him to stop him coming again.

I then ended up having a fight with Louise in the street a few weeks later, not that I blame her for wanting to kill me. Egged on by Saul she attempted to grab my hair but I kicked her into the road. Saul punched me in the face, making my lip explode and some onlookers had to split us up. Kerry sent her boyfriend and brother round to sort Saul out. More fights followed that one, then their kids, now teenagers began harassing me and my old fears I had suffered as an adolescent began to resurface; despite my beginner's kickboxing skills, I wasn't a fighter at heart back then.

My fears became irrational and I obsessed constantly about seeing them in the street; I could fight Louise and I had people to deal with Saul but the teenage intimidation tactics were more terrifying to me than anything. I couldn't hit back because of their age but it went deeper than that. I needed to get away from Wallasey. I was also desperate for Rhiannon not to have to grow up in the area where I had suffered so much as a child before going into care; neither did I want her to find out about her parentage or brothers and sisters.

In the summer after she had turned three, (August 2002), I moved to Derby to be near Teresa. I enrolled in Derby College to do Sport Therapy Massage, Anatomy and Physiology, Nutrition and Diet and Reflexology. Although I had grown apart from Jane a little by then I stayed in contact with her and Kerry who was my best friend and if anything the distance made us closer. A new start.

Chapter 37
Borderline Love

I had been in Derby a couple of weeks when Adam, Kirstie's ex-boyfriend, got out of prison and contacted me on my mum's number while I was visiting home - he had often used my mum's landline to call Kirstie while inside until they had finished one year into his sentence. Apart from that one guy I had been seeing casually, my only other romantic liaisons since becoming a mother had been nothing more than kisses with various guys from kickboxing who I had refused to sleep with as I was this whole new person, full of self-respect. However, that didn't stop the feelings of rejection and abandonment when they didn't show further interest, *obviously after one thing only* but at least I had the knowledge that they hadn't had the chance to use me sexually. I didn't ever want to fall in love again, it hurt too much.
Adam changed all that.

We 'fell in love' within two days of our first meeting in Liverpool. He was still as charming as ever although he had lost a lot of hair. His eyes were hypnotic like the ocean and he was the bad boy I had always wanted. *Smooth criminal.* After just one night of wild passionate sex, one day apart in which we both suffered total longing for each other, he told me he wanted to be with me forever. I felt the same. Kirstie hadn't been a part of my life for years and those crazy speed days of our past were far behind us. I loved the fact he was so obsessive and emotionally passionate with me, that way I didn't have to feel the fear of rejection and abandonment. His insecurity meant I could feel secure. We got intense very quickly. Declarations of love, arguments and accusations of being unfaithful followed by passionate sex and fervent reassurances we were only true to each other. *Perfect!*

He came down to Derby and stayed with me for a week, took Rhiannon on as if she was his own and the two quickly developed a strong bond. He was still on probation in Liverpool or he would have moved in with me there and then. He was a cigarette smoker, I was soon smoking at least ten a day again due to my frazzled love nerves. Relationships always made me lose control and self-destruct. Kickboxing went out of the window and I centred it all onto Adam.

Within a few weeks, he was sent back to prison for breaking his license conditions. I was devastated and promised to wait faithfully. I spent the next ten months writing daily, visiting fortnightly, and being on the receiving end of his beautiful obsessive love. He was on the hospital wing for much of his sentence as he had cracked up inside last time - he had served five and a half years all in all and had seriously self-harmed, leaving his arms covered in scars. He had a diagnosis of Post-Traumatic-Stress-Disorder due to various crises in his younger life and one of Borderline Personality Disorder. I remember reading the Borderline Personality Disorder criteria and totally shutting it out. It was Adam who was unhappy; I was the strong one, his saviour.

I supported him in every way I could through that prison sentence and even wrote a letter to the sentencing judge to get him a lighter sentence. I dreamed of our life together when he got out. There was nothing I wouldn't do for him.

He promised me when he got out he would marry me, become Rhiannon's daddy, leave his life of crime behind and we would have our own baby together. At the time, this was a dream come true for me, *how little I aspired to be.* I just wanted to be loved, have the perfect family and live a stable life, still desperate to escape the remnants of my rocky, tarnished past.

He fulfilled it all. Before we married, we changed Rhiannon's surname to his so that when we had a baby she wouldn't feel left out. We married in Liverpool on the 6th December 2003 and we became prisoners to each other. We owned each other. After the novelty of our relationship wore off, I became abusive and angry towards him, loving that he was so desperate for my love. He stopped me having any male friends and also banned me from smoking weed at all; my mood swings hit full force all over again. *Break up, make up, total apathy, boredom, pulsating anger, tearful depression.* Sometimes, he would go into a pure state of paranoia and accuse me of all sorts, convinced I was having affairs, making me promise I would never leave him. I wasn't allowed out of his sight during these episodes. Sometimes I would be patient and reassuring but then I would get fed up of his insecurity and tell him to fuck off and get really cold towards him. Other times, I would wake with those horrible, empty Eye of the Storm type moods, like a caged tigress, mean and angry, just looking for trouble. I would hurt him verbally, pushing him until it all escalated. I would end our marriage, tell him to get out then throw myself in front of the door should he try to go. Later I would cry inconsolably and he would hold me and we would

tell each other how much we loved each other.
Forever babe, I love you forever, never let go.
For his part, he became evermore insecure and clingy,
demanding explanations whenever I was two minutes
late home from a friend's house and constantly
checking my phone, accusing me of looking at other
men if we were in a bar, totally convinced of my non-
existent infidelity. Ironic, we had survived his prison
sentence, fought the system, probation workers and
social workers who had tried to keep us apart, now
we had what we wanted we fought constantly. *Love,
hate, get out, don't leave me.*
I needed to do something with my life and began
volunteering with a women's refuge where I offered
free reflexology to the women in their care. I also
started a health and social care course with
Addaction, a local drug treatment agency and
volunteering at their centre a couple of times a week.
Adam was very jealous and insecure about this - he
had already stopped me kickboxing at all as he
wanted me all to himself. He would question me
endlessly when I came home about where I had been
and who I had been with even though he knew I
worked at the needle exchange and with Addaction's
outreach team to support female sex workers addicted
to crack and heroin. I was so passionate about giving
something back that he had to tolerate it and his
cognitive behavioural therapist also worked with him
on some of these issues.
I got pregnant while on this course and Jade, my
second beautiful daughter was born in November
2004. I suffered a lot of depression while pregnant
with her and this went full blown within months of
her birth. She was such a beautiful child but apart

from breast feeding her, I left her all to Adam, Rhiannon too. I was horrible with postnatal depression; that on top of an undiagnosed personality disorder saw me go from this strong survivor girl to a suicidal young mother. I was prescribed anti-depressants which removed the suicidal thoughts and reduced the endless crying episodes but also stole my sex drive and any sense of passion I had once had.

I suffered with a lot of migraine headaches as a result of the anti-depressants and got a prescription for Dihydrocodeine from the doctor and was soon taking 150/200mg daily. I was addicted but didn't really see it as problematic as I could still always get more whenever I liked; I had a very prescription happy GP. Adam was on anti-depressants too and had managed to get himself all sorts of disability living allowance benefits for his mental health problems, which he played on a lot, making our dole supported lives a little more luxurious. Rhiannon was happy to have a Mummy and a Daddy and a baby sister but our fights used to really affect her emotionally.

One time he left me and went back to Liverpool after a huge fight due to him staying out and drinking, something which was becoming more and more regular. I was so devastated Kerry had to come and stay with me for the weekend and then when she went home and Teresa had been and gone, I left my girls with a friend then went home and cut my arms up. Hysterical, I drove myself to the hospital despite only having had a few driving lessons and being totally illegal. I sat with the crisis team for about four hours crying until they released me back into the care of my sister.

The next day, Teresa drove me to Wallasey where I could stay with Kerry. Adam, by that time as desperate to have me back as I was him, kissed my cuts better and told me he knew how much I had hurt in order to do that. After a fight, we loved each other so intensely all over again; after that one we clung together physically for days.

He stopped drinking and I tried harder not to hurt him with my abusive words. He attempted to keep me calm and help me with my aggressive temper and abusive outbursts; I made more effort to make him feel secure and even went to cognitive behaviour therapy with him to support him to deal his deep-rooted issues. We were the same; intense, sensitive, extremely damaged products of our past and unable to heal each other. How long can a marriage built on that type of love and attachment last?

When Jade was about fifteen months old and my depression had abated enough for me to get back some of my ambition, I managed to get a paid contracted job as a learning disability support worker. Adam hated it at first and phoned me constantly while at work, demanding to know who I was on shift with; it didn't help that the majority of my team were male. After a while I managed to persuade him to get a job so that he wouldn't feel as empty and obsessive. He surprised me and his entire family in Liverpool by getting a job as a male carer. He was really good at it and for quite a few months we were relatively happy. We both had a new finance car each– he had ensured I stuck at my driving lessons and passed. Wide screen TV, top of the range computer, laminate floors, designer clothes; a two point four life. Meals out, holidays, and regular weekends in Liverpool with our families, a happy stable life. We also made big days of every birthday, Christmas, Valentine's and any other special occasions by spoiling each other rotten with presents and treats.

We tried hard to be good parents to our girls and they wanted for nothing. Rhiannon went to the local catholic primary school where she was a confident, popular, outgoing and intelligent member of her class and Jade went to baby clubs every week. Both girls were always dressed adorably and Adam doted on them as much as much as I did. We had everything we wanted and needed.

It wasn't enough.

We stayed together for almost four years until a disastrous family holiday in the September of 2007, along with a pregnant Kerry, her husband and four children to Tunisia. Adam became unbelievably paranoid, way more so than normal, accusing me several times a day of looking at other men. He then kicked me out of our hotel room so I had to bunk in with the girls on the opposite side of the adjoining door. It was also very obvious, even to Kerry, that he had begun treating both the girls very differently. Jade, at almost three years old, could do no wrong by him, Rhiannon, by then eight, could do no right and a lot of our arguments were about this.

On that holiday it all came to a head. For the first time ever in our marriage, I kissed another guy and I could never go back after that. Even though we only kissed I had fantasies of running away with my girls and him. Borderline 'love' develops very quickly. Luckily that guy did not share my emotions! I told Adam our marriage was over.

Back home, I stuck with my decision to separate. I had recently been promoted to deputy team leader in my learning disability team and knew I could manage alone financially. Regardless of the fact it was my decision, it was the hardest thing I ever did. I just couldn't breathe with him anymore. I hated the fact that Rhiannon had woken crying most nights in the last few months of our marriage due to our fighting and that Jade thought living in a battleground was normal. Adam never raised a hand to me but the emotional stuff we did to each other was appalling. I also stupidly presumed that Adam would share custody of the girls despite the fact he had already abandoned his three older children that he had with two other women. Of course, he abandoned mine too. He did have them overnight one time after much pushing on my part but brought them back in such a dirty state that I didn´t push the issue again.

I was working full time, totally alone with two small children. I had to drop the girls with the child minder at seven o'clock in the morning, sometimes not getting home til six that night. I was horribly depressed, the anti-depressants could not penetrate this pain and I was also still on high amounts of codeine. It didn't help that I managed to totally fall out with Teresa and my parents at the same time as the break up. In Derby, I had no one but my sympathetic work colleagues. I used to come home from work, put the girls in front of the telly after collecting them from the child minder's and just chain smoke myself stupid in the kitchen, drinking endless cups of hot sweet tea.

Two months after I split with Adam, I begged him to come back and he wouldn´t. I had just turned thirty and he had met a stunning young twenty year old. Why would he have wanted me back? I smashed his new car up after he dumped his finance one (in my name) outside my house) leaving me in thousands of pounds worth of debt and spent a week on Kerry's couch crying, not showering or even brushing my teeth. She let me wallow for a while then kicked me up my ass big time and reminded me who I was. That girl has always given me tough love but her support has never wavered.

Despite the fact I had always offered him visiting rights and access, Adam resorted to sending nasty solicitor's letters to me demanding to see the girls - each time they came from a new solicitor so I knew he was just using his First Appointment Free Card. He also started turning up at the swimming baths when he knew the girls had lessons, waiting for my childminder at the school bus stop in the mornings, telling Rhiannon terrible things about me and saying he had a right to take Jade. It was all games and in the end I took out an injunction although I cancelled it again after a few weeks. Neither did he pay a penny towards Jade's upkeep. Once the child support agency took the first payment, he drove his car into a knee high lake in Alvaston Park, got himself temporarily sectioned and then went on the sick to make himself exempt from child maintenance payments.

The emotional intensity of that break up hurt me as much as when my parents put me in care. At the end of that awful year, my auntie Rose died, I had a car crash which wrote my car off while driving up to Wallasey to comfort my mum and became very ill with a horrible virus that knocked me off my feet for two weeks at my parents' house - at least I managed to make up with them and Teresa and I made our differences up too. I literally spewed the last of my marriage breakup out in the vomiting caused by the virus. I returned to Derby in the New Year determined to get strong again.

To this day, I don't know how I survived it, managed to keep my full time job as a deputy team leader and my children relatively well cared for. It was emotional hell. Rhiannon suffered the brunt of my mood swings more and more, sometimes physically and I began to cause trouble in work with my managers, always finding corruption within the company and things to complain about. Conflicts happened wherever I was. I ended up on a performance management which was trumped up but now I look back and realise the manager in question, although in truth very corrupt herself, also probably struggled greatly with my negative aggression. I took six weeks off work, fully paid for my trouble and ended up having her investigated.

In those paid sick weeks I began smoking weed daily again, huge big fat bud spliffs. All my symptoms and emotional pain subsided and switched off into blissful, stoned oblivion. I met various guys who I would sleep with and not allow myself to feel a thing for. One night stands, sometimes a few days, never anything lasting or resembling a relationship. I kept it all out of sight of my girls.

After returning to work, this time as deputy manager of a different team, I began to flourish in my job again. However, as soon as I stopped smoking weed, gave up tobacco and reduced completely off my anti-depressants, it all went to hell again. I seemed to spend my life trying to escape, becoming addicted then striving to beat my various addictions but never ever finding inner peace or happiness. Building myself up just to press self-destruct all over again.

To my credit, I got Rhiannon a mentor in school so she had someone to offload to, not only about her dad abandoning her but also about me. Jade was too little to really suffer and after I split with Adam I began to bond more and more with her. Like Rhiannon had, she sucked her thumb and carried a teddy everywhere with her, angelic and beautiful with huge blue eyes just like Adam and dark curly hair like I had had as a child. For some reason Rhiannon became my trigger but Jade never did.

My life was about looking for people/circumstances to blame. I never dealt with the underlying cause because I did not know what it was. The closest I came to it was admitting I was depressed but I put that down to postnatal hormones and then my marriage break up. The overwhelming and intensely tearful episodes that I suffered now, I put down to quitting the anti-depressants the doctor said I should never quit as well as the withdrawal from cannabis and tobacco.

There was always an explanation for how I was. People generally knew me as emotionally erratic, dramatic but also as a tremendous survivor who had overcome a lot. My past was a great way of explaining it all, my recent marriage break up, my being a single full time working mum with so much work stress. All these factors camouflaged the underlying demon.

Just as I felt unable to cope anymore, I got offered a way out.

Chapter 38
Living the Dream

May - 2008

Mary, a woman on my team at work who had been like a mother to me ever since my bitter separation, told me she was moving to Spain with her husband, grown up children and her little grandchildren who lived with her. She offered me a couple of rooms in their new rented villa in a tiny village in the Valencia region of Spain. Mary had helped me with child care while I worked the obligatory Sunday on my rota and my child minder wasn't available and had always supported me emotionally too, giving me hugs when I couldn't hold back the tears anymore and always being on the other end of the phone whenever I needed her. Her offer was literally a Godsend. Teresa had gone off travelling to Thailand the year before and was now in Australia with no plans to come back any time soon and a month later, I packed up as many of my belongings as my car would carry and drove to Spain with Rhiannon now ten and Jade, four. Rhiannon really hadn't wanted to go - her only security amidst the entire bitter separation and my mood swings was at school where she was very happy. Jade was young enough to be happy anywhere I was happy.

We lasted three months living at Mary's before the clash between Rhiannon and her grandchildren blew our friendship up in our faces. I rented my own house in the village. I had saved money while in the UK and was able to support us for a while before needing to find work. Sadly, Mary and I never got over our differences where the children were concerned and we stopped speaking. She later moved back to the UK with her family. I remained very close friends with one of her adult daughters though.

Spain was a far happier, healthier place than Derby. I was managing to live my life drug and tobacco free although I did begin drinking in the local bars in a bid to socialise. In a totally foreign country with no counselling or professional support, no weed or escapes and not writing at all I felt unhappy, empty and depressed. I would fly into rages about the girls' homework, frustrated to death with myself as much as them for not understanding it, throwing their books across the floor and screaming and shouting. Sometimes, I would lash out and smack them and although Jade had to deal with this at times, it was Rhiannon who bore the brunt.

Rhiannon went from a happy, outgoing school girl to a withdrawn, depressed one. She had found it hard to get on with Mary's grandchildren over the summer and impossible to mix with the kids in a village school where she didn't know the languages – two languages are spoken in Valencia, regular Spanish and Valencian – she knew neither and withdrew into a shell, made worse by me.

I enrolled on an intense Spanish course at the official language school determined not to be a typical Brit who never learns the language. Where I lived there were only two other English speaking families so it was also necessary to learn the language. I joined a gym in the local village and tried hard to make friends but while the guys were friendly towards me, their girlfriends did not like me at all.

My natural insecurities and feelings of being different were amplified by living in a village that seemed to look down on us. The village was a safe place, but it was so close minded. It didn´t matter how strong I was in the gym, how fit I was or how much I mastered the language, I was just never accepted. They didn´t like foreigners but I just could not see that and personalised it all into being about me not being good enough. Jade got on okay as they kids in her class were too young to understand she was an outsider. Rhiannon really suffered with her classmates although the teachers were lovely.

It wasn´t all bad, there were lots of local fiestas that went on all night in the streets and I was soon buying codeine over the counter, drinking every weekend, smoking weed again, all bids to switch off from the demons inside me and to fit in with the village people. *Living the dream, not quite.* Caroline, an English woman who had lived in the village for a few years with her husband and two children became my only true friend but I fixated quite a lot on our friendship and used to suffer overwhelming feelings of rejection if she went out with anyone else and didn't invite me.

I met another English woman Gretel who I became close friends with too and therefore let go of the need for so much of Caroline´s attention. Her boyfriend was the local headmistress´s son and he loved her so fiercely that the whole village including his mum had no choice but to accept her. I could only dream of a love like that. All I had to boast of since living in Spain was a year of seeing this nineteen year old village guy from who always told everyone we were just friends. Then when we finished I had this nasty few months of being some other village guy´s secret little fuck. I actually used to think he cared because he called me every weekend at four o'clock in the morning. *Total commitment!*

My money ran out and I ended up taking various jobs such as teaching English, cleaning houses, doing massages at various local salons, whatever I could to put food on the table. Cleaning work was tough and sometimes demeaning; sweating hot days spent scrubbing filthy toilets and hairy holiday apartments. However, typical of my life, I always had my polar opposites and found some self-employed positions in a couple of salons where the owners, Heather and Eileen, both childless women, treated me as the daughter they had never had. The pay was excellent from them and even though work was sporadic I always managed to survive albeit on a strict budget. I began writing again but my dramas continued. Not even my own daughters could fill that empty space inside me, the broken part that was always hurting. I lived in that village, drifting around inside my head and surviving life outside for three years gradually relapsing more and more on to coke, alcohol, codeine, weed and tobacco; I even managed to get hold of methadone tablets. I was heading right back down the slippery slope. Heather found me a little apartment by the beach near Denia. I escaped the village and once again began a recovery.

2011 Onwards

I had been lucky enough (through Caroline) to find a charity called Guardian Angels, an English organisation run by a single mum, Tricia, to help single parents struggling in Spain. There are no benefits here, no dole and hardly any financial help schemes and Tricia had very recently set up the charity to offer emotional support as well as helping us to find adequate work. Through Guardian Angels I had found the work with Heather and the other salons and I also met various reiki healers and therapists who would treatment swap with me.

I started to see one of their counsellors, Margaret, when I moved out of the village. She helped me drag myself back from the brink, offering me free weekly face to face sessions and was there for me twenty-four hours a day on the phone, well above and beyond the call of duty. She told me she saw something in me worth all her efforts.

With her support, I began to write again and become aware of my twisted thought patterns and violent mood swings. It wasn't just anger and sadness anymore, since moving to Spain, I also experienced really over excitable happy moods too where I couldn't stop talking and laughing then would some tiny little thing would happen all hell would break loose. This was heightened especially when I stopped smoking weed. I began writing a mood diary and this led me to suspect maybe I was bipolar but when I researched the symptoms they didn't fit. I can always sleep, my moods cycle very quickly whereas bipolar moods go high and manic for days, weeks even, before crashing into a low that no external factor can penetrate.

Once again, I put it down to my past, my recent relapse, hormones, being a single mum, something, anything, *give me a reason and find me a cure*.

Once again, I gave up smoking along with weed, coke, codeine and alcohol. I even came off my contraceptive pill and began looking for natural cures and remedies for my hormones, something which definitely did affect my mood swings and my on-going acne. I took milk thistle, starflower oil, zinc, magnesium and calcium. I did reflexology on my hormonal reflexes every night, went for reiki treatments but the moods never went away completely.

I addressed my terrible rages triggered by the girls' homework by playing dance games on the Wii with them to burn off my energy before getting their homework out. This did help somewhat. I phoned Margaret daily with all my highs and lows and managed to stay totally straight for four months. Teresa returned from Australia and came over for a holiday. My girls had their auntie back. I had my sister. She brightened everything up and we all felt happier. She moved in with me right before Margaret had to leave me to go back to the UK. Thank God! I would never have been able to cope alone. With Margaret gone, along went my recovery. Weed came back as did recreational coke. I just failed myself over and over but the restless energy combined with my raging angry or hopelessly depressed days me sometimes became too much.

I got with various guys during the summer of 2013 when Teresa was first here. Some good looking, some not, they were never guys who wanted to date me. *Come round for a smoke. Come and have sex more like.* They weren't guys I particularly wanted to date either but I didn't like suffering that Used For Sex Feeling and I began doing the using. I would sleep with one and then the next day pick another so that I didn't get attached to anyone. I had this little list in my phone of various fuck buddies. If I slept with one straight after another I wouldn't feel for either of them. I had to do this. I had to protect my heart. The nice guys that did want to take me out for dinner, I just didn't fancy.

I used to say to Teresa I knew there was something missing inside; something not right, something broken, irreparably damaged.

In the September of 2013, after ten years without any form of training, I took up kickboxing (K1) again, twice a week. Within a month I was going daily sometimes twice a day. My new addiction. I could switch off from anything and everything while training. For that first year, K1 replaced everything. My need for sex with undesirables, my tendencies towards addiction and my angry outbursts all subsided, I thought finally I was cured.

In April 2014, I finished editing the memoirs I had begun writing while living in the village. I called them Expelled from Grace and Through the Furnace, and by some miracle I managed to get them signed with the famous Andrew Lownie Literary Agency under a pen name, Maddy McGuire. However, by the end of the story I still had no answers and neither did the books as to why it had all happened.

Despite having a top selling literary agent and them being called in by several large publishing companies such as Ebury, Random House, Harper Collins and Headline, my books just did not sell. The editors were all intrigued by my story but said they needed to be together as one shorter book and that although my story was gripping, they were missing their unique selling point.

I am glad of that now. They really were missing their vital ingredient and those editions were way too wordy. My Borderline diagnosis was the missing link and it still hadn´t arrived.

The fact is, when I write, I do well in life and when I stop, life takes me over, twists me up and spits me out. I was so focused that first year of training and during the marathon editing of my memoirs, then I just lost it all again.

Despite having won my first fight in the ring at thirty-six years old I began falling back into my old enemy clutches again. Weed - the death of my creativity. Regardless of my intense level of training, my anger returned. I could train for two solid hours, go home and still explode over trivial little things like a sink full of dishes, or a bad school report from Rhiannon. I had to smoke weed again to switch me off.

My gym (my sanctuary) shut down and I don't know why but my moods started showing themselves more and more in the new gym. I had conflicts with the other people training there, lost my temper easily, sometimes fought tears for no apparent reason and I would write long complaining messages to my trainer about why I was dissatisfied. It was really embarrassing and I did begin to get a reputation as being a little weird and unnecessarily moody.

Despite this, I kept training, had more fights and built up a reputation for myself as an amateur fighter in Valencia. It was like a constant inner fight, the writer and the fighter versus the addict and the unknown inner demon.

I was also terrified of getting involved with anyone seriously although part of me craved the security and love of a relationship. I continued sleeping with younger guys who didn't really attract me either mentally or physically. Sexual impulses just took over but now I was harder and colder than I had ever been. I would dump them, making them chase me but if they accepted it, I would be the one feeling abandoned. I found myself sleeping with guys, swearing them to secrecy, feeling really turned on at the time then totally disgusted with myself later.

The self-disgust followed by the next impulse made me know with total certainty, something was not right inside me. I had been single for eight years. I trained more than most people, aggressive, hard training yet was angrier than anyone I knew. I slept with disgusting people, made myself feel horrible then repeated my behaviour all of two days later.

My mood swings had no reason to them. I had my hormone levels tested, no problem there at all. Although my fight career had started off promisingly well, I began losing all my fights and along with them my confidence. I stopped writing altogether. *Gerbil stuck in a wheel, going nowhere fast.*

January 2016

Rhiannon, now sixteen, had been through a stage of depression and self-harm. With some support from Teresa and me and also a psychologist who volunteered for Guardian Angels, she came out the other side and was now very interested in analysing the whys and wherefores of suicide and self-harm in teens. She would often ask me my opinion. For my part, I was unbelievably hypocritical and hard, replying that suicide was for selfish weak people. How I had forgotten my own past.

She gave me a book to read about this kid with bipolar. This, for some reason, was my undoing. I cried when he committed suicide at the end. So many similarities in his character and mine. Maybe I suffered a mild form of bipolar? I looked up mild bipolar to see if there was such a thing and kept finding all these links to Borderline Personality Disorder, which I eventually clicked on. Oh my God! The Light Bulb Moment! I felt like someone had written a list of behaviours that pertained specifically to me. I suffered Borderline Personality in practically every way. Relief mixed with horror.

I have Borderline Personality Disorder and have done since I was about twelve years old.

Chapter 39
A Borderline in Recovery

June 2016

I am determined to recover! Totally, completely, one-hundred per cent recover. No medication, no more drugs, no more escapes, it is time to deal with who I am and make myself the best I can be. I have never been more determined in my life to do anything. This memoir is a huge part of my recovery.

Since January, I have educated myself as much as I can about Borderline Personality and what it takes to recover fully. Of the nine symptoms I present seven regularly although over the years and through the counselling and writing, I have managed to live a relatively normal, even successful life although many have either written me off or accepted me as extremely dramatic and emotionally immature and unstable.

Part of my nature demands instant fixes but there is no easy cure for this. I have learnt that BPD does not necessarily warrant medication although a lot of sufferers are prescribed various mood stabilisers, anti-depressants and tranquilisers to calm the horrific mood swings. I was advised by my doctor and my psychologist at first to take medication. I firmly refused. My psychologist remarked that if I could smoke weed, why was I so adamantly against pills? She made a good point. I stopped weed that day of my first appointment two months ago and I have not looked back. She is now positive that I can and will recover without medication. Although mild compared to my past hard drug addictions, weed is something that has held me prisoner for years and even just two months clean is a huge achievement for me. It makes my symptoms worse even while appearing or pretending to switch them off. No more! It has messed all my fights up and I truly believe if I relapse one more time I will end up sectioned. The last withdrawal sent me into panic attacks I have never before experienced.

I only get to see my psychologist once a month as resources are limited here but I also have various other forms of professional support. Clair, my mentor from Guardian Angels, an ex-psychologist who has left her traditional training in order to practice something called The Three Principles, comes to see me every week and is there for me daily on the phone. I also have a social worker who sees the girls and me every couple of weeks – we were referred to her by the school after one of my many aggressive outbursts. I also practice Mindfulness which helps repair the damaged neurons. The logical part of the brain is apparently very underactive in BPD sufferers while the emotional part is very over active. Mindfulness can actually improve this and there have been studies done to prove it.

In addition to this, I have signed up for a Dialectic Behaviour Therapy (DBT) online class. They send a lesson each week, I read it and complete the task then they send feedback. There a quite a few participants in this group and I learn from reading their work as much as from doing my own. I write my positive achievements every day and utilise natural spiritual practices such as reiki.

I have continued training and my moods in the gym have really calmed down already. Funny how much better my trainers and gym mates respond to me now I smile rather than flip out and I have since learnt to shut my mouth, not argue and just train hard.

I have a lot of good friends and two very understanding, wise daughters who adore me, even more so if anything since we found out what was affecting me so much. Rhiannon finally got an answer as to why her mother who loves her so much some days, also blames her for everything on other days and why I get more triggered by her than Jade. To my horror, this is a typical aspect of BPD parents - they can hold one child in high esteem while holding the other responsible for everything bad that happens This is one of the things I am most ashamed of doing where my girls are concerned but Rhiannon and I do talk openly and honestly about how she has been affected, how Jade has been affected and it isn´t all just about me.

This particular behaviour is also known as "splitting" or "black and white thinking" and it affects how I see various people not just my daughters. All good or all bad, never an in-between. I am also aware that I sometimes experience splitting as rapidly and passionately changing my viewpoint on a subject.

I apologise for my outbursts, look at the triggers with both my daughters and take responsibility for my moods. I have educated them about BPD and have also been to their schools to ensure as much help for them as I can. It hasn't all been bad for them. They love my funny, happy, excitable moods, they love the fact I am a local fighter. They believe in me and in this book. They also tell me that I am strong, brave and that I have been a mother and a father to them and have always done my best.

I have amazing support in my sister, who, despite being a new mother now herself, is always there for me offering me emotional and practical support. In turn, I translate for her so our relationship is not one sided with me all needy like I used to be. I have Kerry, my absolute rock who is there for whenever I need her despite being in the UK. Without these two I don't know how I would cope at times.

I have many other female friends too who love and support me and then I have a lot of male friends, totally platonic nowadays. I am finished with the promiscuous casual sex; that is a part of my past, albeit recent, that I would have preferred not to mention but this memoir needed to be true in every aspect. I now love myself too much to let myself be used by anyone and I really can´t be bothered with the little using games I used to play.

I cannot stress enough how important it is to have all of these various forms of support and outlets. There is not one thing alone that I can say has helped me but all these people and various activities combined are helping me become whole again. Even my diet affects my mood. Too much coffee can take me to the total limit of anxiety and too much sugar definitely makes my moods swing faster and further.

I have studied my disorder thoroughly and there does seem to be a typical predisposition to it as well as the nurture side which usually involves various forms of childhood trauma ranging from emotional coldness to physical and sexual abuse. The typical nature of Borderlines is intelligent, sensitive, creative or talented in some way. The saying "Genius is akin to madness" sums this up perfectly. The Three Principles to which Clair introduced me have also helped explain Borderline to me and why some abused children will go on to develop BPD and others will not.

There are so many books out there that can help, so many different ways of tackling the same problem. Every person is different and what works for one will not necessarily work for another. Personally, I have found these ways are my tools, my weapons, my ways of fighting BPD and my pointers on my journey to self-healing.

Epilogue - May 2017

So now, here I am, over a year into recovery and still drug free. This last year has been a huge journey and I could probably write another memoir about where it has taken me. I am better now than what I have ever been. Although my moods still jump at times and my emotions still go to the extremes, especially when I have PMT, I am aware of it and my BPD demons are far more under control now as I employ various skills and tools to help me through the stormy times when my mind has flipped into horror movie mode just because I take something out of context.

I can never smoke that "one spliff," never drink alcohol or do anything that changes my brain chemistry adversely. Always at the extreme in one way or the other, I now strive for perfect physical and mental health.

I still suffer irrational thinking about someone's actions towards me however now I am aware of it and can take a step back from myself, switch off my Wi-Fi before sending truly awful WhatsApp messages to the person I am demonising and walk away from a situation before it gets too far. I am learning not to trust my thinking especially if I am feeling bad. The most important thing to remember when I am feeling like that is that the storm does and always will pass. Romantic involvement is something I am working on still as this is always one of my biggest triggers and my temper still needs to become calmer. I think it is better to remain single for now as I have too much going on to make room in my life for a relationship. I am strong now but that awful abandonment fear...well let´s just say I need to work on that still. One step at a time.

I am a fighter, a warrior but the biggest demon I have ever fought is this one inside me. Knowing the demon I am fighting means I can conquer it once and for all.

Now, as I am about to publish this book, I am happier and healthier than I have ever been in my entire life. I am a recovering Borderline and will probably always have these aspects to my character. They make me unique and I am loved despite of or maybe even because of them. I need special care and attention and that is okay. We all do but I have been lucky enough to find out exactly how to care for myself in exactly the way I need to keep me in full holistic health. I have found a way to inner peace and happiness that I never used to believe even existed.

I don´t participate much in the DBT online group nowadays although the skills are very useful to have and learning them really helped me calm down my reactions to external circumstances. I stay mindful and nourish myself with a good diet, lots of exercise, positive affirmations and I write memes for my BPD Writer - Learning to Fly page on Facebook. I also write a blog although I have really neglected that recently as I have been so centred in the fine tuning of this memoir.

I have had a couple of very valuable hypnosis sessions from a trusted friend, Zoe, and these helped me become aware of the different "rooms" inside my mind as well as taking me to a place of deep peace inside myself. I would recommend hypnosis to every Borderline trying to break free of self-sabotage tendencies.

The Three Principles understanding helped me look at the world from a different viewpoint. Watching The Secret and then later, The Magic, has enabled me to colour in my black and white thinking.

I incorporate into my daily routine what I have learned in The Magic and this has brought untold blessings to my life. The daily practice of gratitude that I learned in this book has brought me a multitude of blessings as well as filling in my empty spaces inside; I look to no one for help now.

My skin is finally clear. I don't argue in public anymore, I have good relationships with all those around me and handle conflict calmly and assertively. I am training for another fight in June (you can see my fights on YouTube, just type in Marie Mix Fight) and for the most part, I have a happy and positive outlook.

I have finally discovered the magic of life. I believe that anyone can recover from Borderline Personality given the right support, awareness and tools. Many of us go on to live rich and fulfilling lives and to contribute a lot to the world.

I thought of my life as cursed, now I see it was blessed from birth. On some level I believe I chose this path and my life has been exactly as it should have been. I am grateful for my life story, for my experiences, my diagnosis and my recovery and I am grateful to everyone who has contributed in one way or another to my life story, the good, the bad, the angels and the demons; every single person played their role to perfection.

Thank you for reading.